T0369897

Additional praise for *Kant's International Relations*

"Molloy provides a new reading of Kant for our more troubled times. His sophisticated, wide-ranging and provocative account seeks to reclaim Kant from the liberal cosmopolitans and to emphasize instead the political-theological dimensions of Kant's understanding of International Relations."

—Andrew Hurrell, University of Oxford

"Kant remains one of the most influential thinkers about world politics. He is also one of the most misunderstood. Seán Molloy's penetrating assessment challenges both old and new orthodoxies surrounding Kant's political vision, and his robust insistence on the theological dimensions of that vision presents fundamental questions for thinking about international politics in theory and in practice. By re-examining the relationship between Kant's philosophy and his thinking about international politics, this book makes an important contribution to our understanding of both—it deserves wide attention and should generate substantial and important debate."

—Michael C. Williams, University of Ottawa

"Provides an in-depth and careful reading of Kant as a figure who has largely been misinterpreted by theorists of international relations. Molloy demonstrates a familiarity with not only Kant but the secondary literature in both philosophy and political theory."

—Anthony F. Lang, University of St. Andrews

Kant's International Relations

Why does Immanuel Kant (1724–1804) consistently invoke providence and other theological ideas in his most prominent texts relating to international politics? This question animates this study of one of the preeminent philosophers of modernity. In this wide-ranging book, Seán Molloy proposes that texts such as *Idea for a Universal History with Cosmopolitan Intent* and *Toward Perpetual Peace* cannot be fully understood without reference to Kant's wider philosophical projects, and in particular the role that *belief* in God plays within the critical philosophy and Kant's inquiries into anthropology, politics, and theology. The broader view that Molloy provides reveals the political-theological dimensions of Kant's thought as directly related to his attempts to find a new basis for metaphysics in the sacrifice of knowledge to make room for faith.

This book is certain to generate controversy. Kant has repeatedly been hailed as "the greatest of all theorists" in the field of International Relations (IR); in particular, he has been acknowledged as the forefather of cosmopolitanism and democratic peace theory. Yet Molloy charges that the common understanding of Kant is based on less than careful interpretation, neglect of core texts, and failure to recognize Kant's ambivalences and ambiguities. Molloy's return to Kant's texts forces devotees of cosmopolitanism and other "Kantian" schools of thought in IR to critically assess their relationship with their supposed forebear: ultimately, they will be compelled either to seek different philosophical foundations or to find some way to accommodate both the complexity and the decisively theological aspects of Kant's political ideas.

Seán Molloy is Reader in International Relations at the University of Kent.

Kant's International Relations

THE POLITICAL THEOLOGY
OF PERPETUAL PEACE

Seán Molloy

UNIVERSITY OF MICHIGAN PRESS

ANN ARBOR

First paperback edition 2019
Copyright © by the University of Michigan 2017
All rights reserved

This book may not be reproduced, in whole or in part, including illustrations, in any form (beyond that copying permitted by Sections 107 and 108 of the U.S. Copyright Law and except by reviewers for the public press), without written permission from the publisher.

Published in the United States of America by the
University of Michigan Press
Printed and bound by CPI Group (UK) Ltd, Croydon, CR0 4YY
First published in paperback January 2019

A CIP catalog record for this book is available from the British Library.

Library of Congress Cataloging-in-Publication Data

Names: Molloy, Seán, author.
Title: Kant's international relations : the political theology of perpetual peace / Seán Molloy.
Description: Ann Arbor : University of Michigan Press, 2017. | Includes bibliographical references and index.
Identifiers: LCCN 2016049898| ISBN 9780472130405 (hardcover : alk. paper) | ISBN 9780472122943 (e-book)
Subjects: LCSH: Kant, Immanuel, 1724–1804—Political and social views. | International relations—Philosophy. | Peace (Philosophy)
Classification: LCC JC181.K4 M65   2017 | DDC 327.101—dc23
LC record available at https://lccn.loc.gov/2016049898

ISBN 978-0-472-03739-1 (pbk.)

To
My Wife (and expert bibliographer and indexer),
Deborah Molloy.
The Book Beastie Is Slain!

Contents

Preface

This book began in earnest on a particularly gray Edinburgh morning with a single question: Why does Kant persistently employ the term *providence* in his IR-related works? Two passages in particular attracted my attention: Kant's declaration in *Idea for a Universal History with a Cosmopolitan Aim* that "a *justification* of nature—or better, of *providence*—is no unimportant motive for choosing a particular viewpoint for considering the world," and a similar pronouncement in *Toward Perpetual Peace* in which the persistence of the concept of right throughout unremittingly violent human history leads Kant to the conclusion that "[p]rovidence is thus justified in the course of the world."[1] These statements raised my curiosity as the central significance that Kant attributed to providence in *Toward Perpetual Peace* had not garnered much, if any, attention in the various texts of the cosmopolitan and democratic peace literature I had read prior to my sustained engagement with his work. Digging deeper into the Kantian corpus revealed that these passages were by no means anomalous, e.g., Kant contends in *On the Common Saying: That May Be Correct in Theory* that "it can be considered an expression not unbefitting the moral wishes and hopes of people (once aware of their inability) to expect the circumstances required for [peace among states] from *providence*, which will provide an outcome for the end of *humanity* as a whole species, to reach its final destination by the free use of its powers as far as they extend, to which end, the ends of *human beings*, considered separately, are directly opposed."[2] This passage is particularly important in that it juxtaposes humanity and human beings, with the former closely associated with peace and providence and the latter with the pursuit of inclinations ("from which evil arises") and conflict.

The research took a somewhat meandering route from this initial identification of the key role played by belief in providence in Kant's political essays:
from the moral philosophy of *The Groundwork* and the *Critique of Practical
Reason*, to the importance of reflective judgment, aesthetics, and teleology in
the *Critique of the Power of Judgment*, to Kant's work on anthropology and theology, and finally to the text that underpins them all, the *Critique of Pure Reason*. In each case I found providence or other theological principles at the core
of Kant's efforts. As I struggled through this difficult material it gradually became clear that political theology would be the axis around which my interpretation of Kant would turn: the question that remained to be answered was how
best to accomplish this task? An interdisciplinary approach incorporating
methods and concepts familiar and unfamiliar to me was necessary in order to
negotiate the various requirements of the book. I have attempted to incorporate
as seamlessly as possible a critical-historical investigation of Kant's work within
an exegesis of those texts that made possible the articulation of the argument
made in *Toward Perpetual Peace*. As part of the process of getting to grips with
Kant I have had to become *au fait* with "Kantian" IR and political theory, tra-
verse at least some of the galaxies of philosophical literature that Kant has inspired, and explore the fascinating terrain of political theology. I can only hope
that the interpretation contained herein is sufficiently compelling and coherently presented to retain the interest of the reader and perhaps to spark further
inquiries into the ambiguities and ambivalences of Kant and his complex legacy
among those interested in the normative dimensions of Kant's theorization of
human political interaction at the international and cosmopolitan levels.

In light of this legacy I have also attempted to draw out the implications of
this recovery of the broader and deeper dimensions of Kant's thought for the
theorization of international politics, an endeavor in which Kant is often cited
but rarely engaged with beyond opportunistic appropriation of isolated concepts or cursory claims of exalted ancestry. In this regard the value of the book
lies in my discovery that Kant cannot be reduced to the status of occasionally
useful philosophical buttress or rendered as an obsolete prototype cosmopolitan theorist, whose occasionally embarrassing observations on metaphysics
and theology can be dismissed as unfortunate and unimportant ephemera that
can safely be disregarded in our postmetaphysical, more intellectually advanced
era. On the contrary, the very *centrality* of the metaphysical and theological
concepts within Kant's remarkably complete theorization of the international

political environment poses a challenge to those who identify as his successors, i.e., they may consider these elements of Kant's thought antiquated and irrelevant in a secular age, but with what precisely do they propose to replace these lynchpin concepts and ideas? Here the contrast between Kant's critical philosophy and the liberal ideology that underpins contemporary cosmopolitanism becomes clear. Kant's unflinching philosophical anthropology identifies in human beings only the source of problems—this morally compromised species cannot serve as the foundation for its own salvation. Only a rationally justified belief in *purposive* nature can ultimately serve as the basis for the reorientation of the species toward its redeemed form, humanity. Contemporary cosmopolitanism, convinced of the rational capacity of human beings to transform their moral and political natures, falls into a serious logical problem: it recognizes that political life is selfish, callous in the face of human catastrophe, and often brutal, but pins its hopes on those responsible for (and who profit from) this state of affairs becoming the agents of change toward a more just order. Kant recognized that our capacity to create knowledge through observation of ourselves and of what we are capable leads to some dispiriting conclusions, which call forth the necessity of sacrificing knowledge to make room for faith beyond what that knowledge reveals. Kant explicitly states that hope for salvation can only be rationally justified by belief in God having arranged the possibility of such salvation. Contemporary cosmopolitans assume in an uncritical manner that hope can be invested in human beings, a position to which Kant was opposed and many of their own observations would suggest is highly unlikely. The problem is in effect that contemporary cosmopolitans cannot provide a rationally justified basis for the assumption that salvation from the depredations and violence of human beings can be found in human beings themselves. Contemporary cosmopolitanism has not evolved beyond the repeated iteration of its dogma to the point where it realizes that its principles lie on an insufficient basis, and like the rationalists of Kant's era, call forth the skepticism of those who would reject as groundless—or cynically exploit—the principles of cosmopolitanism. Rather than assuming that they have left Kant behind, cosmopolitan theorists must go back to Kant to understand better the nature of their own project. An adequately secular, postmetaphysical foundation for a *convincing* cosmopolitan theory that addresses the problems raised by Kant in relation to human beings may be possible, but it still awaits articulation.

The interpretation of Kant in these pages is at odds with many representations of Kant current within philosophy, political theory, and IR. It presents a

Kant who is fearful of the species he tries to point toward redemption. A Kant who is contemptuous of rationalism yet horrified by the effect of skepticism and worried by the prospect of continual, meaningless cycles of human progress and regression. Above all, it is a Kant whose fear that human existence is meaningless forces him to invest his hope beyond the limits of knowledge in the idea of God as the architect of a universe in which mankind has a role more significant than that of an animal within the mechanism of nature. It is from Kant's fear and anxieties that *Toward Perpetual Peace*, and all the theories that follow in its wake, originates: the implications of those fearful, anxious origins for how we think about, construct, and reconstruct our world must be explored.

Swalecliffe, Kent
May 2016

Acknowledgments

A book has many debts. This book owes its origin to an animated discussion of Kant in the Institute of Development Studies bar at the University of Sussex involving Kamran Matan and Justin Rosenberg, whose curiosity regarding my throwaway interjection that Immanuel Kant was "history's greatest monster" inadvertently started me on this path. Vassilis Paipas has been my most consistent interlocutor on all things Kant and political-theological and has commented on most of the chapters contained herein with good humour and insight. I should also like to thank the following for all their advice and suggestions: Luke Ashworth, Richard Beardsworth, Andreas Behnke, Christina Boswell, Howard Caygill, Charles Devellennes, Mick Dillon, Brad Evans, Cecile Fabre, Harry Gould, Ian Hall, Patrick Holden, Aggie Hirst, Beate Jahn, Bob Lacey, Tony Lang, Andrew Lawrence, Ned Lebow, Jeremy Moses, Andrew Neal, Oliver O'Donovan, Cian O'Driscoll, Adrian Pabst, Stephen Palmquist, Ilias Papagian-nopolous, Mustapha Kamal Pasha, Julian Reid, Nicholas Rengger, Robbie Shilliam, Leslie Stevenson, Scott Thomas, Dara Waldron, and Howard Williams.

I would particularly like to thank the following for inviting me to present papers based on this material: Tom Moore at the University of Westminster; Hugo Slim and Chris Hancock of the Oxford Institute for Ethics, Law and Armed Conflict; Mikko Kuisma and Molly Cochrane at Oxford Brookes; Beate Jahn at the University of Sussex (a most enjoyable return to the scene of the original crime); and the munificent Barry Ryan at Keele University. In 2010 I was honoured to be a guest of the Hungarian Academy of Sciences to give a paper on Kant and benefited from the useful insights and extraordinary hospitality of Gábor Gángó and his colleagues.

Xavier Guillaume, Cian O'Driscoll, Andrew Neal, Brona Murphy, and Mo Hume (and their respective families!) came to the rescue of the Molloy clan more than once over recent years and we are very grateful for all their assistance during very trying times.

I am very grateful that Taylor and Francis have granted permission to use my article, "An 'All-Unifying Church Triumphant': A Neglected Dimension of Kant's Theory of International Relations," *International History Review* 35, no. 2: 317–36. The original article can be found at http://www.tandfonline.com/doi/abs/10.1080/07075332.2012.761148/

A very special word of thanks must go to my former editor Melody Herr who steered me through the process of publishing with the University of Michigan Press. After Melody's departure Mary Francis, Meredith Norwich, Danielle Coty, and Kevin Rennells have been extremely helpful and supportive. I am especially grateful for the patience you have all shown me over the years.

Above all, though, I must thank my long-suffering wife Deborah. She has endured years of erratic behavior, nocturnal note taking, and frequent splenetic outbursts directed toward Kant and Kantianism in general. She has done so with great understanding and good humor, and when necessary has brought her cataloguing skills into play when compiling the bibliography for this volume. I also have to thank her for making the last ten years the most rewarding of my life. Sam, Maebh, and Liam must also be thanked for all their efforts in the fields of laughter, wonderment (often shading into bafflement), and sleep deprivation.

Introduction

In 1795 and 1796 Immanuel Kant wrote two essays that reference in their titles the desire for the permanent cessation of hostilities in philosophy and international politics. The first of these essays, *Toward Perpetual Peace*, argues for peace among states as both a political necessity and a moral requirement. The second, *Proclamation of the Imminent Conclusion of a Treaty of Perpetual Peace in Philosophy*, proposes an end to the intractable dispute in philosophy between dogmatic and skeptical factions. Although Kant continued to publish significant material after these essays there is a sense in which they indicate the final horizons of thought in politics and philosophy of a thinker who by 1796 was beginning to show the signs of mental deterioration.[1] The crystallization of Kant's thought in relation to the ultimate pacification of international politics was probably linked to momentous events affecting Europe at the time, events that simultaneously pointed to the limits of what was achievable in the immediate context, but that also held promise for the future that Kant was determined to explore. One such event occurred on April 5, 1795, when François Barthélemy, the ambassador of the French Republic to Switzerland, and Karl August von Hardenberg, the representative of the Prussian king Friedrich Wilhelm II, signed the first Treaty of Basel to end Prussian involvement in the War of the First Coalition against the revolutionary regime that had transformed France and the face of Europe. The Treaty of Basel is a fairly typical example of a contemporary peace treaty: it comprises 12 articles relating to mundane matters such as the cessation of hostilities, the settlement of territorial claims, the return of prisoners, and the restoration of commercial relations. These articles are followed by a further six "secret" articles known only to the French and Prussian delegates. They concern the conduct of the contracting parties within the context of the ongoing war between Austria and her allies against France. Particularly interesting is the undertaking in the second secret article by Prussia to discuss the modalities of transferring Prussian-held territories to France in return for a French indemnity in the event of France retaining the left bank of the Rhine at the conclusion of the wider war.[2]

Toward Perpetual Peace is Kant's ambitious but guarded philosophical response to the problems of war and peace in a revolutionary era. Published by the Königsberg publisher Nicolovius in December 1795, this essay may be read as a repudiation of the kind of peace represented by the Treaty of Basel. In contrast to the "solid" peace by which France guaranteed to respect the interests of the Prussian king on the right bank of the Rhine for the limited period of three months, Kant's peace would establish peace in perpetuity.[3] Toward Perpetual Peace is composed of six preliminary articles, three definitive articles, two supplements, and two long appendices. The preliminary articles outline the conditions necessary for peace to be achieved: that peace should be concluded with no secret reservations for war in the future; that states and their populations should not be subject to acquisition by other states; that standing armies ought to be abolished; that debt should not finance the conflicts of states; that the principle of nonintervention should be maintained; and finally that in any war the combatants should not act in such a manner as to make the trust of its current opponent impossible to obtain in the future. The definitive articles concern what is necessary in order to maintain peace: domestically, the establishment of a republican constitution; internationally, that the law of nations should be based on a federation of free states; and finally, that cosmopolitan law should be restricted to hospitality. The first supplement argues that the "great artist nature" guarantees the eventual achievement of perpetual peace. The second, secret supplement contains Kant's plea that sovereign authorities seek and consider seriously the advice of philosophers regarding war and peace and allow those philosophers to speak freely to each other in relation to these matters. The appendices concern the conflict between morality and politics as an impediment to perpetual peace and how this conflict might be resolved. The primary difference between Kant's theoretical enterprise and its real-world equivalent signed in Basel is that Kant's treaty extended the concept of right in global politics from the great powers to all states and, through the concept of cosmopolitan law, to individuals. Deftly weaving together politics, law, philosophy, and theology, Kant outlines a path to peace that acknowledges the powerful claims of rational morality within a framework that also accommodates the self-interested motivations of human beings, arguing that the former will only be achieved after the latter have reached a point whereby human beings are restrained by the fear of extinction in war or loss of commercial earnings, or both.

Although often viewed as a relatively minor piece by one of the most influential philosophers in history, *Toward Perpetual Peace* has secured for Kant a prominent position within International Relations (IR), a discipline that would not exist in its own right for over a century after his death. The influential normative theorist Chris Brown, for example, has singled Kant out as "the greatest of all theorists of international relations."[4] Brown is not alone in his estimation of Kant's significance to the discipline. Howard Williams makes the claim that "[b]y any standards Kant is a major international theorist. Indeed in so far as it is possible to speak of a history of international political theory Kant would have to be regarded as one of its founders."[5] Williams's claim is borne out as, in addition to his primary disciplinary significance as a "founding father" of democratic peace theory (DPT) and cosmopolitanism, Kant also plays a role in the English School as the key representative of the revolutionist tradition, while constructivists have dealt with Kant in terms of cultures of anarchy and the legacy of republicanism in international relations.[6] Poststructural and critical theorists have also engaged either directly or indirectly with Kant or the Kantian legacy in IR, with Andrew Linklater claiming that "Kant's decision to place the problem of community in a world historical framework of analysis that was concerned with the development of humanity from the beginning of time made him the first great theorist of the international relations of modernity."[7]

Despite the wide-ranging nature of Kant's presence across the spectrum of IR, however, the philosophical positions that underpin his theory—and their implications—remain relatively underexamined.[8] This book explores these deeper and wider aspects of Kant's international theory and the various areas of his work from which it grew. Perhaps this book's primary aim is to demonstrate that *Toward Perpetual Peace* does not exist in an intellectual vacuum, but rather should be seen as the product of decades of wrestling with some of the most important aspects of human existence.[9] To understand Kant's work as a theorist of "International Relations" it is important to examine the various stages of its development, from the critical philosophy to his synthesis of politics, philosophy of history, theology, and morality in *Toward Perpetual Peace*. It should be made clear at the outset that Kant will be primarily treated throughout this book in terms distinct from those of IR as such, which, as a twentieth-century discipline, he obviously predates, and to whose themes it would be anachronistic to expect him to address directly. While commonly employed terms such as "International Relations" and "global politics" are used throughout the book, this is solely for the sake of convenience: the development of Kant's thought will be treated sui generis and only *after* a final position is reached on what constitutes his theory of mankind's social relations shall the implications of his thought to IR and international political theory be investigated. This book is not "Kantian" in the sense of being a celebration of or even being sympathetic toward his project, and it certainly does not cleave to the "Kantian" approaches current within IR and international political theory. It is Kantian, however, in the sense that the spirit that animates it is one of critique, that Kant's own theories about human existence in general and international relations in particular should be subjected to sustained scrutiny, and that there is "nothing," including Kant's work, "so important because of its utility, nothing so holy, that it may be exempted from this searching review and inspection, which knows no respect for persons."[10]

Kant has risen to prominence relatively recently in the history of IR primarily through the efforts of democratic peace theorists and the emergence of cosmopolitanism within the discipline, movements whose success is closely related to the end of the Cold War.[11] Such has been the influence of cosmopolitan and democratic peace discourses in relation to Kant that they have overshadowed important aspects of Kant's theory of international society, obscuring the full complexity of a theory that incorporates several dimensions or aspects of human existence. Another element explored in this book that is often ignored or downplayed by contemporary Kantians is the extent to which parts of Kant's project are frequently in apparent conflict with each other. Kant's antinomies, ambivalences, and ambiguities are at the heart of his project and his attempts to resolve the various tensions between elements and perspectives within his theory are the keys to understanding it. As Kimberly Hutchings emphasizes, Kant's is a more "volatile legacy" than is often realized or admitted.[12] To take elements of his theory without reference to how Kant developed those elements within a wider philosophy is to take only a part of a more complex system and risks misrepresenting both part and whole. This book is intended to go beyond such a reading by arguing that one better understands the parts of Kant's theorization of international society by reference to the various dimensions—critical, moral, political, psychological, anthropological, and theological—that compose it.

For a non-Kantian theorist to enter the Kantian thought world is to embark on a strange and disorienting adventure, not unlike Alice's in Wonderland or Dorothy's in Oz. Like those intrepid females, one enters an odd, often counterintuitive world governed by its own peculiar internal logic that is baffling to the uninitiated. Such is the complexity of Kant's world that it makes sense only if we pull back from the intricacies of the exotic flora and fauna and look at how the various layers, dimensions, and aspects interrelate. It is also necessary to recognize that the language and concepts employed by Kant are particularly ambiguous and it can be difficult, if not impossible, to discern what his position actually is on any given subject, e.g., sincerity is a moral good, but politically a handicap; war is a moral evil in his political works, but he claims in the *Critique of the Power of Judgment* that war produces nobler people than peace, which leads to the degradation of both moral and mental abilities.[13] It is for this reason that I agree with Geoffrey Waite's observation that "the serious philosophical and hermeneutic problem throughout *Toward Perpetual Peace*, and indeed in all Kant's major texts, remains. We simply *cannot* know what his full stand was."[14] Such ambiguity invites constant interpretation of his texts and revision of what Kant "means" for the theoretical study of international relations.

Kant as Progenitor of Peace Theory and Cosmopolitanism

The first task is to understand how Kant came to be understood in the manner he is today. In a review essay written during World War I, just before the emergence of IR as a discipline, Leonard Woolf commented on the "ruinous condition" of "the temple of Perpetual Peace." Observing the history of the "projects and schemes and dreams" of perpetual peace, Woolf stated that "none is more curious and original than Kant's *Zum ewigen Frieden*." Woolf's analysis of *Towards Perpetual Peace* is startling to contemporary eyes given the somber seriousness with which this text is treated in political and international theory: "Most people who have written about this difficult little essay do not seem fully to grasp the import of its design. It is a philosophical joke, a transcendental satire . . . there is a flavour of irony over the whole treatise." Despite the satirical intent, however, Kant's treatise "is full of political wisdom and far the most 'practical' work ever written upon the subject." The true significance of Kant's tract, according to Woolf, is the realization that Kant's purpose cannot be dismissed as utopian fantasy. The remarkable issue for Woolf is that human beings have *not* effected what is an achievable set of clearly laid out objectives—this failure haunts the philosopher concerned with questions of war and peace. Woolf can only ask: "Is the answer to be found still in the answer of Leibnitz: 'The mightiest among the living have little respect for tribunals?'"[15]

The intriguing fact in relation to Kant's influence on Woolf and other leading figures at the dawn of International Relations theory is that they did not seek answers to the questions of war and peace in Kant's work. Kant may have been present at (or slightly before) the birth of IR, but his work had little visible impact on those who would shape the discipline. The second generation of IR theorists, dominated by realist thinkers such as E. H. Carr and Hans J. Morgenthau, also proved remarkably resistant to Kant's theoretical charms.[16] The only theoretical approach to afford Kant a significant—and even then a secondary, or perhaps tertiary—role in IR theory during the Cold War was the English School, with Martin Wight identifying Kant with the revolutionary tradition of international thought. For Wight, Kant is a revolutionist because of his cleaving to a "revolutionary presumption" that "international society as it exists at present must be renovated, revolutionized."[17]

Kant's comparatively recent rise to prominence in IR is attributable largely to two movements: first, Kant's promotion as a peace theorist; second, the linkages forged between Kant's work and contemporary cosmopolitanism. Despite their relative novelty, the literature produced by these movements is immense and it would not be possible to do justice to the sheer size and complexity of the literature in this introduction—another book would be required for that purpose. As a means of coping with this problem of scale I concentrate on the major positions of certain key theorists within these movements rather than attempt to synthesize the voluminous amount of material that has proliferated about Kant.[18]

Kant as Peace Theorist

The representation of Kant as a peace theorist began to gather pace with F. H. Hinsley's treatment of Kant in *Power and the Pursuit of Peace*. Hinsley's argument centers around the claim that, in contrast to the simply mechanical and organizational efforts of writers such as the Abbé St. Pierre, Kant's theory of perpetual peace is essentially a product of a particular philosophy of history predicated on the eventual unfolding of peace as the result of the interaction *between* the mechanical course of nature and the demands of rational morality. The key to understanding Kant's argument, according to Hinsley, lies in the concept of freedom being fulfilled within the system of nature. Hinsley's read-ing of Kant stresses that it is the freedom of states that creates the conditions whereby the human being's "unlovely qualities—his love of glory, power, and possessions" create the conditions for the emergence and development of the human being's better qualities and his use of reason.[19] According to Hinsley, it is the natural competition of states that will create the conditions for "[t]he es-tablishment of a completely just civic society in which alone the faculties of men could be fully developed."[20] This "completely just civil society," governed by the rule of law, fosters the internal and external development of both domes-tic and international order.

W. B. Gallie acknowledges the achievement of Hinsley in providing the first thorough analysis of Kant's approach to IR and adds to his analysis a series of important insights regarding Kant's role as a philosopher of peace. The most important of Gallie's observations on Kant is his identification of the legalism that underpins the project of perpetual peace.[21] Gallie also stresses the impor-tance of recognizing the nature of Kant's "guarantee" of perpetual peace. This is not a guarantee in the conventional sense, but rather an argument proceeding from the recognition of the very fragility of maintaining peace within a federa-tion. The guarantee has two significant aspects. First, Gallie suggests that it is the *"persistently remembered possibility, if not the actual danger or threat"* of war breaking out among its members that serves as the motivation to preserve the peace. Second, the guarantee reconfigures objections to the possibility of per-petual peace rooted in human nature as spurs to rational human effort neces-sary to overcome these obstacles.[22] The "guarantee" in effect makes perpetual peace possible in principle and by extension in practice if the necessary politi-cal will is present. The problem with Gallie's analysis is that the nature of this guarantee is not probed in sufficient detail, especially in relation to who, or what, underwrites the guarantee and the implications of this underwriting for the rest of the project.

Drawing on Hinsley and Gallie, Michael W. Doyle's highly influential two-part article "Kant, Liberal Legacies and Foreign Affairs" established Kant as the primary precursor of liberal theory in IR. As Doyle's liberal peace morphed into democratic peace theory (DPT) Kant's reputation as a systemic peace theo-rist was copper-fastened and inextricably linked to a major research program in IR. Like Hinsley, Doyle reads Kant as professing a theory of "natural" evolution toward harmony.[23] Kant's significance for Doyle lies in the fact that he offers the best understanding of the "exceptional nature of liberal pacification." Doyle claims that Kant argues that "Perpetual Peace will be guaranteed by the ever-widening acceptance of three 'definitive articles' of peace."[24] Doyle makes the intriguing claim that it is the very indistinctness of Kant's projection of conflict creating the conditions for the emergence of republicanism that is one of its more important features:

> [T]he argument is so indistinct as to serve only as a very general hypothesis that mobilizing self-interested individuals into the political life of states in an insecure world will eventually engender pressures for republican participation. Kant needs no more than this to suggest that republicanism and a liberal peace are possible (and thus a moral obligation). If it is possible, then sometime over the course of history it may be inevitable.[25]

The emergence of republics is important because they foster both rational self-interest and a culture based on the recognition of rights and caution in the conduct of foreign policy, thereby enabling the emergence of the moral foundations for the liberal peace. The development of cosmopolitan law also "permits the 'spirit of commerce' sooner or later to take hold of every nation, thus impelling states to promote peace and to try to avert war."[26] In the second part of the article, Doyle admits a certain amount of doubt about the Kantian project in the contemporary age when he claims "the Kantian logic of war [as an educative force] may find itself supplanted by a nuclear logic of destruction. . . . a great and long depression or a runaway inflation could create the conditions that lead to authoritarian or totalitarian regimes. . . . technological progress that lowered the costs of transport and that developed rapidly and unevenly—together encouraging international trade—could change direction."[27] It is only if we assume that "these setbacks do not emerge" that the pressure for peace, operating through transnational and international channels, will achieve its ends. It is clear then that in Doyle's analysis perpetual peace is not guaranteed as it is susceptible to major and potentially terminal reverses.

As democratic peace theory has progressed since Doyle's decisive intervention, it has become significantly less interested in Kant per se and more concerned with the empirical proposition that liberal democratic states do not fight each other. To the extent that Kant features, for example in the non-Doyle penned contributions to the important volume *Debating the Democratic Peace*, it is merely as a seedbed for propositions that may be tested against the historical record. The arguments of Bruce Russett in favor of the democratic peace thesis and of Christopher Layne against it are both couched in the language and logic of contemporary American social science.[28] This language and logic, however, are not the language or logic that underpins Kant's analysis. Kant's projection of perpetual peace is not subject to the historical-empirical tests proposed by either the supporters or opponents of DPT. Kant did not think that testing claims against the historical record was a sound basis for making claims about the *possibility* of perpetual peace in the future because human history cannot provide the basis for such an argument. In effect, Kant removes perpetual peace from history by locating it "countless generations" in the future. Kant's appeal is not to history and experience but rather to reason and an abstractly conceived future; his argument, therefore, is, in his own words, chiliastic not experiential or evidential.[29] Any historical analysis in Kant's view is contingent and inherently unreliable as the "progress" made in any historical period is potentially prone to reversion. For Kant, only arguments derived from a practical perspective may legitimately be deployed in relation to the achievement of perpetual peace; when history is invoked it is a history written backwards from an ideal point in the future. DPT is an important research program in its own right, but it is quite separate and distinct from Kant's philosophical consideration of the conditions and circumstances required for perpetual peace. Even Doyle, perhaps the most sophisticated and textually sensitive of Kant's DPT readers, is guilty of taking those parts of Kant's projects that are attractive to twentieth-century liberal IR theorists, the definitive articles of *Toward Perpetual Peace*, and largely ignoring the remainder of Kant's project.[30] The problem, as John Macmillan correctly identifies, is that "as the Democratic Peace discovered Kant it also rewrote him, which is to say it provided a fresh interpretation of his thought and his legacy in the light of the research agenda's own core concerns."[31] As this book is concerned with Kant's normative theory of IR, I do not deal from this point onward with the largely positivist DPT literature.[32]

Kant and Cosmopolitanism

Unlike democratic peace theory, cosmopolitanism does not have a clear moment of crystallization like Doyle's article. The process by which it gained prominence was slower and less obvious—cosmopolitanism seeped into IR from numerous points, e.g., law, sociology, and political theory, forming an inchoate trend as opposed to a distinct research agenda.[33] Cosmopolitanism is therefore much more amorphous, and Kant's role within it is more ambiguous than within the DPT literature. It is possible, however, to trace a distinct Kantian stream within the wider cosmopolitan discourse: as Robert Fine and Robert Cohen state, Kant's "ideas have become a focus of contemporary study among those who see a need to revive the idea of cosmopolitanism for our own age."[34] Opponents of cosmopolitanism, e.g., David Harvey, also begin with Kant "because his inspiration for the contemporary approach to cosmopolitanism is impossible to ignore."[35]

A large part of this stream of Kantian cosmopolitanism is dominated by the impact of John Rawls and his followers' interpretation of Kant.[36] Rawls's primary significance to the understanding of Kant's role as a forebear of cosmopolitanism lies in his method of dealing with Kant's legacy for political theory. For Rawls, Kant's ideas are to be understood in terms of how they may be employed in the service of theory formation as opposed to how they relate to each other. Rawls is also interested in a small number of Kant's texts that he considers relevant to moral philosophy. Rawls is indifferent toward or actively distances himself from large parts of Kant's wider philosophy: in Michael Sandel's memorable description, Rawls wanted to save Kant's system by replacing "Germanic obscurities with a domesticated metaphysic less vulnerable to the charge of arbitrariness and more congenial to the Anglo-American temper."[37] According to Rawls, one can best use Kant's concepts by identifying their core qualities and dispensing with those elements that are not "essential," a position best exemplified in "A Kantian Conception of Equality":

> Much depends on what one counts as essential. Kant's view is marked by a number of dualisms, in particular the dualisms between the necessary and the contingent, form and content, reason and desire, and noumena and phenomena. To abandon these dualisms as he meant them is, for many, to abandon what is distinctive in his theory. I believe otherwise. His moral conception has a characteristic structure that is more clearly discernible when these dualisms are not taken in the sense he gave them but reinterpreted and their moral force reformulated within the scope of an empirical theory.[38]

Rawls expands on this theme in "Kant's Moral Constructivism" in which he argues that "the adjective 'Kantian' expresses analogy and not identity; it means roughly that a doctrine resembles Kant's in enough fundamental respects so that it is closer to his view than to other traditional moral conceptions that are appropriate for use as benchmarks of comparison."[39] In Rawls's account of

Kant, the parts of Kant's theory are akin to building blocks—separable and possible to reassemble in novel configurations. Rawls chooses not to see the parts as indispensable and inseparable from a wider Kantian theory of mankind and its place in the universe. The contemporary Kantian can take what is "useful" from the component parts and apply it within a new framework. The problem from the critical perspective in relation to Rawls's efforts is that such an approach produces a "Kant" shorn of much of his philosophical power pressed into the service of an ideologically driven theory of society: "Rawls draws upon Kant's moral philosophy to help to underpin a particular vision of the just society. In doing this, Rawls neither acknowledges the radical ambiguities of Kant's attempts to legitimate the claims of reason in theory and practice, nor seriously challenges the presumptions of liberal social democracy."[40]

Rawls's somewhat elastic and avowedly selective reading of Kant is also typical of his former student Thomas Pogge's interpretation and employment of Kantian themes in international political theory. Like Rawls, Pogge is unafraid to propose amendments to aspects of Kant's thought that he finds problematic, or which conflict with the "essentials" as perceived by Pogge. Pogge attempts to resolve ambiguities within Kant's texts and is prepared to advocate positions that Kant ultimately rejects, e.g., the establishment of a world state.[41] Pogge proposes replacing Kant's sovereign power system with a global juridical order in which "world law would reflect democratic procedures rather than the distribution of power among national governments."[42] Rawls's doubts about the ability of Kant's philosophy, and especially his metaphysics, to provide part of the basis for practical liberal politics feed into Pogge's attempts to engage with the *Rechtslehre* as a juridical, rational program for liberal government independent of his moral philosophy.[43] Pogge presents Kant almost as a pragmatist, involved in the creation of "practical rules" designed to be applied in a human, political context, hence for Pogge "Kant's question is not whether I can will my maxim to be universally available in any context, but whether I can will this in our world, against the background of the actual laws of nature."[44] The realm of ends serves as the basis for a model world order for Pogge in which each person's moral agency is that of an "ideal rational legislator" and as such part of a "possible harmonious community of human beings pursuing their material ends."[45] In this sense, the categorical imperative is not just a formal principle of moral logic but a prescription for moral and political reformation, which has the effect of greatly reducing moral indeterminacy.[46] Yet this prescription is limited, it is not a design for life, it is not "a real social world to be brought about"; rather, it is a "vivid image designed to secure a unified structure for the individual agent's will."[47]

Pogge presents his idea of cosmopolitanism as an idea for gradual global institutional reform based on the idea of dispersing sovereignty in a multilayered scheme, "in which the political authority currently exercised by national governments is both constrained and dispersed over several layers, and in which economic justice is institutionalized at the global level and thus inescapable."[48] The distinctness of Pogge's project from that of Kant is evident from the lack of reference to Kant's work in Pogge's article "Cosmopolitanism and Sovereignty." On the few occasions in which Kant is cited or mentioned in this article, Pogge is more often than not distancing his position from that of Kant, particularly in relation to Kant's concept of absolute sovereignty. Rawls and Pogge are clear in their position that they are only interested in certain aspects of Kant's moral and legal theory, and where the other dimensions of his work, e.g., the metaphysical, the political, or the anthropological, conflict with these aspects, they reject or ignore those dimensions as irrelevant to their research agenda.

Charles Beitz is another leading international political theorist indebted to Rawls who makes much of his "Kantian" inheritance. Writing in *Political Theory and International Relations*, Beitz describes his book as "a first attempt to provide a political theory of international relations that is more systematic and more consonant with the empirical situation than traditional views. . . . I characterize such a theory as cosmopolitan (in Kant's sense)."[49] Yet for all that the book is conceived as Kantian, Beitz restricts the connection between cosmopolitanism and Kant to a series of brief references and one important paragraph in the conclusion of his book where he presents cosmopolitanism in terms of a third conception of international morality in addition to Realism and the morality of states:

> Following Kant, we might call this a cosmopolitan conception. It is cosmopolitan in the sense that it is concerned with the moral relations of members of a universal community in which state boundaries have a merely derivative significance. There are no reasons of basic principle for exempting the internal affairs of states from external moral scrutiny, and it is possible that members of some states might have obligations of justice with respect to persons elsewhere.[50]

Beitz rarely engages with or reinterprets Kant; rather, he is gesturing toward a cosmopolitan concept that he links to Kant.[51]

As Sandel has argued in relation to Rawls's use of Kant, the major issue at stake in such an approach is whether or not "Kant's metaphysics are detachable 'surroundings' or inescapable presuppositions of the moral and political aspirations Kant and Rawls share—in short, whether Rawls can have liberal politics without metaphysical embarrassment."[52] In the epilogue of this book, once the intrinsic significance of the metaphysical and theological elements of Kant's theory of IR have been investigated, an assessment will be conducted of "Kantian" cosmopolitanism from which those elements have been largely excised. If metaphysics comprises an *essential* part of Kant's project for perpetual peace, have his contemporary heirs successfully replaced this *pudenda origo* with more "respectable" or reliable foundations? And if they have not, what are the implications for contemporary Kantianism, which claims kinship with Kant but through the filter of Rawls? It may well be the case, as Hans Blumenberg asserts in relation to the theological origins of modern philosophy, that despite its claims to the contrary, cosmopolitanism remains embedded within its "prehistory, which it considers itself to have 'overcome', it is bound to the frame of reference of what it renounces."[53]

Interpretive Strategies in Relation to Kant's Theorization of the International

The issue of how to engage with such an icon animates this book. Of several interpretative strategies two seem the most persuasive. One is to immerse oneself in a "tradition" of Kant scholarship and attempt to locate Kant within it as a touchstone or a source of legitimacy or authority, and thereby to tease out from Kant's work those elements that "speak to" the contemporary concerns of that tradition. The other approach is to regard these traditions with a certain amount of suspicion, to see the source, in this case Kant, as being quite distinct from the theoretical "legacy."[54] For this second strategy one must consider interpreting the original theory as something valuable and important in itself, and that such a theory is distinct from the layers of conceptual accretion that cling to it as discourses coalesce over time. This is not to insist on an antiquarian mummification of theories, to believe that they should remain solely rooted in their historical context. It is in fact the opposite of mummification in that the ideas of a theorist are once again brought out into the open, albeit in a context different to his or her own time and the context in which a tradition places the theorist in relation to its concerns. In this vein, "[o]ne of the advantages of going back to the formulations of Kant and Weber, and staying away from writers such as Habermas, who now so happily celebrate the potentials of modernity," writes R. B. J. Walker, "is that they are far more direct, and honest, about the contradictions that arise from the affirmation of the modern subject. These remain contradictions that ought to be taken very seriously indeed."[55]

Kant's texts are certainly read in both DPT and cosmopolitan traditions primarily in *their* terms rather than his—i.e., they read Kant in terms of a putative ancestry, reading back into Kant their own identity. As a consequence Kant is always rendered as deficient in some respect, and his inheritors as somehow purified of any objectionable or vestigial elements that marred the prototype. A further aspect that they share in common is that they do not adequately address the questions of why and how their projects will succeed in political terms. Kant attempts this by reference to the guarantee of nature and the special role played by rationally justified belief in providence, i.e., a belief that ultimately forces greater than mankind have arranged matters such that the human being will come to accept the insights of both his or her technical practical and pure practical reason and institute a system of peace. Contemporary Kantians do not make recourse to providence, however, and arguably neither DPT nor cosmopolitanism provides an adequate replacement for the role that belief in providence plays. The assumption prevalent among contemporary Kantians is that the solutions to the problems of international politics are to be found in the human being becoming over time more "rational" in political life.[56] This opens up a radical ontological and anthropological disjuncture with Kant's theory, which requires belief in a divine impetus if not direction. Katrin Flikschuh accurately identifies what is at stake in such partial readings of Kant's texts: "doing so can encourage a distorted perception both of Kant's political thought and of contemporary liberalism's relation to it."[57] This is a case in point of what Beate Jahn identifies as the *presentism* of much current interpretation of classical texts in IR theory, which at its worst "entails an unreflected misrepresentation of classical texts as well as of the political issues and intellectual debates at stake in them . . . [and] buries—albeit unconsciously—a more constructive reading of classical authors under layers of 'authoritative' interpretations."[58]

Garrett Wallace Brown's *Grounding Cosmopolitanism* is a good example of best practice within the first interpretative strategy as employed in relation to Kant. This book performs a useful task in that it crystallizes the previously rather nebulous and undeveloped relationship assumed to exist between Kant and cosmopolitanism and places it on a much more secure and firm footing. Brown recognizes that cosmopolitanism is an inchoate and unfixed concept: "there is still considerable confusion regarding what a cosmopolitan stance entails. Although cosmopolitanism is often discussed between academics, it is not always clear what cosmopolitanism is supposed to mean."[59] In this sense Brown's achievement is to go beyond the "passing references" and "obligatory footnotes" that R. B. J. Walker identifies as the hallmarks of a by no means innocent tendency within traditions to "legitimise and circumscribe what counts as proper scholarship."[60] Brown's claim is that "a Kantian form of cosmopolitanism, which is based closely on the works of Kant, can best capture the complexities of a pluralistic global environment while confirming a moral concern for humanity and the normative obligations that we should have towards one another if we are to coexist."[61] Brown's book also has the virtue of making its interpretive stance explicitly clear in that he proposes a "mixed perspective" incorporating exegesis of Kant's texts, but with an overriding commitment to reexamination and reinterpretation of "ambiguous or underdeveloped aspects of Kant's cosmopolitanism in order to provide what could be considered a more coherent and thoroughgoing formulation of Kantian cosmopolitanism."[62] Brown commits to reading Kant in the light of contemporary cosmopolitan theory and indeed makes a virtue of such a reading: "If we were to solely approach the study of Kant as narrow exegesis, to outline what Kant said, the historical context of his work and the logical coherency of his internal philosophy, it would significantly limit his contribution to human knowledge."[63] Brown cleaves to a reading of Kant in which, as Otfried Hoffe claims, "one can still make use of Kant to go beyond Kant."[64]

While recognizing that Brown's position is perfectly acceptable in terms of its own agenda, the important theoretical question from my perspective relates to the remainder of Kant's theory—those parts that either do not serve or that embarrass contemporary Kantians. Are these unwanted parts irrelevant or do they potentially present difficulties in that they are essential to the success of those parts of Kant's work that *are* attractive to contemporary theorists, but which are ontologically, epistemologically, or normatively unacceptable to the theorist who has taken what he or she requires? As a consequence of this problem of the remainder, and a general suspicion of "traditions" of thought, this book follows the second interpretive strategy in that it is committed to returning to Kant's texts in order to distil from them a sense of his approach to the theorization of international politics.[65] I am not claiming to present the *sole* possible truth about Kant and IR as such a claim would not be feasible. This is not to state, however, that all truths are equally valid—it is incumbent on any interpreter to present to the reader a justification of her interpretation and to explain why he or she should persist with this text as opposed to any other reading. Insofar as this project is worthwhile its benefit lies in the sense that it offers a wider and deeper and more holistic engagement with Kant than has been the case in the dominant theories relating to his work in IR and international political theory.

Rather than seek to remove the ambiguities and ambivalences of Kant's writings, I think it is imperative to explore them in order to understand what he considered to be the limits of his theory of IR (insofar as the term IR applies) and how he proposed that those limits might be transcended. Exegesis and interpretation do not have to be narrow; they can instead be revolutionary, as in the works of Friedrich Nietzsche. A radical exegesis can form the means by which Kant's texts can still speak to contemporary Kantian cosmopolitans, for example, but not necessarily in a manner with which they would agree, or to ends that they would endorse.

The aim of this book therefore is not primarily to place Kant in the context of how he is understood in International Relations theory or international political theory, but rather to develop a greater understanding of what *Kant* writes about international relations and politics. Only as a corollary objective do I intend to explore the implications of his thought for the contemporary cosmopolitanism that identifies him as a source for its endeavors. This project requires an interdisciplinary focus that encompasses Kant's ethics, politics, psychology, aesthetics, anthropology, and theology. I argue that understanding Kant's thought on peace and cosmopolitanism in the context of his wider project on the nature of the human being and its potential for moral reformation or social progress, or both, provides a clearer idea about the potential and limits of his theory than cherry-picking elements of his thought and putting them to work in the service of contemporary theory. The interpretation of Kant offered in this book is, therefore, one based on reclamation and theoretical reorientation. The method employed was inspired by the humanist ideal of returning *ad fontes*. The fundamental idea of this approach is to ask from "whence can one draw a draught so pure, so easy, and so delightful as from the very fountainhead."[66] In short, one of the primary aims of the book is to return to an engagement (albeit in translation) with Kant rather than to approach Kant through the "schools" of thought that, in accordance with their respective dogmas, have promoted their interpretation of Kant's legacy. A return to Kant is important because, as Michael C. Williams has argued, works like *Toward Perpetual Peace* are "systematically grounded in Kant's critical philosophy, but this is a foundation unfamiliar to many students of international relations. This has led not only to serious misconceptions regarding Kant's writings on international politics, but also to the general acceptance of confused or ill-founded interpretations of his position."[67]

Once one accepts that "[f]irst and foremost, however, recourse must be had to the sources themselves," the task becomes a matter of how to engage with those sources, in this case Kant.[68] My intention is not to offer a narrowly historical but rather a critical-historical interpretation: in this I follow Nietzsche's observation that "one takes more pleasure in a work, is more astonished by it, and learns more from it" if one reads it as a living text unbound from its time of origin. The return to the source is not a task of restoring "purity" or garnering the "truth" of Kant as he "intended" it. As Karl Löwith states, "History has time and again to be recovered and rediscovered by the living generations. We understand—and misunderstand—ancient authors, but always in the light of contemporary thought, reading the book of history backward from the last to the first page."[69] The onus is on the reader to engage with the text creatively and, in the engagement, to offer something beyond the accepted wisdom, i.e., to use Löwith's formulation, from the last page of the established reading of Kant to the writings of Kant himself.[70] Blumenberg expresses well the critical ethos that underpins the research undertaken in this book: "To see what has become self-evident as something that was not originally self-evident is the task of all historical reflection."[71] This critical commitment is not so much a licence to read a thinker like Kant according to one's own needs, but rather to read the texts concerned with an eye to the relationships between the ideas that underpin those texts, and not necessarily as the author intended. In this sense I am in agreement with Martin Heidegger: "With any philosophical knowledge in general, what is said in uttered propositions must not be decisive. Instead, what must be decisive is what it sets before our eyes as still unsaid, in and through what has been said."[72] Like Heidegger I consider the decisive task of interpretation to be "the working-out of a problem," which is achieved by making the problem visible through the "recollection of Kant."[73] The problem worked out in this text is that of Kant's use of providence and related concepts within his treatment of IR. Why is Kant concerned with justification of providence "in the course of the world"?[74] What is it about Kant's philosophy that compels him to this and similar statements? The answer, I suggest, emerges from a commitment to reading across the corpus of Kant's texts: Kant requires belief in providence because the revelation of the repetitive operation of the mechanism of nature and the meaninglessness of mankind's existence within its confines distresses him to such a point that he has no other recourse than to sacrifice this knowledge to make room for a salvific faith that is only accessible beyond the limits of the understanding and technical practical reason.

I argue that to concentrate on a single part of Kant's work, e.g., elements of his moral theory, without reference to his wider theorization of the human being as a political, anthropological, aesthetic, teleological, and also a theological entity is to miss a large part of Kant's thought on the potential development of international society. It is Kant's ability to develop a holistic, wide view of mankind that qualifies him as an IR theorist of the first rank. In this respect I agree with Jean Elshtain's observation that "Kant's minor works, including his explicit political treatises, must be evaluated with reference to the main body of his thought if one is coherently to reconstruct the inner logic of Kant's arguments by determining how he ties together anthropological, epistemological, moral, and political concerns."[75] Kant's level of analysis is the human species, which he develops in relation to his philosophy of history, with the effect that Kant provides both an unflinching assessment of power politics as they existed (and at least in part, continue to exist) and a solution to the war problem, as well as attempting to develop a more positive concept of peace as more than the mere absence of war. As introduced in the first chapter and developed throughout the book, Kant's distinction between human beings and humanity is the pivotal move that allowed him to both confront the realities of global politics and to promote a reformation of global politics in the image of his philosophical project.

Outline of the Argument

The argument of the book begins with Kant's fundamental distinction between human beings as they *appear to be* to each other and humanity as it ought to be according to the insights of rational morality derived by Kant from the principles of the three critiques and his moral theory. Kant argues that self-interested human beings acting according to the technical practical reason of prudence have a moral obligation to conduct themselves as far as possible as members of the autonomous, moral, and rational species of humanity. This reorientation of self (or perception of self), mind, and society, however, is undermined by the human being's atavistic tendencies toward animality. In attempting to confront the barriers to progress, Kant represents human nature *as it appears to be* in opposition to his theory of human nature as it *ought to be*. Kant's political and international theory is the product of this fundamental distinction between his pessimistic analysis of the *human being* and his optimism that *humanity* as a species ought to be, and therefore can be, redeemed by reason. Kant's efforts to develop a theory of mankind's salvation revolve around whether or not human beings can be reformed, by what means, to what extent, and to what ends. Assessing Kant's success as a theorist of IR is in large part an exercise in determining the viability of the means and the extent to which he proposes to narrow the gap between human beings and humanity.

The second chapter examines Kant's arguments in relation to the potential reform of human beings according to the ideal of humanity as expressed in the *Critique of the Power of Judgment*. Kant makes the human mind itself an essential theater in the conflict between the natural and the rational. The argument put forward by Kant is that within the wider faculty of cognition there operates a faculty of understanding, which makes sense of the world by reference to technical practical principles, including prudence as the technical practical means to understand the *art* of politics, and a faculty of reason that reveals the rational laws of freedom. The faculty of the power of judgment is an intermediary faculty that allows "the transition from the domain of the concept of nature to that of the concept of freedom."[76] The faculty of the power of judgment enables this transition by systematization through the *assumption* of purposiveness in nature. The power of judgment legitimizes the recourse to faith and justified belief, especially in the absence of ontological certainty. To propose that purpose and order may be imputed to nature also enables the claim that this order is the result of an "artist's hand." Kant argues that although the determining power of judgment cannot assert this as *fact*, the reflective power of judgment can, and indeed must, make this claim, as otherwise existence would be meaningless—a condition of being Kant finds intolerable. Bridging the gap between nature and reason has to proceed from *belief* in God in order to determine the end of nature. This end is revealed to be the ideal of humanity— although it must be stressed that this is an end to be believed, not known. Kant does not make an ontological claim at this point (i.e., he cannot claim that this ideal will be achieved), rather he posits his resolution in the terms of the more permissive, but still necessary, category of belief.

The focus of the third chapter is Kant's most important political text: *Toward Perpetual Peace*—a work that in many respects is a sequel to themes explored in the *Critique of the Power of Judgment*. If the *Critique of the Power of Judgment* argues the possibility of human evolution in general terms, *Toward Perpetual Peace* offers a much more precise and narrowly political account of how this process might play out in the international context. The argument of this chapter is that Kant recasts the difficulty he encounters as a moral theorist, i.e., the human being's reliance on technical practical reason and its attendant politics of power and confrontation, as the foundation and impetus for perpetual peace and the possible achievement of a cosmopolitan order. Kant in effect offers two phases on the path to perpetual peace: first, he highlights the powerful technical-practical incentives to peace, rooted in self-interest, fear of death, and desire for commercial gain; second, Kant argues that pure practical reason also promotes a more positive peace, one based in moral, rights-based legislation affecting all elements of human life. These competing impetuses to peace are brought together in Kant's scheme by his teleological projection of a point in time when both push and pull incentives might force mankind into establishing genuine peace. This teleology, however, requires faith for *practical* (not ontological) reasons—Kant's projection of a harmonious order requires belief in an orderer, "a being who rules the world according to reason and moral laws." Belief in God is necessary because without such belief human existence would be meaningless and there would be no incentive to achieve goals established by rational morality. This chapter is a gateway to the rest of the book in that the centrality of anthropology and theology are revealed as essential to understanding Kant's attempt to narrow the gap between human beings and humanity in that analysis of Kant's political philosophy lays bare its central problem, i.e., that without faith human beings are restricted to the status of political animals that cannot be expected to transcend or escape their environments. The problem is revealed to be anthropological, and the putative solution to be theological in nature.

The fourth chapter engages in more detail with Kant's writings on anthropology in order to determine to what extent Kant considers mankind *capable* of reform within the limited autonomy granted to it, a capacity that is crucial to the success of Kant's theory of global politics. Kant locates this reform not in a discourse of rights but of experience. The starting point of Kant's anthropology is the "deep abasement" of human nature—Kant claims that good men are few in number. Surprisingly perhaps in the light of his moral theory, Kant considers this a political *positive* in that the pursuit of self-interest is the key to human progress. Only over time, as the capacity for comprehension changes nature from empirical to reflective cognition, can a reform of human beings potentially occur. Kant develops a theory of politics based on "illusions," especially the illusions of civility, propriety, and politeness. It is this illusion of civilization that enables the eventual emergence of at least some genuine element of civil society. Eventually, after the passage of countless generations' suffering, Kant *hopes* a cosmopolitan system will be established. This hope is underwritten by belief in a plan of nature initiated by a wise creator of which man is the beneficiary. The historical record offers no hope for Kant, so he appeals instead to a chiliastic vision of the future in which successive civilizations rise and fall, but leave behind enough to act as a step in a speculative progressive history written from the cosmopolitan future backwards into the past and present. The positive role of human beings in securing this future lies in their ability to foster culture and civilization through education, but even education is subject to a paradox based in human insufficiency that can only be resolved ultimately by belief in "education from above."

The final chapter brings to the fore the theology that underpins the argument of the rest of the book. The importance of belief in God is a crucial theme of Kant's ethics, politics, aesthetics, teleology, and anthropology. The only theme that secures anywhere near as much attention as the necessity of belief in God is the insufficiency of the human being and what may be hoped in terms of its reformation. These two themes predominate in Kant's writings on theology, especially *Religion within the Boundaries of Mere Reason* and the *Conflict of the Faculties*. Kant's thoughts on evil in human nature bring into focus his ambivalence regarding the possible moral development of human beings and their reorientation toward humanity—a revolutionary shift in species perception that he admits is "inexplicable." Kant argues that the existence of "radical evil" as an innate propensity in human nature may be overcome, but only through "a revolution in the disposition of the human being."[77] The restoration of what Kant argues is the human being's more fundamental, original predisposition to good is the focus of Kant's theology as directed toward the human being. The crux of the issue is, however, whether or not the human being is capable of effecting this restoration. Kant comes to the conclusion that the magnitude of this problem is too great for the means of human beings on their own in that "[t]o found a moral people of God is, therefore, a work whose execution cannot be hoped for from human beings but only from God himself."[78] Belief in the existence of God then becomes a crucial issue not simply in theology but also in political and ethical terms.

Kant's Theorization of International and Cosmopolitan Politics as Political Theology

Kant's biographical details reveal a complex, ambivalent relationship to religion and theology. Born into a Pietist family in 1724, Kant credited his devout parents with inculcating within him a strong respect for morality, asserting "late in his life that the education he received from them 'could not have been better when considered from the moral point of view.'"[79] Kant's experience of formal Pietist education, however, was less positive. Kant resented the fanaticism of his teachers and the "terror and fear" they inspired, but also recognized that the education he received was "useful and not objectionable."[80] Kant certainly seems to have thoroughly rejected Pietism, and according to his friend Pörschke in his old age he lost faith in Christian dogma.[81] Yet this is the same philosopher who could write to Heinrich Jung-Stilling in 1789: "it is quite right of you to seek in the Gospels the final satisfaction of your striving for secure foundation of wisdom and hope, since that book is an everlasting guide to true wisdom, one that not only agrees with a Reason which has completed her speculations but also sheds new light on the whole field surveyed by that reason, illuminating what still remains opaque to it."[82] Kant's attempt to rescue the grounds of belief from ecclesiastical obscurantism in *Religion within the Boundaries of Mere Reason*, his consistent employment of theological ideas, and insistence on the importance of belief demonstrate that, although his personal Christian faith might have diminished or even vanished in the end, these elements are essential within the overall Kantian system. God may or may not exist, but belief in God is essential to hold together the various parts of Kant's social and political theory. Whether God is "real" or "virtual" is of secondary importance for Kant; what is crucial is that belief in God is necessary.

The extent to which belief in God plays such a central role in Kant's analysis of political and international interaction came as something of a surprise, as most contemporary readings of Kant tend to ignore or deny the significance of the relationship between Kant and the divine. Nietzsche's reference to Kant as a "cunning Christian" in *Twilight of the Idols* was, however, a partial steer to my eventual conclusions. In *The Anti-Christ*, Nietzsche attributes Kant's significance to his articulation of "a secret path to the old ideal," the previous faith; "Kant's success," he claims, "is merely a theologian's success."[83] In IR and international political theory, few have made much of the connection between Kant's theology and his politics. David Boucher dedicates a small part of his analysis of Kant to the importance of God in that he claims that "the presupposition of the rational providence of God, or nature, in a non-naturalistic sense, permeates the whole of his philosophy."[84] Howard Williams also identifies the importance of the role played by a divinity (not necessarily the Christian deity): "Only by an act of divine grace for which there is no empirical evidence can we hope finally to attain eternal peace. The supposition of divine grace is not one which flows from the facts but rather one that is required as a necessity of our moral inclinations."[85] The prevalence of God across Kant's various attempts at understanding the human being suggests that his work may best be understood as a species of political theology.

Mark Lilla's depiction of political theology as "a primordial form of human thought," which provides a "deep well of ideas and symbols for organizing society and inspiring action," expresses the powerful hold that theological concepts still have on political theory.[86] While acknowledging that modern "political philosophy is not religious today, nor is it exclusively or even primarily concerned with the social effects of religion," Lilla argues that "[r]eligion, however, is its original problematic." In this context, "Kant provided an utterly novel account of religious experience and its relation to politics."[87] Reading Kant's IR theory as political theology opens the connections between ethics, politics, anthropology, and aesthetics in his work. The concept of political theology is useful in that if Kant's politics are a function of his moral philosophy, then political theology is a means by which both may be understood in relation to each other in the context of a theological understanding of the universe, and, in theory at least, reconciled as dual aspects of an eschatological mode of thought.

It is illustrative to contrast Kant's political theology with that of Carl Schmitt, who is often credited with developing political theology as a specifically modern concept.[88] Schmitt's political theology revolves around the idea that "all significant concepts of the modern theory of the state are secularized theological concepts." This is historical, both in the sense of a conceptual role transfer, e.g., the omnipotence of God being transferred to the omnipotence of the sovereign lawmaker, and in terms of the deep "systematic structures" of theological concepts playing an important role in the development of modern theories of politics.[89] Schmitt makes the claim that in the case of Jean-Jacques

Rousseau, for example, the "politicization of theological concepts is so striking that it has not escaped any true expert on his writings."[90]

Schmitt's own political theology is particularly unpleasant, as befitted a future *Kronjurist* of the Third Reich.[91] For Schmitt, the sovereign is "he who decides on the exception." In this decisionist reading of political life, all things revolve around authority and especially the authority to make direct interventions in political and legal systems. Drawing on both Thomas Hobbes and the Spanish Catholic theorist Juan Donoso Cortés, Schmitt concludes that law is ultimately derived from authority: *Autoritas, non veritas facit legem.*[92] In Schmitt's analysis the sovereign ought to be absolute, a secular mirror image of God. Cortés's recognition of the death of kingship as a concept becomes for Schmitt the metaphysical context in which the embrace of dictatorship is legitimate.

Kant's political theology is more complex than Schmitt's apologia for dictatorship.[93] In Schmitt's terms, Kant exhibits aspects of both the rationalist tendency, "which ignores the exception," and the "natural law tendency which is interested in the emergency and emanates from an essentially different set of ideas."[94] Kant as a theorist of humanity is a rationalist, while Kant as a theorist of human beings is closer to being a natural law theorist, although in many respects he is harsher in his analysis of mankind than the members of a tradition he described as being no more than "sorry comforters." Kant is a rationalist in Schmitt's terms as he wishes to ignore the exception, or excise it by depoliticizing political life by means of legislation, as Schmitt writes: "[e]mergency law was no law at all for Kant."[95] God is necessary as a supreme legislator—the author of both the physical *and* the moral laws of the universe. The machine does not start by itself in Kant's analysis: mankind must believe that God has designed and given impetus to a creation that has man's redemption as its culmination. In this sense it may be useful to understand Kant's conception of God as a constitution writer of the moral law—involved in the creation of the rules of the system, but not responsible for directly overseeing the system, which explains why the system does not conform to the rational ideal. God should be believed in as a lawmaker, not as a law enforcer. It is mankind's responsibility to realize the law. It may be useful to consider Kant a deist in terms of the operation of the mechanism of nature (of which human beings are merely an unremarkable part) and as a theist in terms of the critical and practical philosophy in which it is to be believed that God has provided for our salvation as an integral part of purposive nature.

In relation to the technical practical reason of the natural world, Kant accepts the validity of politics (domestic and international) based on sovereign, decisionist power—that authority, not truth, makes the law. This, however, is a provisional arrangement rooted in the power of the sovereign, which is necessary to maintain civil order. Regarding how humanity ought to be, Kant wishes to remove the exceptional power of the sovereign, to remove arbitrariness by subjection to the law—to institute in effect Rousseau's dictum, that society should "imitate the immutable decrees of the divinity." Kant's is also a political theology of the legislator, or the idea of legislation, and not the sovereign in that it is based on removing the exception, rather than deciding it. In this sense, Kant's is a political theology of salvation through reason. Kant's is a political theology that depends on acknowledging, but ultimately removing, the political from politics. In this sense, Kant's exercises in teleology, as explored in *Perpetual Peace* and other works, are understood as eschatology, a study of the end of the current world (the natural world) and the contemplation of the next (the pure practical world): as Jacob Taubes observes, "the metaphysical statements of Christian eschatology become the as ifs of the transcendental eschatology" that undergirds their formulation.[96] The human being is an insufficient entity as currently constituted. Reason allows the human being to grasp both its insufficiency and the means to secure the eventual salvation of the species by realizing its humanity, thus fulfilling its role as the end of nature. Jürgen Moltmann stresses that "Kant was aware that the fundamental ideas of the teleological philosophy of history—development, progress, goal—were derived from the salvation-history theology of chiliasm, and are translations of salvific plan, economy of salvation, world aeon, and the reign of Christ as the completion of history," even to the extent that Kant "saw the French Revolution as a 'historical sign' of the inherent moral trend of the human race towards improvement, and an eschatological sign of the times which he described in Thomist sacramental terminology as a *signum prognosticum.*"[97] God therefore is the artist, nature the medium, and the humanity immanent within the human being the artistic product of God's design. In this light, Simon Critchley is correct in his assessment that Kant does not simply secularize, but rather transforms the sacred: "What occurs in Rousseau and Kant is not some assertion of the secular. It is rather a metamorphosis of the meaning of the sacred."[98] Whether the process is one of secularization or metamorphosis, the implication is clear: Kant derives the bases of his thought from theology. A political-theological reading restores God to the center of Kant's project in the sense that belief in God acts as a foundational part of his *practical* philosophy. Belief in God enables Kant to resolve his politics and ethics in the idea of a purposeful nature and a rational morality emanating from the same source and by doing so adds meaning to existence: it is in this sense that Lilla is correct in observing that "[a] century after Hobbes, Kant found a way of returning theology to the center of political thought."[99] Perhaps the most important aspect of Kant's political theology to Kant himself is that it allowed him to confront, and in part repudiate (at least to his own satisfaction), what he saw as David Hume's projection of nature as a mere fecund cause, what Kant calls *Natura Bruta*, and the prospect of humans existing forever within a universe dictated by "hopelessly playing chance."

A political-theological reading of Kant also allows us to understand Kant's transposition of Christian theological concepts and structures into deistic or theistic forms and the later transposition of Kant's concepts and structures into a contemporary liberal, secular form. The latter in particular is a process of de-theologization, which according to Schmitt also implies a depoliticization of life.[100] This de-theologization, however, proceeds without regard for the past, as those committed to formulating concepts do so without sufficient regard for the foundations of their theory, and those older parts of the new discourse will be caught up in its progress and either consumed within the new or "ignored as unusable or annihilated as invalid."[101] It is for this reason that Schmitt claims that the "transposition from the old political theology into a pretentious and totally new, purely secular and humane humanity needs to be watched closely and critically."[102] This is all the more necessary in the case of contemporary Kantian approaches that eschew the metaphysical and theological aspects of Kant's work as "[a]ll de-theologised concepts carry the weight of their scientifically impure origins," whether they wish to or not.[103] Understanding these transpositions allows us to understand the problematic association of Kant with cosmopolitanism. By cleaving to Kant's project, however remotely, the cosmopolitans unwittingly commit themselves to the labyrinth composed by the deep theological structures of thought that lay in Kant's mind; they operate in the ruins of his metaphysics and anthropology, but cannot properly escape this terrain because they do not recognize that it forms part of their own theoretical landscape. God is in the very grammar of DPT and cosmopolitan theories of IR—although they lack the necessary insight to recognize the importance of this aspect of their inheritance from Kant. The cosmopolitan order is an attempted secularization of the idea of the New Jerusalem, and cosmopolitanism its faith.

If cosmopolitanism is a faith, and Kant its problematic prophet, then the remainder of his philosophy *is* important. Of particular significance is the question of the guarantee of perpetual peace. As part of the transposition from Kant to "Kantianism" the nature of the guarantee changes from an explicit and specific invocation of providence in the case of Kant to an implicit assumption that the guarantee of perpetual peace is within the gift of human beings or simply a product of the operation of the mechanism of nature. The Kantian simultaneous avowal/disavowal of Kant here opens a problem as Kant rejects the possibility of humans achieving the transition to perpetual peace solely by their own power—they require faith in God in order to realize their humanity and transform society in the fundamental manner Kant espouses.

Kant then becomes a problem for the Kantians. The project of perpetual peace is a question of *which* agency one chooses to believe in—is this process underwritten by faith in God or is it within the capacities of the human being alone? If it is to be restricted to the human being alone, what factor can replace Kant's faith in God as the deus ex machina to be appealed to or invoked at those crucial moments when the system threatens to break down due to human insufficiency? Kant's own writings leave little room for doubt: left to their own *natural* devices, human beings by themselves are simply incapable of achieving peace other than the "negative" peace constituted by the absence of war, i.e., a peace that is contingent and unstable at best, and degenerate at worst. It is only by means of a moral reformation, underwritten by belief in providence, that perpetual peace in the fullest sense, according to Kant, can be achieved. Contemporary Kantianism has forgotten, or chooses to ignore, that one of Kant's primary representations of cosmopolitanism is that of an all-unifying *church* triumphant.

An additional critique derived from political theology that may be directed at both Kant and the Kantians is that the idea of perpetual peace itself may be merely a product of the "immensely polymorphous realm of political theology," which Schmitt states "contains naïve projections, numinous fantasies, reflective reductions of the unknown to something that is known, analogies between being and appearances, ideological superstructure over substructure."[104] In other words, the project of perpetual peace may be nothing more than a political-theological mirage.

It is important to stress that I am not endorsing Schmitt's political theology with its varying emphases on apocalyptic confrontation and *katechontic* restraint over Kant's political theology of eventual salvation by reason.[105] My aim instead is to highlight that both are political-theological thinkers and by doing so to confront the political-theological legacy of Kant's vision—a legacy, like that of Schmitt's, that may be read as rooted in "totalizing projections" and as "reductive and excessively foundational."[106] One can legitimately ask whether or not Kant's political theology, rooted in his almost mystical metaphysics, does not fall prey to what Ernst Kantorowicz identifies as "the danger" inherent in any mysticism, i.e., "of losing its spell or becoming quite meaningless when taken out of its native surroundings, its time and its space," all the more so when the elements of this political theology are used by his successors in a less than careful manner.[107] To move forward it is necessary not to ignore the political-theological nature of Kant's work but to understand it, and only after the acknowledgment of its importance to Kant can we confront the ultimate problem: Without belief in God, is there any *compelling* incentive to act in the political sphere other than according to pure self-interest or in satisfaction of our emotional or instinctual desires?

CHAPTER 1

Unholy Human Beings and Holy Humanity in Kant's Critical and Practical Philosophy

> A human being is indeed unholy enough but the *humanity* in his person must be holy to him.[1]

To begin to understand the positions undertaken by Kant in his IR-relevant works such as *Toward Perpetual Peace*, one must first recognize that these essays are products of a much wider project, i.e., Kant's advocacy of a reorientation of mankind's perception of itself. This chapter concerns itself with what might be called the anthropological implications of the critical philosophy, which in turn lay the ground for Kant's political and international theory. In the reading offered here, I employ "mankind" when referring to the human race as a whole without any attribution of a moral or political character. Following Kant's distinction, the term "human beings" is used in instances where Kant details how members of the human race view each other within the "sensible world" of the mechanism of nature, i.e., primarily as politically prudent, self-seeking actors. "Humanity" is mankind viewed in terms of its moral character, i.e., without reference to the impulses and incentives that pertain to the mechanism of nature.

The anthropological implications of the critical philosophy eventually find themselves at the heart of Kant's project. In *The Critique of Pure Reason* Kant claims that "[a]ll the interests of my reason, speculative as well as practical" combine in three questions: "1. What can I know? 2. What ought I to do? 3. What may I hope?"[2] Kant claims that the *Critique* itself answers the first question as far as possible. The second question relates to the "purely practical," which Kant deals with primarily in *The Groundwork* and *The Critique of Practical Reason*. The answer to the third question is tied to the second, i.e., what can I *hope* for, if I do that which I *ought* to do? Kant maintains that the answer is both practical and theoretical, reflecting both morality and interest, in that hope is directed toward achieving happiness, which is best attained by allowing hope to arrive at the conclusion "that *something is* (which determines the ultimate possible end) *because something ought to happen*," which is arguably the ultimate basis and justification of the practical philosophy.[3] The importance of the anthropological implications of the critical philosophy becomes clear by the addition in the *Lectures on Logic* (1800) of another pivotal question—"what is man?" This fourth question, Kant stressed, was the *master* question: "[f]undamentally . . . we could reckon all of this anthropology, because the first three questions relate to the last one."[4]

It is in the context of the centrality of the anthropological implications of his philosophy that Kant develops perhaps his single most important political-theological theme: the conjunction of humanity and holiness, and, conversely, that of human beings and unholiness. If political theology can be understood as "the collection of stories we tell ourselves about our nature as humans, our aspirations for order and justice in light of the sacred, and what, thereby, constitutes and limits legitimate rule over our collective lives," then Kant's twofold investigation of mankind, viewed from the standpoints of the profane "human being" and sanctified "humanity," marks him out as perhaps the most significant political theologian of the modern era.[5] The human being/humanity distinction has important implications for Kant's answers to the defining questions relating to what mankind can know, how it ought to act, and for what it may hope. The answers of the human being are distinct in each case from those of humanity. As a participant in the "world of sense," the human being "knows" his or her environment through the use of understanding and technical practical reason. The human being perceives herself and others as acting according to the insights of prudence, a worldview in which the second question, "what ought I to do?," is answerable solely in terms of achieving security and material well-being, while hope is restricted to survival and, at best, the extension of rational self-interest on a universal basis in the political and economic spheres. By contrast, when viewing himself as a citizen of the world of understanding, a member of the rational species humanity can *know* nothing of this world, but is entitled to *think* about its possible foundations and to hope for an ultimate and beneficial arrangement of human affairs derived from pure practical reason. This study begins therefore with Kant's primary task as a political and IR theorist: advocating the reorientation of what it *means* to be human.

Kant's attempt to provide human existence with *meaning* results in a dual reality: mankind is representable *simultaneously* as both humanity and human being, but what are the implications of this discovery? A persistent theme emerges in Kant's work of the requirement for reorientation according to the ideal of humanity: "A human being has a duty to raise himself from the crude state of his nature, from his animality (*quoad actum*), more and more toward humanity."[6] While human beings are unlikely to ever achieve a *total* reorientation, they *can*, and, Kant argues, therefore must, be able to reform themselves sufficiently to attain at least an approximation of humanity. The key question for Kant is then, given the onus on human beings to effect this reform, can they be expected to do so? It is in relation to this point that the second political-theological element of Kant's practical philosophy becomes vital as Kant is quite clear that corrupt and inadequate human beings cannot be expected to achieve this reform without incentives drawn from elsewhere: reason alone will not be enough. Kant finds his incentive in the *belief* that nature is purposive, a purposiveness that in turn is the product of a divine author. It is in the light of this finding that Kant postulates belief in the afterlife, in order to provide human beings with sufficient opportunity to achieve some genuine measure of humanity's perfection. These postulates allow the individual to reach conclusions about himself or herself that are not available to an animal occupying a precarious niche within an indifferent mechanism of nature. It is rational belief, not reason per se, that permits mankind to think of itself as a product of purposive nature and to have faith that its salvation is at the heart of existence.

Existence Viewed from Two Standpoints: The World of Sense and the World of Understanding

In the Transcendental Aesthetic of the *Critique of Pure Reason*, Kant establishes and justifies the division of objects into *phenomena* and *noumena*—and from this distinction derives two ways of thinking about existence: "a world of the senses and a world of the understanding."[7] These "worlds" of sense and understanding are points of mental orientation, or, to employ an ocular analogy, two sets of lenses that provide the mind with two coherent, if very different, perspectives on existence that represent the world according to (respectively) sensible concepts and intellectual ideas.[8] As a consequence of the formulation of these worlds, a rational being "has two standpoints from which he can regard himself and cognize laws for the use of his powers and consequently for all his actions; first, insofar as he belongs to the world of sense, under laws of nature (heteronomy); second, as belonging to the intelligible world, under laws which, being independent of nature, are not empirical but grounded merely in reason."[9] The difficulty for Kant is that within the world of sense all events—including those involving human beings—"stand in thoroughgoing connection in accordance with unchangeable laws of nature."[10] The primary question for Kant is whether or not freedom, the most essential characteristic of rational morality, "is completely excluded by this inviolable rule."[11]

Kant's answer to the question lies in recognizing that freedom is a nonapparent, intellectual *idea* contained *within* an object of appearance (the human being) and hence in the category of the intelligible, not the sensible.[12] Freedom, however, can have effects in the world of sense, which leads Kant to the finding that "[r]egarded as the causality of a thing in itself, it is *intelligible* in its *action*; regarded as the causality of an appearance in the world of sense, it is *sensible* in its *effects*." This leads Kant to an important conclusion, namely that freedom must be thought in two ways: "We should therefore have to form both an empirical and an intellectual concept . . . and to regard both as referring to one and the same effect."[13] Stephen Watson correctly identifies the significance of this *first* phase of Kant's development of the idea of freedom in that the successful resolution of the third antinomy of the *Critique* "discovers the paradigm which will form the structure and limits of the development of the ethical domain."[14] That mankind is free opens the door to the twofold characterization of mankind as being conceivable in terms of both sensible appearance (human beings) and as possessed of intelligible freedom (humanity). In each case, mankind possesses a faculty that allows greater insight into both its phenomenal nature (understanding) and its quite distinct capacity for acting according to its own volition (reason).[15]

The distinction between understanding and reason becomes crucial in relation to the development of practical philosophy (and by extension, Kant's theory of global politics) as the understanding is limited in that it "can know in nature only what is, what has been, or will be. We cannot say that anything in nature ought to be other than what in all these time-relations it actually is. When we have the course of nature alone in view, '*ought*' has no meaning whatsoever."[16] Prudence, a form of thought that incorporates aspects of both the understanding and technical practical reason, typifies the political and natural state of human beings:

> [I]n the precepts of prudence, the whole business of reason consists in uniting all the ends which are prescribed to us by our desires in the one single end, happiness, and in co-ordinating the means for attaining it. In this field, therefore, reason can supply none but pragmatic laws of free action, for the attainment of those ends which are commended to us by the senses; it cannot yield us laws that are pure and determined completely a priori.[17]

It is because of the limits of nature and the understanding that the human intellect seeks to go beyond both—leaving behind knowledge and employing reason instead. Reason itself is divided into two types: technical and pure practical. Technical practical reason—prudence in the political arena—is employed in order to make sense of the natural world and to complete the tasks raised by the understanding's attempts to grasp phenomena. Technical practical reason does this through systematizing the data it receives from the understanding in as complete a manner as possible. This theoretical reason, however, "in its quest for the unconditioned, produces antinomies; in the end, the kind of unconditional explanation that would fully satisfy reason is unavailable." Kant's resolution of the antinomies, away from the search for cause to a perspectival method based on the possibility of considering both the theses and antitheses of the antinomies in terms of causality, opened the door to practical reason, which as Christine Korsgaard notes, "in its quest for justification is subject to no such limitation," and eschews the search for certainty of knowledge in favor of a practical foundation for freedom.[18] "It is the faculty of pure practical reason," according to Eric Sandberg, "which first allows us to consider ourselves from a different point of view and which gives the only possible determinate content to this view of ourselves. . . . there is a whole different order and system of nature in accordance with which we ought to determine our actions in the empirical world."[19] At this stage of his thinking, Kant was content to view *human beings* as essentially being determined from one perspective, but humanity as being free from the other, thus permitting the simultaneous consideration of mankind as it "is" and as it "ought" to be.

The fact that mankind is capable of thinking in terms of "ought" implies that pure practical reason *can* inform human freedom to act in a manner distinct from the dictates of nature and the insights of prudence.[20] This faculty in turn can generate its own set of principles developed according to "the *possibility of experience* . . . such actions as, in accordance with moral precepts, *might* be met with in the *history* of mankind." As reason "does not have causality in respect of nature as a whole . . . [it] cannot give rise to laws of nature"; it is only in the practical realm of morality that "the principles of pure reason have objective reality."[21] Kant was, however, not content to distinguish between the worlds of sense and understanding, or to develop an abstract morality solely for its own sake. Kant is perfectly clear that the intelligible world *can* and *ought* to influence the world of sense:

> This world is so far thought as an intelligible world only. To this extent, there-
> fore, it is a mere idea, though at the same time a practical idea, which really can
> have, as it also ought to have, an influence upon the sensible world, to bring that
> world, so far as may be possible, into conformity with the idea. The idea of a
> moral world has, therefore, objective reality, not as referring to an object of an
> intelligible intuition (we are quite unable to think any such object), but as refer-
> ring to the sensible world, viewed, however, as being an object of pure reason in
> its practical employment, that is, as a *corpus mysticum* of the rational beings in
> it, so far as the free will of each being is, under moral laws, in complete system-
> atic unity with itself and with the freedom of every other.[22]

The idea of the moral world as a *corpus mysticum* of rational beings allows Kant to propose that the human being is "subject to . . . reason, which contains in the idea of freedom the law of the world of understanding," that the individual should think of himself "as subject to the autonomy of the will; consequently the laws of the world of understanding must be regarded as imperatives . . . and actions in conformity with these duties."[23] It must be remembered, however, that the world of understanding remains simply a standpoint "that reason sees itself constrained to take outside appearances in order to think of itself as prac-tical," but this standpoint is necessary for the human being "insofar as he is not to be denied consciousness of himself as an intelligence and consequently as a rational cause active by means of reason, that is, operating freely."[24] We cannot *know* anything about this *pure* world, but it remains "always a useful and per-mitted idea for the sake of a rational belief, even if all knowledge stops at its boundary . . . for producing in us a lively interest in the moral law."[25] In the absence of knowledge, one must turn to faith, or, more precisely, to a rational belief that there exists beyond nature an order and set of rational-moral laws analogous to the laws of nature. The question becomes then, if there is such a law, what would reason have us believe that it would be? In the *Critique of Practical Reason*, Kant argues that the moral law is the "fundamental law of a supersensible nature and of a pure world of the understanding" that requires an approximate counterpart in the "sensible world but without infringing upon its laws."[26] In the absence of direct revelation by intuition, the human mind has to create this approximation to the best of its abilities according to the reason it possesses, but in the context of a sensible environment in which its imperatives do not find a perfect home. It is notable in this context that *Toward Perpetual Peace* endorses a negative surrogate, as opposed to a pure ideal, in order not to infringe upon the laws of sensible nature.

The development of these worlds is the essential backdrop to Kant's theorization of global politics in *Perpetual Peace* and elsewhere. The simultaneous theorization of "is" and "ought," and the argument that the moral ideal can, and therefore ought to, have an impact on the sensible world provides a powerful means to understand existing society and power relations and yet also to present a rational alternative distinct from, but arguably immanent within, the world of sense. Once the limits of the understanding have been reached Kant argues that it is inherent within the human mind to seek to go beyond these limits, which can only be done legitimately by recourse to pure practical reason.

Human Beings and Humanity

Having identified the worlds of sense and understanding and the special role of reason in legislating for the world of understanding, the question of whether or not mankind is capable of ending its "self-incurred minority" is of utmost importance as only a perspectively reoriented mankind can approximate the ideal of legislative reason by becoming enlightened.[27] The question therefore refers back once more to the ultimate Kantian query: "What is man?" At the most fundamental, ontological level it is impossible to elaborate on what man *is* other than to state that he exists: it is not given to human beings to *know* any more than this most basic fact. Instead of professing knowledge of themselves on inadequate bases, human beings must, according to Kant, accept "the strange though incontestable assertion of the speculative *Critique, that even the thinking subject is* in inner *intuition a mere appearance to itself.*"[28] Kant's point is not that our existence is illusory, but rather that "although my existence is not indeed appearance (still less mere illusion) . . . I have no knowledge of myself as I am but merely as I appear to myself."[29] As a collection of impressions, the self is inherently unstable, and no "fixed and abiding self can present itself in this flux of inner appearances."[30] The apparent self, although by definition merely a representation of an object—the true self—by its very inadequacy to present the whole draws attention to the fact that the self is "an object which cannot itself be intuited by us, and which may, therefore, be named the non-empirical, that is, transcendental object."[31] Again, we cannot *know* the transcendental object, but are permitted to think about it according to the insights derived from both appearances—human beings—and as to what it might be as a thing in itself (as revealed by pure reason), i.e., as humanity.[32]

A picture of what human beings appear to be (that is convincing in its own terms) may be constructed by reference to the character of their actions when viewed as products of the understanding and technical practical reason. That the self is unstable and in flux, and hence malleable and alterable, provokes consideration about the character of the transcendental object beyond the apparent human being and by extension the social and political environments that ensue from the theorization of the transcendental object. The transcendental object that is mankind may be formulated not according to empirical character, but rather through reason, and in particular pure practical reason. The transcendental object's practical content, however, is not something that can be known; rather, it must be formulated by reference to the moral law, itself something that has to be accepted ultimately on a basis of faith in a purposive order of existence. That the formulation of humanity in this manner is merely an idea does not, however, detract from its significance within Kant's system: "As the idea gives the *rule*, so the ideal in such a case serves as the *archetype* for the complete determination of the copy; and we have no other standard for our actions than the conduct of this divine man within us, with which we compare and judge ourselves, and so reform ourselves, although we can never attain to the perfection thereby prescribed."[33] This significance, however, must always be filtered through the obstacles of human nature "to the degree of which there are no assignable limits."[34] The major issue for Kant then is whether technical practical *human beings* can alter their self-perception to such an extent that they approximate the ideal of pure practical *humanity*. What is at stake then in Kant's practical philosophy is the salvation of mankind through its reorientation via pure practical reason.

Human Beings

The human being plays out her life as a being of inclination, understanding, *and* reason—the question of practical philosophy for Kant revolves around which of these modes is and ought to be primary in terms of determining human behavior. The human being is incapable of achieving moral and rational purity, yet is possessed of enough reason to recognize that he cannot be solely a creature of inclination. Kant proposes a process of moral development that is achieved through several stages: the human being, becoming aware of good and evil, uses reason to move beyond a prudential ethic toward a more rational understanding of good and evil derived from the world of understanding. Given the limits of human cognition a division manifests itself in practical reason between pure practical reason and technical practical reason: very different ways of comprehending mankind's moral and political essences, one rooted in what *ought* to be the case (pure practical reason) and the other in what Kant argues *is* the human being's defining lack of "true" morality (technical practical reason). The lack of true morality is due to the dominance of the inclinations, as a result of which the human being makes happiness for its own sake his end. In the *Groundwork*, although happiness is necessary to avoid temptation from duty it is generally understood in opposition to the "true" foundation for morality in reason and duty.[35] If prioritized as an end in itself, happiness represents "a powerful counterweight" to the observance of duty and morality, corrupting them at the source and undermining the strict laws allowing their formulation.[36] Insofar as there is a role for happiness in Kant's system it lies in achieving the condition of being worthy for happiness.

Within this environment, Kant is clear that human understanding reduces "everything to more or less refined self-love," and finds its satisfaction in the fulfillment of the "dear self" in happiness, itself a value not of reason but of imagination, resting on empirical and hence subjective grounds.[37] The human being in this condition may make claims to morality based in experience and happiness but these claims are false:

> human reason in its weariness gladly rests on this pillow and in a dream of sweet illusions (which allow it to embrace a cloud instead of Juno) it substitutes for morality a bastard patched up from limbs of quite diverse ancestry, which looks like whatever one wants to see in it but not like virtue for him who has once seen virtue in her true form.[38]

The "sweet illusions" of happiness and other human inclinations are identified as being the very things from which "rational beings" must strive to be free.[39]

Human beings have as their primary aim the realization of ends. The problem for Kant is that human beings do not prioritize reason in deciding their actions, but rather favor desire—or, more accurately, the lower faculty of desire.[40] Desire accounts for the power of the natural over the human psyche, yet any end that desire puts forward, ethical or otherwise, cannot serve as the basis for a law pertaining to *all* rational beings as desire produces only subjective interests that cannot be made the basis for a universal law based on absolute necessity derived from reason.[41] Even universal concepts devolved from desire, particularly pleasure and displeasure, cannot serve as the basis for universal laws pertaining to rational beings as each person's pleasure and displeasure remains merely subjective and empirical.[42] Pleasure and displeasure lead to the development of what Kant calls "material practical principles"—which are simultaneously part of the world of sense as the locus of their operation and source of their original stimulus, but also part of the practical world as ideas active in (and in many cases determining) the will. Kant argues that material practical principles can serve as the basis for universal laws for the gaining of ends based on the concept of happiness (perhaps better expressed as satisfaction), but they can only culminate in happiness for a section of mankind as they cannot be "universally directed to the same objects."[43] This recognition by Kant of the power of happiness and the lower faculty of desire constitutes a certain form of reasoning (if not rationality). Elsewhere, Kant goes so far as to afford this kind of reasoning its own status as a doctrine—"the technical (subjective) doctrine of ends . . . the pragmatic doctrine of ends, containing the rules of prudence in the choice of one's ends."[44]

The single greatest problem with happiness for Kant is its heterogeneity. Having no single purpose decided in advance by pure practical reason, the general rules of happiness, rooted in the empirical, and consequently contingent and shifting environment, demand endless judgment.[45] Nature furnishes the human being with the means to judgment in prudence, from which maxims of "self-love" can be derived, thus prudence adapts the practical law to the ends of life.[46] Desire, through prudence, can even give rise to concepts such as good and evil, desire for good and aversion to evil being bases for the practical laws of prudence, thereby leading to the determination of causality. Good and evil emerge through experience, which determines their natures and consequences. Kant's objection to this original formulation of good and evil is that "good" is then reduced to being "merely the useful."[47] This is insufficient ground for a foundation for genuine good for Kant, who insists that there can be no truly moral good derived from merely sensible intuition.

The universal quest for happiness in nature is a consequence of human beings viewing themselves as parts of the mechanism of nature, the actions of which are determined by necessity. From this perspective, the human being is the plaything of his environment, a puppet tied by the strings of inclination to his predetermined, animalistic role. In this sense, human beings are degraded by their adherence to a self-image predicated on the inclinations.[48] Reason offers a way of escaping the animal dependence on sense and the crude logic of prudence to another world of freedom realized by reason, as once good and evil are identified, in the appraisal of good and evil "reason is needed in addition to sense."[49] Reason, once provided with the concepts of good and evil, can work from *apparent* good and evil, the domain of prudence, to true good and evil, the domain of pure practical reason—a shift in perception from the natural to the practical in mankind's conceptualization of the moral universe.

Humanity

The ideal representative of humanity is a "rational being" and as such man must "regard himself *as intelligence*" not simply as a product of nature.[50] If the human being as a natural or technical practical entity, or both, is characterized by her lack of freedom, then humanity is defined by the use of its freedom.[51] The shift from the *primacy* of the natural and the understanding (technical practical) to rational (pure practical) being is effected through reason, which must be allowed to define the terms of freedom. This shift does not represent a repudiation of the other elements of mankind, which always retains its natural elements and faculty of understanding—what Kant advocates is a shift in the primacy of relations among the elements that constitute the human. Where technical practical human beings' choices appear determined in advance by necessity, humanity makes use of its rationally informed volition to discover and submit to laws of reason. Kant therefore describes the "true vocation" of reason as being "to produce a will that is good, not perhaps *as a means* to other purposes, but *good* itself."[52] Good then has to be understood not in terms of intended ends or consequences but as a quality determined in conformity with reason.[53] Where the human being bases her actions on "self-love" and derives prudence from self-love, humanity bases its life on duty to moral principles derived from reason. The will is in itself undetermined and according to Kant "stands between the a priori principle, which is formal, and its a posteriori incentive, which is material," yet the will must be determined in order to act and "since it must be determined by something, it must be determined by the formal principle of volition."[54]

The advantage of basing moral life in the a priori is that it avoids the constant political and social judgment required of prudence. There is in effect only one judgment required, to follow the dictates of reason as expressed in the moral law: "reason by itself and independently of all appearances commands what ought to happen."[55] What Kant proposes is replacing self-love with love for the moral law, to orient the human being away from "melting sympathy" toward respect for and observance of the law.[56] This search for the moral law ultimately concludes with the various formulations of the categorical imperative. The laws of reason allow for the coexistence of objective and subjective morality in that imperatives express "the relation of objective laws of volition in general to the subjective imperfection of the will of this or that rational being, for example of the human will"; in this coexistence, however, the subjective must bow to the objective.[57] This conditioning of the will through reason has as its logical end the reformation of the human being as a moral entity as the will and the moral law converge in "an accord of will with the pure moral law becoming, as it were, our nature, an accord never to be disturbed."[58] Kant concedes that mankind cannot achieve this "holiness" of will-law convergence, but insists that observance of duty can still provide a means of moral reformation.[59]

The concept of freedom allows mankind to cognize itself within both the world of sense and the world of understanding, but *rationally* the latter is preferable:

> For we now see that when we think of ourselves as free we transfer ourselves into the world of understanding as members of it and cognise autonomy of the will along with its consequence, morality; but if we think of ourselves as put under obligation we regard ourselves as belonging to the world of sense and yet at the same time to the world of understanding.[60]

The autonomous will is obliged to follow the moral law, but another problem presents itself in that the autonomous will is ultimately responsible for deriving universal moral law via reason, and reason must do this in a context in which freedom and nature are both legitimate categories. Kant cannot allow a "true contradiction" to exist between freedom and natural necessity as philosophy "cannot give up the concept of nature any more than that of freedom."[61] Kant resolves the seeming contradiction by claiming that the laws of nature pertain only to the *appearance* of human beings, while the universal law applies to the human in itself that exists beyond appearance, but which in itself is only perceived or known through appearance: "things in themselves (though hidden) must lie behind appearances as their ground and that one cannot insist that the laws of their operation should be the same as those under which their appearances stand."[62] Thus we have two parallel laws governing human behavior: the laws of apparent behavior and the laws of "true" behavior, with human beings enjoined by Kant to discover and follow the latter as closely as possible because *"what belongs to mere appearance is necessarily subordinated by reason to the constitution of the thing in itself."*[63] The individual has not merely to follow the moral law, he has to internalize it to such an extent that he lives according to the maxims of freedom as if they were laws of nature.[64]

The Problem of the "Crooked Wood"

In contrast to the ideal of humanity, Kant's attitude to human beings in his works is typically contemptuous or hostile. At best, human beings are characterized as "domestic animals," "placid creatures," and infants in "walking carts" who have not left the state of minority.[65] This minority is "woven together from folly and childish vanity and often even childish malice and destructiveness."[66] As it appears from observation of its empirical character, the species is mired in self-incurred immaturity, is tied to inclination, and does not act in a truly moral fashion—that is to say, in a manner determined by a priori reason. This manifest failure of the human being in appearance to act in a rational-moral manner appropriate to its humanity condemns "the human being to contempt for himself and inner abhorrence."[67] Kant presents the relationship between human beings and the moral law in this context as one based inevitably on abasement: "the moral law unavoidably humiliates every human being when he compares with it the sensible propriety of his nature."[68] To be good then is to accept reason and the moral law it provides and to submit to the authority of "holy law" without question, as to question is "already to defect from it in spirit."[69] It is for this reason that the human being is, according to Kant, "unholy enough" in himself but he must learn to recognize the holiness of humanity within him.[70]

The human being must also recognize that without the moral law, he must conclude, "on self-examination, that he is worthless and contemptible in his own eyes."[71] This becoming aware of his worthlessness and contemptibility is the precondition for moral growth because "every good moral dispensation can be grafted onto it, because this is the best, and indeed the sole, guard to prevent ignoble and corrupting impulses from breaking into the mind."[72]

In contrast to the sublimity of humanity as a principle, Kant stresses the insignificance of the human being as a *natural* entity in terms of the human being's cosmological irrelevance in that "the multitude of worlds annihilates . . . my importance as an animal creature."[73] Life itself is irrelevant in contrast to observance of the moral law, in that Kant's moral agent should have no desire for life or happiness in himself, he should be concerned merely with the observance of duty: "in comparison and contrast with which life with all its agreeableness has no worth at all. He still lives only from duty, not because he has the least taste for living."[74] The only way to live a life beyond animality is through the purposive determination of existence via reason and the moral law, which allows mankind "to reach into the infinite."[75] Kant's hostility toward human beings, as opposed to his redeemed-through-reason humanity, is clear in that in the absence of moral reorientation "we should have to hate or despise" the human race.[76] Although the means and purposes of God are unknown to human beings, Kant is baffled by the very creation of humans as they appear to be: "that such a race of corrupt beings should have been put on earth at all cannot be justified by any theodicy (if we assume that the human race will never be or can be better off)"—it is only on the assumption that mankind can be redeemed that it has any value.[77]

Kant comes to the conclusion that the best that can be said of a potential reformation of the human being and his or her environment is that it is a "reasonable hope" to be professed against the "despairing denial" of its possibility.[78] Ultimately, we are forced to accept on *faith* that human beings can ultimately achieve consciousness of themselves as pure practical entities and at least approximate the moral law: "to admit that the moral law within us is itself deceptive would call forth in us the wish, which arouses our abhorrence, rather to be rid of all reason and to regard ourselves as thrown by one's principles into the mechanism of nature as all the other species of animals."[79] Kant's *faith* is invested in the *telos* of coinciding reason and nature, which may be desirable in its own terms, but has as its true ground a practical interest born of the fear that, in the absence of this *telos*, "we no longer have a lawful but an aimlessly playing nature and hopeless chance takes the place of nature's guiding thread."[80]

The Postulates of Practical Reason I: Freedom and Mankind

In addition to the problem of human insufficiency, freedom, the basis of Kantian morality, is also problematic—as he states, "freedom is only an idea of freedom, the objective reality of which is in itself doubtful, whereas nature is a concept of the understanding that proves, and must necessarily prove, its reality in examples from experience."[81] Kant attempts to reconcile freedom and nature by claiming a difference between laws of nature and universal law. The laws of nature pertain only to appearances while the universal law applies to the thing in itself.[82] Kant freely accepts that his notion of freedom has little or nothing to do with how human beings conduct themselves: "nothing in appearances can be explained by the concept of freedom and there the mechanism of nature must indeed constitute the only guide."[83] In the face of appearances and the mechanism of nature, Kant offers only the *hope* of redemption through reason. Human freedom can be properly comprehended only when the human being is viewed as a "rational agent engaged in a process of deliberation regarding what I ought to do," in which case freedom may be understood "in the negative sense of being independent of determination by natural causes; while qua bound by the moral law I must regard myself as free in the positive sense of possessing autonomy."[84] In order to preserve hope and meaning for human existence, freedom must be assumed as a postulate of pure practical reason, i.e., "a principle that one must premise, for moral reasons, to be true even though pure speculative reason can only confirm that such a postulate is not contradictory to other known truths."[85]

This perspective on freedom may work in terms of a rational agent when all other sensible and nonrational incentives are abstracted away, but it does open another problem with the concept of freedom, which is the issue of time and circumstance in relation to autonomy.[86] Kant's theory requires, at least at one level, the free actor to be autonomous in order to develop a good will, and to act according to duty and obligation. This actor would have to exist outside of space and time (which is the case at the noumenal level, if not at the phenomenal level of appearances), as Kant accepts—"since time past is no longer within my control, every action that I perform must be necessary by determining grounds that are not in my control, that is *I am never free at the point of time in which I act*" (emphasis added). Kant can only save the concept of freedom by in effect placing it safely out of harm's way in the noumenal sphere or in the afterlife, but in doing so he concedes that it has limited or no effect in the world of sense. Kant therefore insists on a transcendental freedom, "which must be thought as independence from everything empirical and so from nature generally."[87] This has wider implications, as "without this freedom [from nature and the sensible] . . . which alone is practical a priori, no moral law is possible and no imputation in accordance with it."[88] All Kant can do is to claim that all determining factors outside pure practical reason for a person should be regarded as "nothing but the consequence and never as the determining ground of his causality as a *noumenon*."[89]

Kant's moral project therefore depends on whether or not one accepts the existence and the primacy of the *homo noumenon* as revealed by pure reason, and the possibility of an afterlife in which successively greater degrees of moral perfection, and hence "true" autonomy, may be thought possible. If one does believe, then the project holds, at least in principle; if one does not follow Kant in this belief; then without this other, more "fundamental" perspective, the problems of autonomy observable in the sensible world become insurmountable. If one does not follow Kant, he insists we must conclude that "the highest good is impossible in accordance with practical rules," and "the moral law, which commands us to promote it, must be fantastic and directed to empty imaginary ends and must therefore in itself be false."[90] This leads to the ultimate difficulty for Kantian morality: as long as human beings perceive themselves as technical practical entities operating in a natural environment, Kant's practical morality cannot be instituted or even approximated. This problem is particularly acute in the realms of political life and international relations, where Kant's champion of pure practical reason in *Toward Perpetual Peace*, the moral politician, must be both astute political strategist and tactician, while simultaneously acting in strict accordance with pure practical reason and the moral law, and so successful in all these endeavors that his means *and* ends become universal templates.

The problem of political existence calls forth a further problem: How can and should human beings engage with pure reason itself? As Kant recognizes, "it is quite beyond the capacity of any human reason to explain *how* pure reason, without other incentives that might be taken from elsewhere, can be of itself practical. . . . it is impossible for us to explain, in other words, *how pure reason can be practical*, and all the pains and labor of seeking an explanation of it are lost."[91] The crucial issue becomes, therefore, what are these other incentives that might enable the possibility of pure reason? Kant argues that the existence of the moral law and practical reason in addition to political necessity and social pressures "force" the issue of freedom (and thereby transcendent and pure reason) onto the agenda of human existence, thus allowing the transcendent into the practical, and it is on this basis that Kant argues that pure reason is practical of itself alone, i.e., that it serves as a model for human thought.[92] Even to the extent that this is the case, however, "the utmost that finite practical reason can effect is to make sure of . . . unending progress of one's maxims toward this model"; to do so is virtue, but "virtue . . . as a naturally acquired ability, can never be completed."[93]

The Will

The final difficulty that Kant's theory presents in relation to the perceptual shift in orientation from the primacy of human beings to that of humanity is the extraordinary contortions he has to undertake in order to link pure and practical reason in the concept of the will. Kant asserts that pure reason contains the practical and hence is "sufficient to determine the will," but this will is not the will of human beings as they appear to themselves, but rather the will of "rational beings," from which human beings are excluded until they are redeemed by reason and achieve the requisite shift in consciousness to enable them to recognize their "true" nature.[94] Kant accepts this exclusion by admitting that within a "pathologically affected will . . . there can be found a conflict of maxims with the practical laws cognized by himself."[95] Kant opposes this by stating that the will is at least in part independent of the pathological/sensible world.[96] Kant, according to Jennifer Uleman, "insists on envisioning will as something other than a mechanism determined from without and instead as another kind of thing, belonging to an order outside nature, outside space and time, which can begin its own unconditioned beginnings."[97] Kant attempts to provide a means by which pure reason can influence the world of understanding and the world of sense in the *Critique of Practical Reason* to the extent that he insists that the moral law, "to which all our maxims are subject," achieves "objective reality" through reason. Kant concedes, however, that in nature, "insofar as it is an object of experience," the free will of the actor is not determined by maxims but rather by "private inclinations" that constitute a natural whole in accordance with pathological laws.[98] Kant sees as the end point of moral evolution "the stage of thoroughly liking to fulfil all moral laws," but crucially allows that "no creature can ever reach this stage of moral disposition . . . never be altogether free from desires and inclinations."[99]

The various distinctions that Kant makes in his work between the two primary meanings of the will—*wille* and *willkür*—are helpful in determining just
what roles each aspect of the will plays in the articulation of human freedom.
Wille itself has two meanings, "a broad sense in which it connotes the faculty of
volition, or will as a whole, and a narrow sense in which it connotes the legislative function of this faculty."[100] J. B. Schneewind sees the essential difference
between *wille* and *willkür* lying in the fact that *wille* is "simply identical with
practical rationality and is therefore the home of the moral law," while the
willkür is "a power of choice, whose task is to choose between the promptings
of desire and the imperatives stemming from the will." The crucial importance
of this difference between *wille* and *willkür* is that it "is in the power of choice
that our freedom, properly speaking, resides. The will itself is neither free nor
unfree."[101] By means of this distinction Kant can address the persistent failure
of human beings to choose to act according to the rational-moral requirements
of freedom, while retaining intelligible freedom in principle for humanity.

The Postulates of Practical Reason II: Immortality and God

Along with freedom, God and immortality are "unavoidable problems set by
pure reason" and much of the first *Critique* revolves around how best to think
about these central concerns of human existence.[102] Kant argues that pure
reason "furnishes the idea for a transcendental knowledge" of both God and
the soul, which, together with freedom, enable human beings "to pass beyond
nature."[103] Returning to the question "what may I know?," the immortality of
the soul and knowledge of God lie outside what may be known, which impacts on what human beings ought to do and for what they may hope. Kant
sets *knowledge* aside and sets about reestablishing the grounds on which *belief*
in both God and immortality might be reformulated in a way to serve as elements of practical and moral philosophy. According to Paul Guyer, Kant simply has no option but to postulate on the basis of faith both the afterlife and a
benevolent God.[104]

Kant's starting point is to assert that we simply cannot know what happens
to human beings after death—neither the proponent of practical philosophy
nor "the speculative opponent" has any insight into what happens to human
consciousness after death, allowing Kant to posit that it is thereby permissible
"to hope for an independent and continuing existence of my thinking nature."[105]

The "refusal of reason" to permit knowledge of that which lies beyond death, Kant continues, is "reason's hint to divert our self-knowledge from fruitless and extravagant speculation to fruitful practical employment," which "determines us to regulate our actions as if our destiny reached infinitely far beyond experience, and therefore far beyond this present life."[106] The material composition of the human being may in fact not be the totality of human life and cause of thought, "but merely a restrictive condition of it," useful in the physical phase of human existence, but "a hindrance to the pure and spiritual life."[107] This leads Kant to the transcendental hypothesis of human life beyond the physical.[108] The practical requirement of faith in the afterlife established in the first *Critique* enables the vital postulation of the afterlife in the second *Critique*. Immortality is necessary as a practical idea, according to Kant, because it provides "a duration befitting the complete fulfilment of the moral law," i.e., the moral reformation required by the moral law could only be achieved in a timescale greater than the physical phase of human existence. It is only by means of postulating immortality that the amount of time "required for conformity with the moral law" is possible, and then only on a practical, not a speculative, basis.[109]

That life exists, that the afterlife is possible, and that the moral law applies to humans in both conditions, is closely linked to Kant's most fundamental transcendental hypothesis of pure reason, namely that we must believe in God (although never have *knowledge* of Him) as the wise author of a purposive order. Kant deals with the question of God in the fourth conflict of transcendent ideas in the first *Critique*. Here two equally plausible propositions are made, the thesis, "There belongs to the world, either as its part or as its cause, a being that is absolutely necessary" and the antithesis, "An absolutely necessary being nowhere exists in the world, nor does it exist outside the world as its cause."[110] Kant's ultimate finding is that both positions are equally true, depending on which perspective is employed.[111] The antithesis, however, leads to a *moral* dead end: "If there is no primordial being distinct from the world, if the world is without beginning and therefore without an Author, if our will is not free, if the soul is divisible and perishable like matter, moral ideas and principles lose all validity, and share the fate of the transcendental ideas which served as their theoretical support."[112] While both thesis and antithesis are pursued to their utmost conclusions, Kant argues that "the architectonic interest of reason—the demand not for empirical but for pure a priori unity of reason—forms a natural recommendation for the assertion of the thesis."[113] It is for these reasons, namely the practical interest of mankind and architectonic systemic unity, that knowledge, understood as speculative reason, must be sacrificed to make room for belief in both God and humanity as *practical* ideas. It is only by taking the leap of faith that practical reason represents that human beings can in effect escape the tyranny of nature by means of belief. The error of previous versions of religion and rationalism was to assert that God exists: for Kant the metaphysics of morals is tied not to this ontological claim, but to a *practical* claim that God must be believed to act as the author of nature; otherwise, although the moral law would still be valid in itself as an idea, it would have no chance of being actualized or approximated by human beings. Empirical reason itself can make no real objection to belief in the regulative principle of God's authorship as long as this position is a regulative, as opposed to constitutive, claim. By severing speculative reason and faith, Kant allows both to prosper in their proper spheres—it must be recognized, however, that Kant's practical philosophy is contained within the sphere of faith (what ought to be) and not science (what is, and what can be known about what is).

Having distanced himself from the ontological claim about the reality or otherwise of God, Kant seeks to reground practical reason in the "merely possible":

> [T]he real contains no more than the merely possible. A hundred real thalers do not contain the least coin more than a hundred possible thalers. For as the latter signify the concept, and the former the object and the positing of the object, should the former contain more than the latter, my concept would not, in that case, express the whole object, and would therefore be an inadequate concept of it. . . . By whatever and by however many predicates we may think a thing—even if we completely determine it—we do not make the least addition to the thing when we further declare that this thing *is*.[114]

God, as an ideal entity, can play as important a role as if it was possible to prove He exists, i.e., as "a regulative principle of reason, which directs us to look upon all connection in the world as if it originated from an all-sufficient cause."[115] Kant admits that even though any profession of faith in a supreme being is a mere ideal for speculative reason, "it is yet an ideal without flaw, a concept which completes and crowns the whole of human knowledge," and proposes a moral theology based on a transcendental idea of God. The regulative belief in God as the source of systematic unity allows the systematization of knowledge, including the empirical, and makes this belief a crucial component of the architectonic system that Kant proposes.[116] The idea of God enables human beings to view "all connection of the things of the world of sense as if they had their ground in such a being."[117] The utility of the idea of God is such that, according to Kant, the assumption of a "wise and omnipotent Author of the world" not only can, but *must*, be made, albeit without thereby extending "knowledge beyond the field of possible experience."[118] In what will be crucial in understanding the nature of his argument in *Toward Perpetual Peace*, Kant claims that "in relation to the systematic and purposive ordering of the world, which, if we are to study nature, we are constrained to presuppose," we have to assume a role for God if "only in respect of the employment of our reason in reference to the world."[119] For all the caveats about not making ontological claims regarding the existence of God, Kant nonetheless stresses the importance of belief in the "wise Author and Ruler" of the intelligible world; otherwise, Kant argues reason "would have to regard the moral laws as empty figments of the brain, since without this postulate the necessary consequence which it itself connects with these laws could not follow."[120] Kant ultimately restores the ground of metaphysics (i.e., God) by means of reformulating how God may be conceived: "[f]or although we have to surrender the language of *knowledge*, we still have sufficient ground to employ, in the presence of the most exacting reason, the quite legitimate language of a firm *faith*."[121] The centrality of the transcendental and moral theology to Kant's political and ethical projects is quite clear: although it is impossible to make any positive statement as to whether or not God exists, belief in God and the afterlife are requirements for the successful conclusion of each project.

Conclusion

It is important to recognize that the three answers that Kant provides to the three great questions—What can I know? What ought I to do? What may I hope?—have to be divided into two categories: what can be known has only a negative relationship to that which ought to be done and that which can be hoped. As Kant admits, so far as the other two questions are concerned "this much, at least, is certain and definitively established, that in respect of these two latter problems, knowledge is unattainable by us."[122] If anything, knowledge actually poses a problem in terms of what I ought to do as, within its own limits (which Kant urges us to transcend), it proposes that we ought to act pragmatically and with regard to our own happiness. Speculative reason also denies the possibility of hope—things will remain within the parameters set by prudence and pragmatism. There is nothing in speculative reason that points beyond the perpetuation of the political logic of heteronomy.

In the *Groundwork* and the second *Critique*, Kant raises the possibility of a rational, moral alternative to the inclination-driven existence of human beings. An individual ought to reverse the relationship between technical practical reason and pure practical reason, and because she ought, according to Kant, she can do so. Kant couches this reorientation in terms of how the human being ought to act, yet he never provides an adequate reason as to why an individual *should* relegate technical, prudential reasoning to secondary status in relation to pure practical reason other than that it would be in conformity with his idea of moral and rational evolution. The most Kant can offer is the *hope* that the operation of prudential, technical practical reason will ultimately create the conditions in which pure practical reason might gain a foothold and eventually come to dominate human consciousness. These processes—teleological, cultural, political, anthropological, educational, and, in the final analysis, theological—are the focus of the rest of this study. What will become clear as the argument progresses is that Kant continually employs faith and hope as the foundations for human reformation and perpetual peace. Shifting from transcendental idea to postulate of practical reason to subjectively necessary fiction to putative architect of the universe to author of the moral law and designer of purposive nature, it is the idea of God that grounds the "rational" belief that mankind might achieve independence from nature and live according to the principles of rational morality.

In order for a peace worthy of the name, the chasm between necessity and freedom, understanding and reason, human beings and humanity must be confronted. This chasm, and Kant's attempts to solve the problem of the distance between how human beings appear to themselves and humanity as revealed by pure practical reason, is the subject of the next chapter.

CHAPTER 2

Independence from Nature

Preparing the Ground for Perpetual Peace *in the Third* Critique

The third *Critique* represents a shift in emphasis for Kant in that he moves away from a concern with the limits of knowledge and the content of rational morality as explored in the first two critiques toward an approach based on universal subjectivity designed to address those issues of human existence that are outside the purview of the strict domains of understanding and reason. It is this shift in emphasis that allows Kant to enter the final phase of his career, a period of speculation on politics, anthropology, and theology—subjects directly related to the achievement of the final ends of mankind. If human beings are constitutionally incapable of actualizing or approximating these final ends then all that could and should serve as the basis for the reorientation of human beings to humanity—freedom, rationality, the moral law, i.e., the very core of Kant's project— would be the vain delusions of a creature out of tune with nature. In such a condition, human existence would be essentially meaningless. The political theoretical significance of the *Critique of the Power of Judgment* is that it is (at least in part) an attempt to argue the *possibility* of there being a positive *telos* for the human race: that a reformed human species may be thought of as the end of nature. Kant's sacrifice of knowledge enables not only faith in God and humanity but also hope in the future.[1] These elements of hope and faith inform Kant's political project as expressed in *Perpetual Peace*, which in many respects is a sequel to the *Critique of the Power of Judgment* that elaborates on many of its themes in a more specifically political context.[2]

Philosophy, Politics, and Judgment

Kant's first task is to restate what he considers to be the "real system of philosophy itself," namely the division of philosophy into two constituent parts, the
"theoretical," which deals with the philosophy of nature, and the "practical,"
which is the philosophy of morals.[3] These two categories are quite separate, and
Kant stresses the distinction between natural laws (derived from natural philosophy) and laws of freedom (derived from practical philosophy). Kant is particularly anxious to stress the fundamental difference between a moral, practical proposition and a proposition that is merely natural.[4] Given the finality of
this impasse it is imperative for Kant to employ a different kind of thought in
which the natural and the practical are no longer stymied, which is why Kant
revisits and extends the power of judgment that he first outlined in the *Critique
of Pure Reason*.[5]

Philosophy and the Faculties of Cognition:
The Special Role of the Faculty of the Power of Judgment

Kant argues that "the systematic representation of the faculty for thinking is
tripartite," and identifies the three parts as the faculty for the cognition of the
general (of rules), i.e., the understanding; the faculty for the subsumption of the
particular under the general, the power of judgment; and the faculty for the
determination of the particular through the general (for the derivation from
principles), i.e., reason.[6] The faculty of understanding is responsible for yielding the laws of nature, the faculty of reason provides the laws of freedom, and
the faculty of the power of judgment is responsible for transposing the ideas
and concepts of both faculties into a different, discursive realm under a new
rubric, that of subjective relations in the reflective power of judgment. A particularly significant aspect of the faculty of the power of judgment is that it allows the examination of human existence under the assumption of what *might*
be the case if, as is to be believed and *hoped*, nature is purposive.

The category of the power of judgment is designed to act as a thinking space
between and distinct from the two other faculties; its significance lies in the fact
that "the power of judgment makes possible the transition from the domain of
the concept of nature to that of the concept of freedom."[7] Kant proposes to resolve the problem of the space between nature and freedom by transposing it to
the reflective power of judgment, where, in Henry Allison's formulation, "the

requisite *Ubergang* is not from nature to freedom *per se*, but from our way of thinking [*Denkungsart*] about the former (in terms of laws of nature) to our way of thinking about the latter (in terms of moral laws)."[8] In the *Critique of the Power of Judgment* Kant argues that a solution to the problem lies in the capability of the power of judgment to discover general rules for the treatment of aesthetics, morality, and teleology via the foundational assumption of the purposiveness of nature.[9] This purposiveness suggests (although does not prove) the existence of a creator with a purpose for mankind, which provides the ground for the rational belief that the idea of humanity represents the end of nature as well as the fulfillment of reason, which perhaps accounts for the invocation of both nature *and* providence in *Perpetual Peace*.

For present purposes it is important to identify how Kant conceives of politics within the power of judgment. Political theory is composed of "technical" propositions, which instead of seeking to achieve practical ends, i.e., what ought to be the case, belong to the "art" of "bringing about that which one wishes should exist." Prudence and political calculation are "techniques" and belong to the "theoretical knowledge of nature" rooted in the faculty of understanding.[10] Moral precepts, on the other hand, are based on objective propositions rooted in the faculty of reason. Part of the difficulty of understanding the complex relationship between politics and morality, then, is to recognize that our cognition of both derives from two fundamentally different philosophical origins. As a discourse based on the knowledge of nature, political theory reflects the deterministic elements of the natural world as revealed through the understanding; conversely, as a discourse based on reason, moral philosophy reveals the rational requirement of obeying the moral law. Kant's system requires a resolution of this problem in favor of the latter, which the *Critique of the Power of Judgment* and its political sequel, *Perpetual Peace*, aim to provide.

The Power of Judgment and the Purposiveness of Nature

The power of judgment's role is to act as an interface *between* nature and understanding on one hand and humanity's proposed moral destiny and the faculty of reason on the other. Kant gives an early indication as to the ordering capacity of the faculty of the power of judgment in his declaration that the only concept or rule that the power of judgment provides "would have to be the concept of purposiveness of nature in behalf of our faculty for cognizing it, insofar as for this it is required that we be able to judge the particular as contained under the general and subsume it under the concept of a nature."[11] The concept of purposiveness allows the power of judgment to make sense of the infinite multiplicity of empirical laws and the heterogeneity of forms of nature in parallel with the competing requirements of the faculty of reason. The faculty of the power of judgment allows the systematization of nature "right up to the highest empirical laws and the forms of nature corresponding to them, and thus to regard the aggregate of particular experiences as a system of them; for without this presupposition no thoroughly lawlike interconnection, i.e., empirical unity of these experiences can obtain." Kant admits that this lawfulness is contingent and that the power of judgment "presumes" and "presupposes" its existence as "a formal purposiveness of nature." Avner Baz identifies the implications of this recourse not to a *fact* of nature but to an *assumption* about nature: "We cannot reasonably *rely* on nature to assist us in achieving our goal, and yet we have no choice but to *assume* that it will. This assumption is the transcendental principle of reflective judgment, the principle of nature's purposiveness of our power of judgment."[12] The important aspect of the power of judgment is that through its systematization and assumption of purposiveness, it provides principles for the judging and investigation of nature *as if* it were systematic. The decision to argue that nature should be investigated as if it is systematic has the effect of giving a direction to Kant's inquiries.[13] The only alternative, that nature is a random, chaotic environment in which all is merely contingent, cannot be seriously entertained by Kant, not because it may not be an accurate reflection of reality, but rather because such an analytical framework cannot offer the necessary shift in consciousness from the primacy of the natural to the dominion of the practical.[14] Where chaos reigns or even intrudes there can be no permanent and universal moral law.

The reflective power of judgment is defined by Kant as "a mere faculty for reflecting on a given representation, in accordance with a certain principle, for the sake of a concept that is thereby made possible." The reflective power of judgment is contrasted with the *determining* faculty of judgment, which is defined as "a faculty for determining an underlying concept through a given empirical representation."[15] The determining faculty of judgment is close to the faculty of understanding in that its judgments "are objective in the sense that they are judgements valid for the objects about which they are made." Reflective judgments, by contrast, are closer to the imagination, and may be defined as judgements for which no rule can be found in the understanding to determine an object in intuition. We must reflect and seek to discover another rule or principle in us; judgements properly called reflective judgements are judgements in which a principle of purposiveness is employed to account for the given particular. The principle of purposiveness does not determine our representation, that is, nothing is cognized through this principle.[16]

That nothing is *cognized* through the principle of purposiveness is particularly significant—the status of claims made under the aegis of the reflective power of judgment is very important. Kant is clear in this statement that the ground here is not objective in nature, but it is necessary for the formulation of law-like propositions for those aspects of existence that are not amenable to resolution in either the faculty of reason or understanding, i.e., those that proceed from feelings of pleasure and displeasure (aesthetics), the principle of purposiveness and the ends of nature (teleology), and the accommodation of morality within the realm of nature. None of these issues are resolvable in *objective* terms, but may be discussed meaningfully in the context of universally shared aspects of human subjectivity. The reflective power of judgment should be understood as heautonomous, that is, it legislates solely within its own domain and only for its own purposes, i.e., the play of imagination and understanding in order to achieve, in Allison's formulation, "the application of logic to nature."[17] The power of judgment then "makes" sense of the world in a technical, artistic manner performed under the rule of a "general but at the same time indeterminate principle of a purposive arrangement of nature in a system." The power of judgment is characterized by a tendency to systematize nature, as otherwise we would become lost in the "labyrinth of the multiplicity of possible empirical particular laws."[18] Belief in the existence of a "technique of nature" is internal to the faculty of the power of judgment as its fundamental principle—thus the idea that nature is a system is not necessarily a feature of nature, but rather a feature of our *reflection on* nature.

The initial focus of the third *Critique* is on the internal dimensions of human intellect. The presumed purposiveness of nature is revealed as significant in that the end of nature "is not posited in the object at all, but strictly in the subject and indeed in its mere capacity for reflecting."[19] Kant argues that it is the preexisting tendency to systematize within the faculty of cognition itself that is in fact the greatest evidence of purposiveness in nature. The vagaries of contingency, e.g., the failures of humans to organize themselves rationally, are dealt with by reference to nature's workings being mechanical, as being "mere nature." Nature, however, may also be interpreted as exhibiting the work of an artist's hand, where it proceeds technically as an art in producing objects such as crystal formations, flowers, or the inner structures of plants and animals. Explanation therefore may be mechanical, e.g., Kant's analysis of political life in *Perpetual Peace*, but the *judging* of it may be technical *and* aesthetic, i.e., that there is an artistic end to seemingly simple mechanical procedures.

Although the purposiveness of nature qualifies as a transcendent principle, it does not qualify as an *objective* principle; rather, it is best understood as being "derived merely from the subjective relation of nature to a faculty of the mind," in effect as a form of universal will to systematize in human subjects. The power of judgment is directed toward the technique of nature in that it is not so much concerned with the mechanics directing nature as the presumed *purpose* behind nature itself. Nature is represented as being technical, the product of an art, in the power of judgment as a principle because Kant wants to explore the idea of what the ends of nature *might* be. The significance of this way of approaching nature is that it allows us to understand elements of the natural world such as politics as an art, and thereby allows us to make sense of the role that it plays in the reformation of human existence.

Kant's most significant claim about reflection is that it requires a principle, that "for all things in nature empirically determinate concepts can be found. . . . in all of its products one can always presuppose a form that is possible for general laws cognizable by us." This is essential for Kant as otherwise "all reflection would become arbitrary and blind, and hence would be undertaken without any well-grounded expectation of its agreement with nature."[20] Without recourse to objectivity, the reflective power of judgment instead founds its claims to "well-grounded expectation of its agreement with nature" on the existence of a universally shared subjectivity among human beings. This universal subjectivity allows both universal communication and agreement on certain concepts, e.g., beauty. The claim that something is beautiful, Kant argues, is universally understandable, even if there is disagreement as to what is in fact beautiful. The important corollary of the existence of a reflective power of judgment whose grounding is in subjectivity is that it enables a perspective on nature that may incorporate elements decreed illegitimate, inapplicable, or irrelevant in the faculty of understanding. Unlike the determining faculty of judgment, which is "legislated by the understanding," yielding only "a nature experienced as mechanistic in its causality," the reflective power of judgment legislates for itself through its commitment to purposiveness in nature.[21] This fundamental assumption allows (albeit only in a *regulative* sense) "ideas of reason and the postulates of practical reason" to inform the reflective power of judgment's analysis of nature.[22] Thus, by means of transposition, Kant achieves, if not a bridging of faculties, then a translation of the terms of both into a medium where a weaker, but still important, claim can be made regarding the nature of any relationship between the requirements of nature and freedom. It is this making possible of concepts that makes the third *Critique* so important to Kant's international political theory in that it enables Kant to speculate about the issue of perpetual peace from a point outside nature and beyond the understanding via providence. This productive capacity of reflective judgment is a consequence of the role of imagination in loosening the grip of the understanding in terms of what *may* be possible—as Kant writes in the *Lectures on Logic*, "[t]he more universal the understanding is in its rules, the more perfect it is, but if it wants to consider things *in concreto* then [it] absolutely cannot do without the imagination."[23] The issue becomes on what foundation can this kind of claim be made—on what a priori basis can a claim be made within the reflective power of judgment?

This requirement to ground judgment proves problematic for Kant. He resolves the problem of asserting "the idealism of purpose" by arguing that it is rooted in the supersensible in an indeterminate, but grounding, fashion: "we must presuppose this ground a priori, but we cannot assert its existence dogmatically."[24] For Kristin Gjesdal, in the aesthetic sphere, which is one of Kant's leading exemplars of the power of reflective judgment, this is "a purposiveness of a peculiar kind" in that it has no definite purpose, "save that of making human beings feel at home in the world. . . . This purposiveness without a purpose is the a priori principle of the aesthetic principle."[25] Kant's task then is to argue that the aesthetic, and by extension the reflective, claim "is just as legitimate as the objective, cognitive" claims of reason and understanding—the universality of taste in relation to aesthetic pleasure constitutes an "objectively unsupported and yet subjectively necessary assumption of nature's purposiveness for our cognitive power."[26] By extension, working toward the political project of perpetual peace may also be described as subjectively necessary, even if, as Kant admits in the *Metaphysics of Morals*, it is in objective terms "an unachievable ideal."[27] The purposiveness of nature in the political realm, as explored in *Idea for a Universal History* and *Toward Perpetual Peace*, is essential to fulfill the promise of the critical philosophy, i.e., Kant offers an interpretation of the processes of domestic and international political society that posits as their end result making mankind worthy of happiness. The purposiveness of nature leads Kant to posit the existence of a universal, "subjectively necessary" sense common to all human beings (*sensus communis*).[28] The wider political theory significance of the *sensus communis* "lies in its normative character for the attainment of a harmonious social order," i.e., it permits the drawing of a blueprint for reordering human existence along rational grounds.[29] The blueprint is brought to its logical conclusion of world society in various forms in *Perpetual Peace, Anthropology from a Pragmatic Point of View, Religion within the Boundaries of Mere Reason*, and other works.

The Importance of Aesthetics

Kant examines aesthetics as exemplary of the reflective power of judgment and the *sensus communis* in action. Aesthetic judgment is useful in this regard because it "serves as the inventory and archive of the thought process through which critique emerges." Within the reflective power of judgment, "long assumed presuppositions become liquefied, negotiable, and reconstituted."[30] It is in the context of this untethering of certainties that Kant draws the possibility of links between the faculties of cognition, the higher and lower faculties of desire, the feeling of pleasure and displeasure, and the power of judgment.[31] These links are conditioned upon the very indeterminacy of the reflective power of judgment, in which the faculties of understanding and imagination are in free and harmonious play instead of the understanding directing the imagination, as is the case in the determining faculty of judgment. It is this experience of undetermined harmony that is the occasion of aesthetic pleasure as the mind works from the manifold of sensual experience through the imagination and the understanding to make sense of the object that caused the chain of contemplation. Kant is very clear, however, that the significance of this process is purely subjective; the focus is on the feeling of pleasure in the subject. Nothing about the object itself is explained through the power of judgment.[32] It is this ability to feel pleasure (or displeasure) within the subject as a result of experience that constitutes for Kant the universality of aesthetic judgment.[33] Although that which causes aesthetic appreciation may differ from person to person, every subject engages with each cause similarly, which permits the principle that taste is a form of universally shared subjectivity and that aesthetic judging and taste are species of common sense. This commonality explains the importance of stressing the difference between the merely agreeable on an individual basis from the aesthetic on a universal subjective basis, i.e., that the latter category is characterized by the justified belief that others *ought* to agree that the object under consideration is universally, albeit subjectively, beautiful.[34] This requirement of universality is perhaps why Kant primarily directs his analysis to the products of nature, not craft or culture, as nature itself is universal; unlike the products of any given culture, its products are likely to have universal aesthetic significance as causes of pleasure.

Beauty and Nature

The importance of nature is that it is interpretable through aesthetics; it is understandable as a work of art, exhibiting what may be read as signs of authorship, design, and ultimately purpose. This is not to claim that there *is* an author of nature, i.e., a God, but rather that nature is rendered understandable in a meaningful sense if it is understood *as if* a God is its author, a case of the understanding bringing order to the manifold of intuitions produced by the imagination.[35] In this regard, the important aspect of beauty is the extent to which it is a symbol of morality, necessary because morality, as an idea of reason, "can only be indirectly exhibited, that is, symbolized . . . to claim that the beautiful is the symbol of the morally good is just to claim that there is a sufficiently significant isomorphism between reflection on the beautiful and reflection on the morally good so that the former activity may be regarded as a sensuously directed analogue of the latter."[36] If beauty can find a home in reflective judgment, morality—its rational analogue—can also be accommodated, and in turn contribute to our understanding of nature as purposive in the sense that nature, by way of beauty, prepares us for reason and morality, by weaning us from sensuousness.[37] In this manner, beauty provides "a pleasing propaedeutic to, or preparation for" morality.[38]

It is by such means that the power of judgment makes sense of the "system" of nature.[39] The reflective power of judgment enables the human being to understand existence beyond the "purposeless mechanism" of nature. The power of judgment does not expand the cognition of natural objects, but rather allows the cognition of nature beyond the mechanical, i.e., the concept of nature as art, which, as Kant argues, "invites profound investigations into the possibility of such a form."[40] In a related vein, if politics is an expression of nature, but also an art, then within the reflective power of judgment its nature is not fixed and its form may be adapted to come closer to the requirements of reason in the context of the purposiveness of nature. The power of judgment makes nature cognizable in a much more malleable manner than the faculty of understanding's deterministic and mechanistic depiction allows under strictly objective conditions. As *Perpetual Peace* demonstrates, politics may come to reflect not the chaotic scrabbling for the individual interests of heterogeneous entities, but the harmonious and ordered beauty of a homogeneous rational form—or its nearest achievable approximation (see chapter 3).

The Sublime

In addition to natural beauty serving as a means to understand the potential harmonization of social and political life, Kant employs the concept of the sublime to argue for the possibility of a supersensible element to aesthetics, and, by extension, to life itself. The sublime is defined by Kant as that which "even to be able to think of demonstrates a faculty of the mind that surpasses every measure of the senses."[41] The significance of the sublime is that it demonstrates the superiority of reason over nature through dwarfing everything in nature by its immeasurability and ineffability: only reason is equipped to begin to comprehend it. This constitutes part of Kant's wider effort to emphasize the rational over the natural, in that only the rational can engage with the sublime. This is in effect an affirmation of the internal world of reason over the external world of nature. The sublime points beyond nature, and reason (in conjunction with the imagination) is the means by which this transcendent category can be thought. In order to progress, the human being must look within his consciousness rather than to his existence as a natural, animal entity in order to begin on the path of reform toward rational morality.[42] In this sense, the faculty of reason provides the means to a "nonsensible standard" for judging human existence.[43] Kant returns in this context to the dual standard of estimation for mankind: on the one hand *human beings* are insignificant parts of the natural world, but on the other as members of humanity they are independent of and superior to nature:

> Likewise the irresistibility of [nature's] power constantly makes us, considered as natural beings, recognize our physical powerlessness, but at the same time it reveals a capacity for judging ourselves as independent of it and a superiority

over nature on which is grounded a self-preservation of quite another kind than that which can be threatened and endangered by nature outside us, whereby the humanity in our person remains undemeaned even though the human being must submit to that domination.[44]

The nonsensible standard then reveals a new kind of self-preservation, a preservation of the practical self, which is rooted in the faculty of reason. The natural self, once again, must submit to the demands of nature, but this nonsensible standard allows the human being to conceive of himself as distinct from nature and mere sensibility, with reason eventually to be understood as dominating sensibility, "in order to enlarge it in a way suitable for its own proper domain (the practical) and to allow it to look upon the infinite, which for sensibility is an abyss." This passage in effect is a declaration of independence from nature and the dominance of the understanding. It also enables the reorientation of the human being to humanity and the reformation of political life. The human being in his natural state cannot tolerate the sublime, which for mere sensibility is an "abyss" and "repellent." Only when prepared by culture can the human being engage the sublime—a stage in human development referred to by Kant as the "organized being."[45] Viewed in this context, being in and part of nature is not merely a stage in human development, but is a ball and chain actually preventing human progress toward a condition in which it can profitably encounter and make sense of the infinite and the sublime.[46] Culture then represents an escape route from the strictures of nature (this point is further developed in chapter 4).

Culture entails the eventual reformation of the members of mankind from a condition of being "merely a human being" to being a "refined human being." This reformation is tied to altering society and promoting sociability in that pleasure in existence is transformed from being concerned with mere satisfaction of our sensible natures to a condition where the faculty of pleasure and displeasure becomes concerned with the achievement of humanity, i.e., the contemplation of rationally informed morality.[47] This reformation is dependent upon culture providing the means by which taste would be informed by moral ideas. In order to achieve this Kant draws a connection therefore between the faculty of taste (aesthetics), morality, and pleasure. Each is tied to the other in order to reinforce Kant's claims. The ability to appreciate beauty within and beyond nature leads to a form of aesthetic pleasure to which Kant then draws a direct parallel to moral judgment. Moral judgment, however, informed by the faculty of reason is superior to any feeling of pleasure, and must direct the feeling of pleasure to "true" beauty, as moral judgment in contrast to mere taste is "grounded in objective laws." Only a society that has discovered these "objective laws" is worth inhabiting. This is an important phase in Kant's development as a political thinker in that he bases his claim not in observation of nature's external aspect, but rather within the internal capacity of the human mind to discover and formulate the laws that lead to the ultimate end of creation, i.e., the achievement of the moral vocation.

Kant is not making the claim of a direct correlation between the idea of progress and the material world. The material world of nature is now merely fodder for the imagination, which as a productive cognitive faculty is "very powerful in creating, as it were, another nature, out of the material which the real one gives it." Thus the potential for altering nature lies within the human capacity for imagining it and re-creating it according to the imagination, which should be directed in this end by reason: as a consequence, claims Kant, "nature can be transformed by us into something entirely different, namely into that which steps beyond nature."[48] The most important element of stepping beyond nature is that taste should be linked to the rendering of moral ideas. These moral ideas produce a pleasure that is universally valid for human beings as it is rooted in the higher faculty of desire and the faculty of reason, as opposed to an individual's subjective pleasure—in essence, duty becomes pleasure. Taste, then, must be grounded in the development of moral ideas if it is to serve its highest function, "for only when sensibility is brought into accord with this can genuine taste assume a determinate, unalterable form."[49]

Teleology and Man as the End of Nature

The potential transformation of nature is a result of altering its representation in the mind. This transformation is related to the postulation of forces outside nature, especially the faculty of reason's ability to think of existence beyond the natural. Perhaps the most significant idea relating to that which is beyond nature is the role that God (at least as a powerful idea) is believed to play in creating the possibility of human beings evolving beyond the natural. Kant makes a special point of gesturing toward "ends that are not our own, and which also cannot pertain to nature . . . [that] nevertheless can or should constitute a special kind of causality, or at least an entirely unique lawlikeness thereof."[50] Nature in itself has no discernable end, no purpose, no meaning—nature only has an end, a reason for being, when viewed from *outside* its mechanical course, i.e., within the less restrictive faculty of reflective judgment. Kant argues in effect that a purpose for life is only cognizable in terms of the mind's ability to discern and apply reason to the natural world, that the material world is something upon which an order must be imposed. The ends of nature must be constructed in the mind and then achieved in nature, not as a consequence of any self-fulfilling aspect inherent to nature but rather as a means of liberation from nature itself—this is essentially the process that underpins perpetual peace in its fullest, final sense. If nature is to be systematized, then the system must have an end, a product, and a purpose. Teleology is a means by which reflective judgment can go beyond mechanistic readings of nature and ask what the purpose of existence might be, if we assume that existence is purposive.[51] That purpose for Kant is the reorientation of mankind: from the aggregate of human beings into the redeemed-by-reason species humanity. In the absence of this purpose, nature would be merely a blind mechanism, a senseless and purposeless environment in which humans live out meaningless lives. Kant embraces teleology as an aspect of the reflecting power of judgment, because it can make some sense of nature by bringing it "under principles of observation and research in analogy with causality according to ends."[52] The alternative is the hopeless scenario where neither knowledge nor faith applies.[53]

Kant's first task is to isolate the significance of mankind in terms *beyond* the natural. Kant does this by making a statement as to what would constitute a natural end: "I would say provisionally that a thing exists as a natural end if it is cause and effect of itself."[54] Kant argues the case that humans represent such a natural end, first by distinguishing them from the rest of nature by designating the human as an "organized being," which "possesses in itself a formative power . . . a self-propagating formative power which cannot be explained through the capacity for movement alone (that is mechanism)." Representing the human as an organized being allows Kant to posit the possibility that mankind is not merely a practical end in itself but also a *natural* end—that the natural and the practical aspects of mankind may harmonize. If mankind is a natural end in itself, this allows a retrospective justification for providing natural science with a teleological purpose, "a way of judging its objects in accordance with a particular principle," that principle being that human beings in their reformed guise as the rational species of humanity constitute the end of nature and that theory should have this resolution of the human question as its fundamental and guiding premise. This conclusion alone is significant in that Kant admits that no such premise is derivable on an a priori basis other than that of the purposiveness of nature. The articulation of the faculty of the power of judgment therefore allows the entry of transcendence into the realm of the natural, not by an unwarranted intervention of reason, but by the intermediary of the power of judgment.[55]

God and Humanity's Telos

As the *Critique of the Power of Judgment* progresses there are several allusions to the importance of belief in God as a creator.[56] It is implied that God is believed to be the source of the purposiveness of nature in which we *must* believe, and that it is God who gives to mankind its faculties of cognition wherein mankind has to eventually realize at least in principle, if not in practice, its moral destiny and its teleological role as the end of nature. Kant tries to tease out the possible dimensions of his teleology by reference to an antinomy between the thesis that the generation of all things may be understood in accordance with mechanical laws and an antithesis that "some generation of such things is not possible in accordance with merely mechanical laws."[57] Kant concludes that the reflecting power of judgment needs an intelligent "world cause acting in accordance with ends although this would be rash and indemonstrable for the determining power of judgment."[58] Because of the nature of the reflecting power of judgment, no claim can be made as to the *existence* of such a world cause, i.e., God. Instead, argues Kant, "we can establish it only subjectively for the use of our power of judgment in its reflection upon ends in nature, which cannot be conceived in accordance with any other principle than that of an intentional causality of a highest cause."[59] This statement is important because it demonstrates the significance of *belief* in the divine cause, as the implication is that without such belief there is no ground for the purposiveness of nature, or any special role within nature for mankind. As Michael Kraft has argued, Kant requires us to believe in the "necessary fiction" of God as a foundation for hope.[60] God therefore is an unproven but necessary postulate in Kant's projected development of human beings toward humanity.[61]

Once one makes the necessary leap of faith, God is believed to be the originator of both the sensible and the supersensible aspects of both the natural and the practical destinies of mankind. The assumption of an intention in nature connects (in the reflecting power of judgment) the mechanical laws with teleological laws in the production of nature, albeit with the proviso that the mechanical laws are subordinate to the teleological ones. God therefore is the higher principle that is necessary for the coexistence of all aspects of life. This is consistent with Kant's claim that only something outside nature (and therefore free from it) could be its cause. Mankind's reflective power of judgment therefore leads it to a situation where it believes that it is the final end of nature in a teleological system under God's guidance. Kant therefore restores to mankind a cosmological significance that had been lost:

> Now if things in the world, as dependent beings as far as their existence is concerned, need a supreme cause acting in accordance with ends, then the human being is the final end of creation; for without him the chain of ends subordinated to one another would not be completely grounded; and only in the human being, although in him only as a subject of morality, is unconditional legislation with regards to ends to be found, which therefore makes him alone capable of being a final end, to which the whole of nature is teleologically subordinated.[62]

Behind the human, if his existence is to have any meaning, however remote and obscured, stands God as the ultimate architect of his destiny. The constitution of our faculty of reason, and the faculty of the power of judgment make comprehensible the purposiveness of nature, which, according to Kant, requires a moral legislator and author.[63] As such Kant affirms that we "must assume a moral cause of the world . . . namely that there is a God."

Independence from Nature

Kant constantly stresses in the *Critique of the Power of Judgment* human beings' potential separation from nature. For Kant, nature is at best preparing the human being for her transcendence of it and at worst acting as a block on human potential. The mechanism of nature is subordinated to the teleological and transcendental principle of the purposiveness of nature and the "intentional technicism" that guides it.[64] The human being, if he is to exit the natural mode of being, must re-create political and social life according to what he can discern of the will of God via reason, while still bearing in mind that it is "rational and meritorious" to comprehend the limits set by the mechanism of nature as far as can be plausibly done.[65] The proviso "as far as can be plausibly done" is significant in that the condition of plausibility is set by the limits of rationality, which should not be exceeded.

The historical record and the faculty of understanding contradict the idea that the human being is the end of nature, as he has been and remains a natural creature that is subject in every way to the constitution and demands of nature—thus the human being's status as an end of nature is contingent:

> If nature is regarded as a teleological system, then it is his vocation to be the ultimate end of nature; but always only conditionally, that is subject to the condition that he has the understanding and the will to give to nature and to himself a relation to an end that can be sufficient for itself independently of nature, which can thus be a final end, which however, must not be sought in nature at all.[66]

Kant tries to argue the case for a synthesis of ends and means in the relationship between the culture of skill (including political skill): "the foremost subjective condition of aptitude for the promotion of ends in general" and the rational determination of what those ends should be according to reason—an alliance of prudence and rational morality that recognizes that rational ends must employ technical means, albeit technical means informed by rational morality (this is the modus operandi of the moral politician in *Toward Perpetual Peace*).[67] This synthesis finds expression in the concept of civil society, which, extended to its logical limit, includes the conceptualization of international relations as a cosmopolitan whole. Kant, however, is adamant that the human being as he *currently* constitutes himself ultimately only has recourse to war.[68] It is only post-Enlightenment man, "the organized being," who can live according to Kant's plan.

Conclusion

By outlining the rational possibility of human beings and humanity being the end of nature and the realization of freedom, respectively, the *Critique of the Power of Judgment* informs Kant's later works on politics and international relations.[69] Kant claims that nature "can be transformed by us into something entirely different, namely into that which steps beyond nature."[70] Kant's project may be summed up as the *denaturalization* of human beings, a form of declaration of independence from nature itself. The culmination of the book is the depiction of the human being as a moral agent who steps outside of nature, which is now "teleologically subordinated" to mankind.[71] This is essentially a "have your cake and eat it, too" solution for Kant in that he sees no final contradiction between the natural and the rational in the long term as the rational is (at least potentially) immanent within the natural.[72] Kant proceeds as if he has solved the problem of human social conflict by displacing his analysis from the external, political terrain governed by the faculty of understanding to the reflective judgment's assumption of purposiveness. The failure of human beings to correspond in their actions to "rational" order therefore is no longer a major problem, as the assumption that nature is purposive and humanity is its end point allows the rational *belief* and *hope* that humanity may attain (or approximate) its end, despite the "crooked timber" of human beings. If there is no rational impediment to this end, then, argues Kant, it is incumbent on human beings to work toward it.

CHAPTER 3

The Problem of International Politics

Human Beings within the Mechanism of Nature

[I]n the end one does not know what concept to make of our species, with its smug imaginings about its excellences.[1]

In a manner that demonstrates the intertwining of his critical-philosophical works and his international theory, Kant commences his engagement with global politics in the 1784 essay *Idea for a Universal History with a Cosmopolitan Aim* (which itself anticipates many of the themes of the third *Critique* regarding the purposiveness of nature), by means of a distinction between the freedom of the will, viewed as a metaphysical idea, and "its *appearances*, the human actions," which appear to be determined "just as much as every other natural occurrence" by universal laws of nature.[2] If freedom of the will is determined in the realm of appearances, this has the important implication that political activity is likewise determined and subject to universal laws of nature discoverable by observation and the application of understanding and technical practical reason. The results of such observation and analysis are somewhat dispiriting in relation to human beings: the empirical evidence of their activities in nature leads to the conclusion that one "cannot at all presuppose any rational *aim of theirs*" to be in evidence. The metaphysical presupposition of a purpose underlying nature itself, however, permits the observer "to try whether he can discover *an aim of nature* in this nonsensical course of things human," by assuming a rational purpose that can then render human activity meaningful.[3] Although natural forces determine the *appearance* of human behavior, the *history* of mankind, and therefore its possible meaning and significance, is open to interpretation in that "the narration of these appearances, however deeply concealed their causes may be, nevertheless allows us to hope from it that if it considers the play of freedom of the human will *in the large*, it can discover within it a regular course," culminating in the conclusion that "what meets the eye in individual subjects as confused and irregular yet in the whole species can be recognized as a steadily progressing though slow development of its original predispositions."[4] The progressive reading of a purposeful nature must not, however, be mistaken for an ontological position as "any order Reason imposes upon a historical narrative is one which applies to our manner of comprehending history and not directly nor immediately to the historical events themselves."[5] Jens Bartelson's formulation is particularly useful in identifying the relationship between meaning, narration, and history in Kant's work: "Lacking intrinsic meaning, history has to be narrated through a deciphering of its signs; lacking a finished plot, history has to be created by being narrated. Hence, making history and narrating history become two aspects of the same process."[6] The assumption of "a hidden purpose to nature, a purpose that drives toward morality, even if the people who live in the world would not be aware of that mission in their own lives," despite all empirical evidence to the contrary, enables a reading of human existence in which it is possible to posit a final resolution in which politics bends its knee before morality.[7]

Two *perspectives* then are possible regarding nature and mankind's place within it: first, that nature (including mankind) can be read as proceeding according to a rational plan, and, second, that nature is "purposelessly playing," i.e., that it exists without innate meaning in a universe devoid of genuine purpose. The former reading is Kant's preferred one, i.e., that human existence be viewed as if it is subject to a "determinate plan of nature." At the very least, such an assumption of rational nature provides a guideline for understanding human activity that might lead to philosophy being "in a position to compose that history accordingly." Kant draws an analogy between taking this position and that of "Kepler, who subjected the eccentric paths of the planets in an unexpected way to determinate laws, and a Newton who explained these laws from a universal natural cause."[8] In short, the assumption of a rational plan of nature enables the systematic study of human behavior. The antinomy of rational and purposelessly playing nature proceeds to dominate Kant's analysis of international politics from this point onward, with significant implications both for what we can know and what we can believe about what constitutes and what *may* constitute political life.[9]

The first part of this chapter surveys the *problem* of domestic and international politics in terms of how human beings *appear* to operate to each other (and themselves). The second part moves to a deeper engagement with the essay *Idea for a Universal History*, which accepts appearances as its starting point, but proceeds to offer an interpretive exit from the mechanism of nature. The third part of the chapter introduces Moses Mendelssohn's cyclical reading of human history, a perspective that would haunt Kant's efforts to argue the case for politics being more than the operation of the mechanism of nature for human beings. Mendelssohn's theory, that mankind simply oscillates between peaks and troughs of achievement at different times in different cultures, poses an alternative to Kant's theory of progress that is more empirically grounded and equally, if not more, plausible in many ways than the gradually upward ascent of human beings toward perpetual peace. In order to maintain a compelling case for his preferred path to perpetual peace in response to Mendelssohn, Kant had to stake out very specific positions rooted not in empirical facts of history, but rather in an ultimately providential reading of history from the perspective of his practical philosophy.

The fourth part opens this book's consideration of *Toward Perpetual Peace* in the light of the problem posed by the limits of human knowledge with regard to nature and mankind's role within it. The significance of *Toward Perpetual Peace* in Kant's work is extraordinary in that it "is not simply a book commenting from a philosophical perspective on what can be done about politics. It represents a point of culmination of Kant's critical enterprise, at least in so far as its practical aspect is concerned."[10] Kant develops opposing standpoints of anthropological observation, a higher one associated with the moral politician and a lower one related to the moralizing politician or "practical man," that allow two very different interpretations of political activity and its prospective results. From the higher anthropological standpoint, humanity attains perpetual peace through the realization of Kantian moral philosophy.[11] From the lower anthropological standpoint the prospects of mankind are less clear and encompass a range of results from wars of annihilation to a contingent peace based on self-interest. The important role right plays in elevating political activity from the conflict of interests to the acceptance of order is investigated in light of the two anthropological perspectives, with Kant's finding that the rejection of the world state—the most theoretically satisfying resolution of political existence from the perspective of right—playing an important role in determining how ultimately we should understand the nature of peace in international society. Right may be enough to effect progress from the politics of raw antagonism, but it is not enough to create perpetual peace as a *system* of right-based peace. Kant's "negative surrogate" of peace based on a federative union is, Kant recognizes, continually under siege from natural incentives and desires. The precarious nature of peace may be attributed to the imperfect working of the relationship between right, reason, and nature within this surrogate solution. Kant insists that the very concept of right that states hold will not allow them to accept the world republic, which, according to Kant, is reason's *sole* possible conclusion that would enable all three parts to achieve their perfect fulfillment. It is in this very specific context of human imperfection that Kant introduces his "negative surrogate" of peace under the aegis of a federative league of nations. As the league is a negative surrogate for the world state, so also are faith and hope supplementary foundations designed to shore up reason when the necessary requirements of reason for a world republic are rejected by states operating according to human, all too human, will. Hope and faith do not eclipse reason in *Toward Perpetual Peace*, rather they enable it to work *practically* to counter the despairing denial of hope by "practical man."

The chapter concludes with a return to the fundamental distinction between the moral politician and practical man and the higher and lower anthropological perspectives on the nature and conduct of politics. Kant, realizing that this is in effect an anthropological antinomy, couches his vision of political and moral convergence in practical terms: that one may hope for genuine perpetual peace to emerge from the mutual operation of reason, nature, right, and morality and have faith that this purpose has been arranged by an author of rational nature. This perspective of "benign hope" in perpetual peace is only realizable, however, if mankind assumes the higher anthropological perspective, a radical perceptual shift that would in effect require an anthropological revolution. It is at this point that the analysis of *Toward Perpetual Peace* is suspended in order to investigate the possibility of such a revolution and its underpinnings in faith. For perpetual peace to be achieved in the sense held by the moral politician a profound alteration of mankind's collective sense of itself as a species and its relationship with the divine would have to take place, the possibility of which is assessed in chapters 4 and 5. Alternatively, if peace as understood by the political moralist is the other option available, i.e., peace achieved through the prudential operation of the levers of the mechanism of nature, then mankind will not have escaped the possibility of Mendelssohnian devolution within the cyclical reading of human history, and the fate of Sisyphus is all that can be expected for mankind in perpetuity. Such are the stakes in Kant's complex treatment of nature, reason, and faith in relation to the possibility of perpetual peace.

The Problem of Politics and International Relations

Kant's depiction of the human being as a *political* animal is best exemplified in the *Critique of the Power of Judgment*:

> the conflict in the *natural predispositions* of the human being, reduces himself and others of his own species, by means of plagues that he invents for himself, such as the oppression of domination, the barbarism of war, etc., to such need, and he works so hard for the destruction of his own species, that even if the most beneficent nature outside of us had made the happiness of our species its end, that end would not be attained in a system of nature upon the earth, because the nature inside of us is not receptive to that.[12]

It is no surprise that such a flawed creature as the human being creates politics in its own image—a chaotic scrabbling for the achievement of different individual ends. The defining problem of politics *in nuce* for Kant is that the mere presence of other human beings is sufficient to "corrupt each other's moral disposition and make one another evil."[13] In a political existence within the mechanism of nature, wherein survival and necessity are the ultimate ends, human beings must live according to the dictates of prudence:

> No one, therefore, need wait until he has learned by bitter experience of the other's contrary disposition; for what should bind him to wait till he has suffered a loss before he becomes prudent, when he can quite well perceive within himself the inclination of human beings generally to lord it over others as their master. . . . And it is not necessary to wait for actual hostility; one is authorized to use coercion against someone who already, by his nature, threatens him with coercion.[14]

Although he condemns this as *morally* wrong, Kant recognizes that as long as "externally lawless freedom" prevails then the political realm (and especially international politics) cannot be a genuinely rightful environment.[15] Such an externally lawless condition produces a state of affairs in which

> [c]onstant hostility over the ever-possible violation of their rights is also at all times possible, and so here we have a condition of possible enmity and possible infringement of legitimate freedom (*conditio hominum per quam meliorum jurium capaces sunt*). It should be called only a *status belli omnium contra omnes*, a condition of injustice; a legal condition (for every condition must be legal) in which the determining and deciding of what is to be law can occur no otherwise than by violence; so that even in their constitutions, all peoples are prepared for this. It is therefore nothing more than the *status naturalis*, in Idea.[16]

Until such time as reason can effect serious reform of the structure and processes of international politics, first through the establishment of a system based on the right of nations, and ultimately through the moral reformation of the species, the human being must content himself with existing within a state of nature, at best reforming it according to the limits of his ability and the political and moral insights available to him. In the political realm the use of force and the possession of power, not law, are the determinants of behavior. In such a condition a state may use violence when it is of the opinion that

> [i]n addition to active violations (first aggression, which is not the same as first hostility) it may be threatened. This includes another state's being the first to undertake preparations, upon which is based the right of *prevention (ius praeventionis)*, or even just the menacing increase in another state's power (by its acquisition of territory) (*potentia tremenda*). This is a wrong to the lesser power merely by the condition of the superior power, before any deed on its part, and in the state of nature an attack by the lesser power is indeed legitimate.[17]

As a *political* analyst of international society, Kant is concerned with the power dynamics within the state of nature that lead states to preserve "the right to a balance of power among all states that are contiguous and could act on one another."[18] It is in this context of the state of nature that Kant comes to the conclusion that Brennus, who waged war against Rome in a particularly brutal manner, was correct in his identification of "[t]he right of the stronger against the weaker, which is implanted in everyone, from Gods to unreasoning creatures." This sentiment, typical according to Kant of *homo brutus*, leads to a political condition in which the appeal to justice or rights is meaningless: "In this condition, it cannot even be said that one people may wrong another. For the possibility of violating their legitimate freedom is so acutely and continuously present on both sides, that the state of peace seems merely to be an armistice."[19] Andrew Hurrell correctly identifies the echoes of Hobbes in Kant's presentation of a "bleak picture of chronic and unmitigated insecurity."[20]

Kant sees the emergence of civil society as the alternative to such an insecure and dangerous environment.[21] Domestic and international politics are part of the same process for Kant in that they *ought*, albeit at different rates, and from different starting points, to progress from amorality to rational and moral order through the institution of civil society.[22] The achievement of this condition was attained at the domestic level (at least in principle) by the effects of "omnilateral" violence forcing the establishment of public law and the civil constitution. International politics, however, remains in a state of nature in which mankind is revealed at its most unflattering: "Nowhere does human nature appear less lovable than in the relations of entire peoples to one another. . . . The will to subjugate one another or to diminish what belongs to another always exists."[23] Kant argues, however, that a process similar to that in the domestic sphere will occur at the international level: "so too must the need arising from the constant wars by which states in turn try to encroach upon or subjugate one another at last bring them, even against their will, to enter into a *cosmopolitan constitution* . . . [or a] *federation* in accordance with a commonly agreed *right of nations*."[24] This passage is significant because Kant makes it clear that this process occurs *without* a reorientation of human beings' wills; it will happen "even against their will."

Self-love, greed, fear, and the use of violence are revealed to be the *natural* motors of human progress, as through their operation eventually "every commonwealth, unable to harm another by force, must have recourse only to right and has grounds to hope that others similarly constituted will come to its assistance in this."[25] This is true to such an extent that good will (the foundation for Kant's deontological ethics as outlined in *The Groundwork*) is almost irrelevant in the initial stages of the political evolution of humans: "hence impotence must eventually bring about what good will ought to have done but did not do."[26] The intentions of individual persons, however well meaning, are relatively unimportant at this stage as "this immeasurably distant success will depend not so much on what we do (e.g., on the education we give the younger generation) and by what methods we should proceed in order to bring it about, but instead upon what human *nature* will do in and with us to *force* us onto a track we would not readily take of our own accord."[27]

A Universal History with a Cosmopolitan Aim?

Kant's essay *Idea for a Universal History with a Cosmopolitan Aim* is his earliest, and arguably his most foundational, work on the logics underpinning human progress. As they foster the development of natural predispositions, Kant celebrates the progressive effect of activities that are in themselves immoral: "Thanks be to nature for the incompatibility, for the distasteful, competitive vanity, for the insatiable desire to possess and also to rule. Without them, all of humanity's excellent natural capacities would have lain eternally dormant."[28] Kant avoids the problem of the nature of the human being by situating his level of analysis at that of the species, which, unlike the chaotic and unpredictable individual, exhibits predictability and to whom a pattern of rational behavior may be assigned when viewed from the perspective of rational nature.[29] While no history of human beings is in conformity with a rational plan, Kant insists that one has to "hope" in a plan of nature of which humanity is the beneficiary.[30] The *telos* of nature is important as a principle of faith, otherwise the natural predispositions of human beings are purposeless, which would be contrary to an ordered and systematic nature, with the result that nature would be "under the suspicion that in the case of the human being alone it is a childish play." Kant gives a simple choice to his readers—either we act *as if* there is a rational ordered plan to the universe, or we give ourselves up to random chaos, the play of chance, and the necessarily inadequate efforts of human beings to mediate a system of which they are mechanically determined parts, and hence unable to radically alter. By choosing to adopt belief in rational nature, human beings enable themselves to take an active role within nature as they seek to reform it according to what they take to be its rational ends.

Where mankind has an active role is in its responsibility to prove itself worthy of well-being by overcoming a "whole host of hardships" that will assail it during the ascent from crudity to culture. Chief among these hardships is antagonism in society, the product of unsocial sociability, the condition of being simultaneously attracted and repelled by engagement with other human beings in society. The human being, writes Kant, is "driven by ambition, tyranny, and greed, to obtain for himself a rank among his fellows, whom he cannot stand, but also cannot leave alone." Through this desire for rank, talents develop and bloom, taste becomes more widespread, and, importantly, "a beginning is made toward the foundation of a mode of thought which can with time transform . . . a society finally into a moral whole."[31] Cultivation and civilization, however, are not synonymous with moralization; at best, they are interpretable as being preparatory for it, and at worst as contrary to morality. Mankind will remain in a condition of insufficiency until the external politics of violent expansion and the internal politics of repression retarding the inner development of the citizens' minds have ceased, but in order to get to the point where they must cease they will operate to their fullest extent.[32] The existence of these natural incentives and inbuilt drives toward competition—including competition in the arts and sciences of advanced societies—may be interpreted, according to Kant, as betraying "the ordering of a wise creator."[33]

The solution to the problem of unsocial sociability is to institute a civil society in which right is universally observed. Kant portrays this as a self-fulfilling process in that social action allows antagonism, which constrains and contains freedom within the parameters established by the conflicting parties. In such an environment the talents of human beings are fostered to their utmost degree. Social order then is the fruit of managed antagonism, and as human beings get better at managing the antagonism, the establishment of an expanding, evolving, rights-based civil society ensues in which the "germs of nature" can develop.[34] This solution is jeopardized by the fact that the human being remains an animal and as such, according to Kant, requires a master, but the only possible master is another human being—and hence a master certain to misuse his freedom. In what would become a feature of his thought on political existence, Kant claims that a perfect solution to this problem is impossible, as, in his famous dictum, "from the crooked wood of man, no straight thing may be made."[35] Only a constitution based on "correct concepts," informed by "great experience," and a populace with a good will to implement this constitution provides an approximation of the idea that Kant regards as an ideal political community. This approximation, Kant concedes, is remote both in terms of the likelihood of its achievement and in the sheer scale of time required for this success in that if it occurs at all it will come very late in human development and only after many fruitless attempts—a condition that Brad Evans has aptly described as condemning mankind to live in a "temporal purgatory."[36] The possibility of human moral and social evolution is explored in the following chapters—at this point it is sufficient to recognize that even allowing for eons of development, Kant still identifies *belief* in God as a key component of this evolution away from the purgatorial status in which mankind is enmeshed.

The holistic vision of Kant's political theory is evident from his linkage of the creation of a perfect civil constitution at the domestic level with the successful resolution of the problem of establishing a successful lawful set of relations between states.[37] Kant's position is to claim that global politics will follow a similar logic to that of domestic politics because it is similarly based on unsocial sociability, antagonism, and the attendant pressure to develop a system in which this antagonism may be managed:

> Nature has therefore once again used the incompatibility of human beings, even of great societies and state bodies . . . as a means to seek out in their unavoidable antagonism a condition of tranquillity and safety; i.e. through wars, through the overstrained and never ceasing process of armament for them. . . . nature drives them to what reason could have told them even without so much sad experience: namely to go beyond a lawless condition of savages and enter into a federation of nations.[38]

It is important to recognize that Kant fully expects human beings to *reject* reason—human beings will learn only from "sad experience" of war and hardship. Kant forecasts a future in which states form, are destroyed and reconfigured in wartime, time and again in a process where "new relationships" become possible until external and internal political structures are sufficiently developed to preserve commonwealths in their respective spheres.[39] In a position he was later to revise, Kant identifies the balance of power as underpinning hope for the establishment of a peaceful international regime as the operation of the laws of equilibrium of force and counterforce engender the conditions in which, at least in principle, the "cosmopolitan condition of public state security" can attain.[40]

Kant admits in this essay to being a philosophical chiliast, seeking and finding a little, but sufficient, evidence for his thesis "to determine reliably enough" a vision of the human future.[41] The assumption of a plan within rational nature can act as a positive "guiding thread" that helps to make sense of the seemingly senseless activities of human beings—it is a systematization of nature, whether nature is subject to this system or not, that allows the human mind to find meaning and purpose for its existence. Part of the guiding-thread thesis is that as civilizations rise and fall they leave behind "germs of enlightenment" that future civilizations refine and develop in a manner that is both cyclical and ultimately progressive (see chapter 4 for further elaboration). The *belief* in a universal world history, informed by the idea of a rational plan underpinning the operation of nature, is for Kant a "useful idea," in that it not only allows "political soothsaying" but also opens "a consoling prospect into the future (which without a plan of nature one cannot hope for with any ground)."[42] By providing a positive resolution to an otherwise hopeless situation, Kant avers that he has achieved the justification of "nature—or better of *providence* . . . no unimportant motive for choosing a particular viewpoint."[43] This passage marks the beginning of the bifurcation of nature and providence that would become crucial for Kant's political theology.

Kant, Moses Mendelssohn, and the Problem of Regression

The high stakes of Kant's reading of nature become clear in his characterization of rational nature offering "the guideline of reason" while "purposelessly playing nature" entails only "desolate chance."[44] It is clear from Kant's presentation of the implications of both perspectives that we ought to prefer the former to the latter in that "otherwise the natural predispositions" of human beings "would have to be regarded for the most part as vain and purposeless," a condition that would also have the effect of removing "all practical principles."[45] All of Kant's subsequent IR theory is built on this preference for purposiveness and fear of unpredictability, the two factors that ultimately compel Kant to develop a political theology of perpetual peace in order to point a way beyond the impasse of the two perspectives and to tip the balance in favor of pure practical reason and rational morality.

Drawing on the guiding-thread principle, Kant explains the antagonism of human social activity as the product of *unsociable sociability*. The course of human existence is attributable to this form of antagonism, "from which so many ills arise, which, however, impel human beings to new exertion of their powers and hence to further development of their natural predispositions," which, when viewed from the perspective of *rational* nature, betrays "the ordering of a wise creator." The significance of unsociable sociability, however, changes quite dramatically when viewed from the perspective of "purposelessly playing nature," in which the activities of humans are simply antagonistic and effectively meaningless. The question of whether nature has meaning or is meaningless becomes therefore the ultimate battleground of Kant's efforts to develop his thought in relation to the final resolution of human political life. The meaning of human existence is inextricably bound up with the achievement of a cosmopolitan political system that is subject to three philosophical positions.

Kant dismisses the Epicurean position (an expectation of a "concurrence of efficient causes that states, like little particles of matter, should seek all sorts of formations through their chance collisions, which again are destroyed through new impacts, until finally by chance there succeeds a formation that can preserve itself in its form") as "a fortunate coincidence that could hardly ever take place!"[46] Turning to his own position, Kant asks "whether one should assume that nature here follows a regular course, leading our species from the lowest step of animality gradually up to the highest step of humanity." It is the third interpretation that causes Kant the most anguish, in that its findings are at least as logically sound as his own, but do not offer the hope of lasting salvation embedded within the principle of "rational nature." In this, the Mendelssohnian reading of nature, the teleological principle is replaced by a cyclical principle. For Mendelssohn, "many a nation will alter its form of government as often as changes take place in its culture, way of life, and convictions, and, in the course of centuries, will pass through the whole cycle of forms of government, in all their shades and combinations."[47] The species does not progress in Mendelssohn's reading of human history as "the material is always the same," and despite its wandering through the "cycle of ideas" the "quantity and weight of its morality may, perhaps, remain, on balance, about the same during all these various epochs."[48] Although some nations may be in a fairly advanced stage at one moment, others are not, and in the event of the other states progressing, the advanced states will have regressed from the heights they had achieved.[49]

The Mendelssohnian reading of human history, according to Kant, predicts that

from all these effects and counter-effects of human beings nothing at all will result in the large, or at least nothing prudent, that it will remain as it always has been, and that therefore one cannot say ahead of time whether the discord that is so natural to our species will in the end prepare a hell of ills for us in however civilized a condition, in that nature will perhaps annihilate again, through barbaric devastations, this condition and all the previous steps of culture (which cannot be excluded under the government of blind chance, which is in fact the same as lawless freedom, if one does not ascribe secretly to a guiding thread of nature as attached to wisdom).[50]

Mendelssohn opposes the idea of a divine education (a principle that plays an important role in Kant's anthropology; see chapter 4) in Gotthold Lessing and offers instead a vision of mankind in which "'[w]e see . . . the human race as a whole make small oscillations, and it never takes a few steps forward without soon afterward sliding back twice as fast into its former state.'"[51] The Sisyphean fate of constant struggle with the limits of its own nature that awaits the human species within the Mendelssohnian reading of human history has important consequences for Kant in that although he does not dispute its possibility, he rejects it as a "sight most unworthy . . . even of the most common but well-disposed human being to see the human race from period to period taking steps upward to virtue and soon after falling back just as deeply into misery. To watch this tragedy for a while might be moving and instructive but the curtain must eventually fall." Kant's rejection is couched in explicitly theological terms in that Mendelssohn's reading of human history is "contrary to the morality of a wise creator and ruler of the world."[52] For Mendelssohn, however, providence is inscrutable and its designs cannot be divined or presumed. Mendelssohn's position is—crucially—rooted in the *experience* of human history, the study of which leads him to conclude that one should not "frame hypotheses" regarding providence: "only look around you at what actually happens and, if you can survey history as a whole, at what has happened since the beginning of time," study of which reveals that "as far as the human race as a whole is concerned, you will find no steady progress in its development that brings it ever closer to perfection."[53] Perhaps in response to Mendelssohn, Kant realizes that his argument regarding possible human advance can only be expressed in practical terms and surrenders the empirical history of mankind (see chapter 4) to skepticism. Kant develops his theory of teleological salvation by reference to a time so distant that it is beyond the scope of empirical inquiry and hence of any objection emanating from that quarter.

In the context of the anthropological implications of the critical philosophy, Kant's interpretation of Mendelssohn's reading of mankind's inability to progress morally is profoundly disturbing.[54] If Mendelssohn is correct, according to Kant in *That May Be True in Theory*, the only appropriate stance to take toward human beings is hatred: "however one may try to extract love from oneself, one cannot avoid hating what is and remains evil."[55] Kant recoils from this finding and instead offers an alternative reading of mankind. It is telling that in his reading of human progress Kant invokes a second *Critique*–inspired duty to work for progress: "so to influence posterity that it becomes always better (the possibility of this must, accordingly, also be assumed)," coupled with hope ("without which an earnest desire to do something profitable for the general well-being would never have warmed the human heart"). The most important element, however, is an identification of the importance of providence: "[f]or only from nature, or rather from *providence* (since supreme wisdom is required for the complete fulfillment of this end), can we expect an outcome that is directed to the whole and from it to the parts."[56]

The identification of the importance of providence as a more apposite idea than nature is significant as it marks an advance in Kant's thought that would prove decisive in his treatment of perpetual peace. Although he offers it only as "an opinion and a mere hypothesis," Kant proposes that "it can be considered an expression not unbefitting the moral wishes and hopes of people (once aware of their inability) to expect the circumstances required for these from providence, which will provide an outcome for the end of *humanity* as a whole species, to reach its final destination by the free use of its powers as far as they extend, to which end the ends of *human beings*, considered separately, are directly opposed."[57] This passage encapsulates the opposition of human beings and humanity, and the close relationship between the realization of the latter status and belief in providence—it is telling that Kant insists on the *inability* of human beings to achieve their moral wishes and hopes *without* belief in a purposeful nature that is the design of a *particular* kind of providence, which in turn serves as the foundation for his progressivist reading of mankind's destiny. Kant therefore implicitly recognizes that from the observation of human beings, Mendelssohn's reading of human existence, i.e., that mankind "continually fluctuates within fixed limits, while maintaining, on the whole, about the same degree of morality in all periods," is correct, but shifts the ground of the differences between them from that of empirical observation to that of faith. Faith guarantees that Kant's New Jerusalem, the condition of perpetual peace, will not meet the same fate as Mendelssohn's *Jerusalem*, which, having achieved a height when "teaching and life, wisdom and activity, speculation and sociability were most intimately connected," soon declined and "within a short period, things took the road of corruption. It was not long before this brilliant circle, too, had been completed, and matters again returned to a point not far from the low level from which they had emerged."[58] In sum, the Mendelssohn/Kant issue devolves to competing readings of the relationship between man and God: on the one hand observation reveals an inscrutable God whose intentions toward mankind permit no hypothesis, and on the other rational morality requires *belief* in an entity that has ordered nature for the sake of our eventual salvation. To believe otherwise is "[t]o conclude that what happens in nature happens entirely as the result of random chance," which "is unthinkable for Kant. The human being must have a purpose to serve within the plan of nature or else reason itself has to be abandoned."[59] In the absence of this essential foundation, the remainder of Kant's project, e.g., freedom, the moral law, the hope for a rationally ordered cosmopolitan peace, also disappear.

Perpetual Peace

In *Toward Perpetual Peace*, Kant is still haunted by the prospect that "if there were no freedom and no moral law based upon it and everything that happens or can happen is instead the mere mechanism of nature, then politics (as the art of making use of this mechanism for governing human beings) would be the whole of practical wisdom and the concept of right would be an empty thought."[60] It is in this context that Kant develops a specifically political formulation of the human beings/humanity dual perspective that emerged from the critical philosophy. The distinction is not as clear cut, but can be discerned through a careful reading of Kant's juxtaposition of "practical man (for whom morals is mere theory)" and the "moral politician." The core difference in this instance is epistemological. Practical men "make much of their knowledge of *human beings*," knowledge built on empirical observations and predicated upon the primacy of power itself.[61] For these practical men politics reduces to the operation of power rather than principle ("it is not their business to reason subtly about legislation itself but to carry out the present commands of the law of the land"), with their motivation being "private advantage." Expedience rather than truth serves as the basis of political life in that "whatever lawful constitution now exists must always be the best and, when this is altered from on high, the one following it, since everything is then in its proper mechanical order." Practical man believes he can solve any constitutional issue empirically, by reference to previous experience within "the hitherto most lasting constitutions . . . even though they were for the most part contrary to right." Ignoring principles of freedom, the practical man expresses his political logic in the "sophistical maxims" of "*Fac et excusa*" (act and justify after the event), "*Si fescisti, nega*" (if you are at fault, blame others for the consequences), and "*Divide et impera*" (divide and rule).[62] The fundamental belief of the practical man is that "a practice that is based on empirical principles of human nature, one that does not consider it demeaning to draw instruction for its maxims from the way of the world, can alone hope to find a sure ground for its edifice of political prudence."[63]

The key move that Kant makes is to deny that the perspective of the practical man is the sole means by which we can comprehend political existence. Practical man's perspective is not as definitive as he believes, and is based, according to Kant, on ignorance of "the human being and *what can be made of him*" (emphasis added). Kant insists that knowing the human being and what can be made of him requires "a higher standpoint of anthropological observation" than the (implicitly) lower anthropological standpoint of the practical man.[64] Central to Kant's argument is the position taken in *That May Be True in Theory*, denying the epistemological primacy of knowledge derived from empirical experience: "it does not matter how many doubts may be raised against my hopes from history . . . as long as these doubts cannot be made quite certain I cannot exchange the duty . . . for the rule of prudence. . . . however uncertain I may always be and remain as to whether something better is to be hoped for the human race, this cannot infringe upon the maxim, and hence its presupposition, necessary for practical purposes, that it is practicable."[65] In addition to being an impediment to the practical purposes of mankind, the empirical is logically unsatisfactory as it ignores the potential future success of actions or principles that had failed in the past: "Empirical arguments against the success of these resolutions, which are taken on hope, accomplish nothing here. For, that what has not succeeded up to now will therefore never succeed does not even justify abandoning a pragmatic or technical purpose (for example, that of flights with aerostatic balloons), still less a moral purpose that, if only it is not demonstratively impossible to effect it, becomes a duty."[66] The reliance on hope, and its explicit opposition to empirical observation, is telling and would become a major feature of Kant's approach to international politics.

Right and the Role It Plays in Toward Perpetual Peace

In *Toward Perpetual Peace* Kant refines and draws out the specific logic and processes that underpin his thinking about international politics. Kant was also able in this essay to draw on important advances within his own philosophy as developed in the second and third *Critiques, Religion Within the Boundaries of Mere Reason*, and *That May Be True in Theory*.[67] *Toward Perpetual Peace* also anticipates important developments within the wider practical philosophy, notably the concept of right upon which he elaborates in the *Rechtslehre* section of the *Metaphysics of Morals*. Kant's decisive move in *Toward Perpetual Peace* is to present international society as akin to the state of nature in previous contract theory in which the mere existence of other nations is presented as being problematic in terms of their external relationships:

> Nations, as states, can be appraised as individuals, who in their natural condition (that is, in their independence from external laws) already wrong one another by being near one another; and each of them, for the sake of its security, can and ought to require the others to enter with it into a constitution similar to a civil constitution, in which each can be assured of its right.[68]

Only establishing a condition like the civil constitution based on "lawful coercion" in global politics can lead to an escape from the "depraved condition" of international relations.[69] Kant stresses, however, that even in the depths of this depraved environment, where the "malevolence of human nature . . . can be seen unconcealed," the appeal to right has not been "altogether banished."[70] Right may be understood as the rules that govern the external freedom of members of society in accordance with an idea of universal law. The pure moral philosophy is not identical to the philosophy of right, and in this margin of difference Kant develops an important distinction between external and internal duties: "External duties derive their force not merely from our sense of duty but also from the possibility that we may be coerced if we fail to comply with the law. Internal duties do not carry the same prohibitive force, relying on our sense of duty alone. This makes for an important difference between the philosophy of rights and ethics. The philosophy of right deals with a compulsory mode of behaviour, whereas ethics deals with a voluntary code of behaviour."[71] The key principle of right is not that actions pass the test of the categorical imperative, but rather that "they allow individuals to live in harmony with each other in society." Rights are formulated in this manner because they have to "take into account man's flawed dual nature. . . . Kant sensibly recognizes that ethical standards are not, as things now stand, enough on their own to hold a society together."[72]

Pierre Laberge adroitly employs Kant's "republic of devils" metaphor to argue that the rational origins of right and justice lie in rational self-interest: "[T]he problem of justice lies in the coexistence of free agents in a common world and in the conflicts which therefore inevitably arise. . . . Such a state of nature is a state of war for Kant, as it is for Hobbes. Everyone is at the mercy of everyone else. . . . An intelligent devil could not but will to abandon this condition. He (or she) could not but will to exchange his freedom to kill for his right not to be killed."[73] In the *Metaphysics of Morals*, Kant provides a three-part characterization of right:

> The concept of right, insofar as it is related to an obligation corresponding to it (i.e., the moral concept of right), has to do, *first*, only with the external and indeed practical relation of one person to another, insofar as their actions, as deeds, can have (direct or indirect) influence on each other. But, *second*, it does not signify the relation of one's choice to the mere wish (hence also to the mere need) of the other, as in actions of beneficence of callousness, but only a relation to the other's *choice*. *Third*, in this reciprocal relation of choice no account at all is taken of the *matter* of choice, that is, of the end each has in mind with the object he wants. . . . All that is in question is the form in the relation of choice on the part of both, insofar as choice is regarded merely as *free*, and whether the action of one can be united with the freedom of the other in accordance with a universal law.[74]

Right serves as an alternative to the pursuit of power and interest in the political sphere: it is, as Katrin Flikschuh argues, "that which gives each their due (which can be determined with exactitude)," an exactitude that "gives it a claim to context-independent, a priori validity."[75] It is important to recognize, however, that "[r]ightful action need not be ethical," and that it admits of "incentives other than duty."[76] This is particularly important in a text such as *Toward Perpetual Peace*, wherein "a much harsher environment" pertains than in the purely moral writings, and Kant adjusts accordingly in relation to this shift in context: "in contrast to the agent-centred perspective of the ethical writings, the essays adopt a historical perspective. Their principal concern is to assess the possibility of humanity's moral progress through gradual reason. While in ethics, it should be no concern to us how others act so long as we ourselves fulfil our moral duties, the adoption of such an inward looking perspective is not possible with regard to historical and political agency."[77]

Both Flikschuh and Ellis identify the important distinction between two forms of right, *provisional* right and *peremptory* right. Provisional right applies in the less than ideal political situations where the enactment of a right in its fullest sense would be premature and have the negative effect of either forestalling or damaging the evolution of the rule of right. For Ellis, "the concept of provisional right applies to institutions that imperfectly mirror their own normative principles; since all existing political institutions do this, pragmatic politics must follow a rule of provisional rather than conclusive right."[78] Kant, according to Ellis, places provisional right "in the intermediate stage between the absence of civil order (the state of nature) and the advent of the ideal republic (the civil condition). . . . Kant's notion of provisional right requires that the norms of the ideal republican state be respected so far as possible without violating current civil order."[79] It is in this context of imperfection that Kant makes a distinction between practices that "constitute unacceptable contradictions to the idea of the rule of law itself, while other practices merely hinder progress but do not contradict lawfulness *per se*. The moral laws that prohibit this second type are permissive (*leges latae*), as opposed to strict (*leges strictae*)."[80] In Flikschuh's analysis, we should read Kant as proposing "the gradual but steady transformation of provisional into peremptory right as a process of reform which will eventually encompass the spherical surface of the earth as a whole."[81] As Ellis stresses, however, there is a serious difference between the prospect of the global extension and intensification of right between that proposed in *Toward Perpetual Peace* and the *Metaphysics of Morals*, where the former "envisions an eventual advent of world peace under the voluntary union of republican governments, while the *Rechtslehre* argues that such an outcome, while desirable, is impossible," before acknowledging that despite this impossibility, "the political principles directed toward perpetual peace . . . which serve for continual *approximation* to it, are not unachievable."[82] For Mark Franke, the declaration of perpetual peace's impossibility has to be seen as rendering this final goal as a regulative principle "that humans necessarily maintain if destiny is to be fulfilled."[83] Right serves as a principle to lift mankind *as far as possible* out of the state of nature domestically and internationally, but also points toward an asymptotic ideal to which it ought to aspire. It is important to remember though that in this situation of provisional right, Laberge is correct to identify that within Kant's theory "devils A and B are still in the state of nature," even if "some improvement has been achieved insofar as they now know what will be the task of public law. Public law should secure everyone's freedom by securing an equal limitation of everyone's freedom, by guaranteeing private law or natural justice."[84]

The foregoing discussion of right in Kant serves to highlight the general context in which Kant's specific deployment of right in *Toward Perpetual Peace* takes place. In the essay, right establishes the moral personhood of peoples and states (Second Preliminary Article), undergirds Kant's objection to standing armies as irreconcilable with the "right of humanity in our own person" (Third Preliminary Article), forms the basis of the sovereign inviolability of states (Fifth Preliminary Article), and allows the theorization of war as "the regrettable expedient for asserting one's right by force in a state of nature (where there is no court that could judge with rightful force)" (Sixth Preliminary Article). The "rule of right" is itself essential to the distinction between *leges latae* and *leges strictae*: the former are laws that take "into consideration the circumstances in which they are to be *applied*," and permit postponement, while the latter are those laws that "hold without regard for differing circumstances, that insist on . . . putting a stop to an abuse *at once*."[85] Kant also employs the notion of permissive laws in order to establish rights in instances where "normal" laws of command and prohibition do not apply, e.g., in relation to the territory of states attained as "*possession in good faith (possessio putativa)* in accordance with a permissive law of natural right" in circumstances that do not pertain in a civil condition, wherein the putative claim to rightful possession would be illegal and "it would have to cease, as a wrong."[86] Kant then carefully employs right to establish what is appropriate before and after the institution of a civil condition (or more likely, an approximation thereof) domestically and internationally.

Kant's projected process of reform itself is also predicated on right. The first definitive article links the concept of right with the ideal, republican form of constitution, which "as far as right is concerned," is "in itself that which every kind of civil constitution has as its original basis . . . having arisen from the pure source of the concept of right."[87] The extension of right throughout the political sphere is also bound up with the idea of a constitutional basis in that "any rightful constitution" reflects "the *right of citizens of a state*," the "*right of nations*," and the "*right of citizens of the world*."[88] The rendering of territory and political relationships into rightful ideas allows Kant to theorize political existence away from a lawless condition of conflicting interests mediated by power and the use of force toward a rational order. Kant advocates that for the sake of the rightful legitimacy of a state its government, if "it is to be in conformity with the concept of right . . . must have a representative system, in which alone a republican kind of government is possible."[89] The Second Definitive Article concerns the *right* of nations based upon the association of states. Federalism is the ideal arrangement as it creates a condition of cooperation without infringing on the rights of the states that comprise the federation, whereas the establishment of a single world state would impinge on those rights.

Kant's treatment of the idea of a world state is extremely complicated, with important consequences for his overall theory of global politics. When dealing with the right of *nations* (plural) it is a contradiction to insist on a world state, as this would be to remove the rights they possess qua states. Replacing the plurality of states with a singular state would result in the erasure of their *particular* legal identities and prerogatives.[90] Kant is particularly adamant that the plurality of separate states independent of one another is "better in accordance with the idea of reason" and that "the fusion of them by one power overgrowing the rest and passing into a universal monarchy" would lead to "soulless despotism . . . the graveyard of freedom," which "after it has destroyed the seed of good, finally deteriorates into anarchy," and in doing so destroys the hard-won principles of the right of nations that had previously pertained.[91] Yet what cannot be denied is Kant's singularly definitive finding that "in accordance with reason *there is only one way* [emphasis added] that states in relation with one another can leave the lawless condition, which involves nothing but war; it is that, like individual human beings, they give up their savage (lawless) freedom, accommodate themselves to public coercive laws, and so form an (always growing) state of nations (*civitas gentium*) that would finally encompass all the nations of the earth . . . the positive *idea of a world republic*."[92] Despite the authority of reason, this solution is rejected by states "in accordance with their idea of the right of nations." The implications of the rejection of *reason's* single path to peace will be examined later in this chapter. What is important to recognize at this point is Kant's avowal in its place of a "negative surrogate," a "*league* that averts war" but which does not aim for any more permanent, constitutional arrangement—although Kant does argue that "if good fortune should ordain that a powerful and enlightened people can form itself into a republic (which by its nature must be inclined to perpetual peace), this would provide a focal point of federative union . . . conformably with the right of nations; and by further alliances of this kind, it would gradually extend further and further."[93]

Whatever its wider merits, this limited pacific league of states in which the rights of each state is respected serves as a more rational means of securing those rights than war, which in any case is subject to an "absolute condemnation" by reason "as a procedure for determining rights."[94] While problematic in terms of the requirements of reason, the right of nations nonetheless forms the bedrock of the latticework of interconnections that constitute relations between the most powerful actors within global politics. The shared identity of statehood based in a common idea of right trumps the appeal of a global republic and forms the basis for external relations between states. Although "the malevolence" of states toward each other is undeniable, right serves as a bulwark against its excesses and the sophistic posturing of natural lawyers such as Hugo Grotius, Samuel von Pufendorf, and Emer de Vattel, whose work merely serves to justify offensive war.

Right's powerful hold over state behavior is demonstrated by the fact that the word right "could still not be altogether banished as pedantic from the politics of war and that no state has yet been bold enough to declare itself publicly in favor of this view"; in fact, states pay homage (or at least verbally declare their adherence to) the idea of right.[95] Kant's "federative union" of states coalescing around a powerful republic is presented as securing "a condition of freedom of states" that is crucially conformable "with the idea of the right of nations." In the absence of a supreme legislative power only "the surrogate of the civil social union, namely the free federalism that reason must connect necessarily with the concept of the right of nations if this is to retain any meaning at all" is the only hope for peace between states.[96] Although weaker than a global republic, the idea of the right of nations nonetheless underpins this league that averts war, a league that "can hold back the stream of hostile inclination that shies away from right," although Kant confesses that it exists in "constant danger" of being overwhelmed by powerful incentives originating from inclination. Without additional supporting components, a system of peace based on the right of nations seems likely to prove contingent and subject to Mendelssohnian reversion.

As a republic establishes rightful relations between individuals as moral persons within a state, and the right of nations creates the possibility (however contingently) of legal interaction between states, cosmopolitan right mediates the relationship of states and individuals from outside that state. Kant argues the case for this minimal but universal right to hospitality, i.e., to visit and seek to conduct peaceful commerce within a state willing to allow access to its territory and citizens, "by virtue of the right of possession in common of all the earth's surface on which, as a sphere, they cannot disperse infinitely but must finally put up with being near one another; but originally no one had more right than another to be on a place on the earth."[97] The extension of the community of the nations of the earth has made the condition of right so prevalent that "violation of right on one place of the earth is felt in all," allowing Kant to conclude that "the idea of cosmopolitan right is no fantastic and exaggerated way of representing right; it is, instead a supplement to the unwritten code of the right of a state and the right of nations necessary for the sake of any public rights of human beings and so for perpetual peace."[98]

Right in Context: Dormant Moral Predispositions and Political, All-Too Political Calculations

Revealing the influence of *Religion Within the Boundaries of Mere Reason* on *Toward Perpetual Peace*, Kant reads the appeal to right (however faintly expressed) as evidence of a "greater, though at present dormant, moral predisposition to eventually become master of the evil principle within him."[99] The problem with this "dormant" moral disposition is how are human beings to act in the indeterminate yet lengthy amount of time that this moral disposition remains inert? The answer—at least at first—would seem to be to give nature its head and in the play of natural inclinations human beings will ultimately cease hostilities, as to do otherwise would risk extermination in war. Perpetual peace therefore is built, at least initially, on the foundation of fear of the ultimate war: "a war of extermination, in which the simultaneous annihilation of both parties and with it of all right as well can occur . . . perpetual peace come about only in the vast graveyard of the human race."[100] Kant's awareness of this is what leads him to declare that "a war of this kind, and so too the means that lead to it, must be absolutely forbidden," but forbidden by what authority in an environment that in Kant's own terms has "no court that could judge with rightful force"? In the absence of good will and an effective framework for legal resolution of rival claims and interests, Kant is forced to conclude that the essential preconditions of perpetual peace (at least in its first phase) lie in technical practical reason, with the human being concluding that war is no longer a *politically* viable option. Kant's problem is to make the case for the viability of such a system given the natural, political impulse toward autonomy (in the international sphere, sovereignty).

Kant argues the potential success of his system by means of a domestic analogy. A republic is the form of government that is most difficult to achieve and maintain, "so much so that many assert it would have to be a state of *angels* because human beings, with their self-seeking inclinations, would not be capable of such a sublime form of constitution." Yet republics are formed by humans because "nature comes to the aid of the general will grounded in reason, revered but impotent in practice, and does so precisely through those self-seeking inclinations." Such is Kant's confidence in prudential reason providing at least the beginning of a solution to the problem of politics that he maintains that the "problem of establishing a state . . . is soluble even for a nation of devils (if only they have understanding)."[101] By extension the same ought to be true of international relations. Indeed, Kant in one of his rare invocations of empirical evidence in *Toward Perpetual Peace*, argues that "[i]t can be seen even in actually existing states, still very imperfectly organized, that they are already closely approaching in external conduct what the idea of right prescribes, though the cause of this is surely not inner morality."[102]

Kant stresses that the first part of the solution to the problem of creating the initial conditions for establishing perpetual peace is not a moral issue, but rather a technical one, akin to that of establishing a state:

> [T]he problem *is not the moral improvement of human beings* but only the mechanism of nature, and what the task requires one to know is how this can be put to use in human beings in order so to arrange the conflict of their unpeaceable dispositions within a people that they themselves have to constrain one another to submit to coercive law and so bring about a condition of peace. (emphasis added)[103]

Kant therefore argues that the establishment of peace is at first the implementation of a rational, ordered international society—he refers explicitly to this phase as "the most beautiful *social* order" (emphasis added) and as the fruit of unsociability.[104] In *Toward Perpetual Peace*, Kant defines the process of pacification in terms of an ideal (i.e., one presupposing a rational purpose and end to existence) relationship between reason, the mechanism of nature, and right:

reason can use the mechanism of nature, through self-seeking inclinations that naturally counteract one another externally as well, as a means to make room for its own end, the rule of right, and in so doing promote peace within as well as without, so far as a state itself can do. Here it is therefore said that nature wills irresistibly that right should eventually gain supremacy.[105]

The problem is that this solution, Kant informs us, is continually assailed and undermined by political agents acting according to inclination, a situation that is the consequence of what Kant identifies as a refusal to accept the solution offered by reason, namely the establishment of a world state.

Hypothesis *versus* Thesis: *The Rejection of the World State and Its Implications*

Kant's treatment of the role of reason in the articulation of a solution to the problem of war and conflict in international politics is very important in terms of understanding his complex analysis of human nature and capabilities. Revisiting a vital passage, it is important to stress that reason's prescription in relation to war is clear:

> In accordance with reason there is only one way that states in relation with one another can leave the lawless condition, which involves nothing but war; it is that, like individual human beings they give up their savage (lawless) freedom, accommodate themselves to public coercive laws, and so form an (always growing) *state of nations (civitas gentium)* that would finally encompass all the nations of the earth.[106]

As already discussed, however, according to Kant nations will not let go of their "idea of the right of nations," i.e., sovereign independence, "thus rejecting *in hypothesi* what is correct *in thesi*."[107] This admission by Kant is extremely important in that it demonstrates the extent to which human beings are *immune* to the influence of reason, and that reason cannot serve as the sole basis for the transformation of human political community. As Howard Williams and Ken Booth acknowledge, "[h]umans are affected by reason, but not determined by it."[108] The rejection of the "positive *idea of a world republic*" in favor of the "negative surrogate" of a "*league* that averts war" is revealing in that this league "can hold back the stream of hostile inclination that shies away from right, though with constant danger of its breaking out," but only does so in the constant shadow of catastrophe.[109] The precarious peace of the negative substitute only calls to attention the fragility of Kant's rights-based order within a political environment. The idea of right allows mankind to see itself beyond the pursuit of self-interest and existence beyond the state of nature, but it is not enough *on its own* to secure peace in anything more than a precarious manner. Clearly, at the point when the ultimate solution of reason is rejected in favor of preserving the right of nations, something else is required in order to secure perpetual peace in the *final* sense that Kant argues can pertain even in the circumstance of the negative substitute of the federative league of states. The ideal relationship of reason, right, and nature acting in unison is unavailable to Kant, but in extremis he turns to faith and hope as "practical" surrogates when mankind refuses to accept in toto the recommendation of reason.

The desperation of Kant's position is evident from his observation that the negative substitution is necessary "if all is not to be lost."[110] To deal with the persistence of politics as the pursuit of self-interest, it is to nature and right that Kant turns in order to argue the possible salvation of human beings despite themselves. Nature as mechanism, which Kant has posited as the condition from which the human being ought to escape, serves as the means by which the conditions of peace (from whence the end of community will *hopefully* emerge) will be achieved as a product of nature, "from whose mechanical course purposiveness shines forth visibly," but only if we choose to see nature as rational, and, ultimately, providential (see the concluding chapter).[111] The purpose of nature when viewed as a rational process is to bring the human being's will and inclination into harmony with his reason such that "the human being is constrained to become a good citizen even if not a morally good human being."[112] What Kant proposes is not inner moral regeneration (at least not at this crucial initial stage), but rather the evolution of the natural mechanism, which nonetheless results in the rule of right as "nature *wills* irresistibly that right should eventually gain supremacy. What we . . . neglect to do eventually comes about of its own accord."[113] Kant's anthropomorphist understanding of nature in this passage demonstrates the extent to which he is reliant on a *hope* that nature (again, when viewed from the perspective that assumes it is purposive) will resolve the political dilemmas that face human beings—possibly because of his anthropological pessimism in relation to human beings when viewed through nonpurposive lenses. Rather than solely being the problem, human inclinations are revealed to be (at least in part) the solution to the development of perpetual peace and the political conditions necessary for the *emergence* of the conditions in which moral behavior might emerge as mankind moves from the politics of naked self-interest and confrontation to that of right and *eventually* to moral politics. The Mendelssohnian problem remains, however, in that the achievement of a rights-based system could devolve from the heights of its achievement back into the dogfight of politics as usual. The establishment of right is still contingent, and the rights enshrined within that system face a precarious fate where their maintenance cannot be guaranteed without moral transformation, but how might such a moral transformation be achieved and Mendelssohn's "road to corruption" be avoided? It is for this reason that "at the international level, Kant has unavoidably to look to the moral improvement of mankind as the only possible element that can ultimately ensure peace. . . . The aim of perpetual peace cannot be achieved by political and legal means alone."[114]

A *just* perpetual peace, if it is to arise at all, will develop only *after* the technical political processes have created the conditions for its emergence.[115] In a two-phase process nature and morality are jointly responsible for perpetual peace in that nature creates *negative* peace, i.e., the absence of war, while rational morality points toward the second, definitive phase of perpetual peace. Right occupies a position between these two points as the means by which external relations between agents can be regulated, but it is doubtful whether this would be enough to preserve peace perpetually. If peace is to be perpetual it requires a genuinely moral character to develop in the space created by right.

A crucial part of Kant's argument regarding the transition from the first to the second phase is the role played by competitive self-regard in creating the *semblance* of morality, which over time allows the development of genuine morality as the product of the social order that emerges from the initial pretense—in other words, nature is preparatory for peace in a positive, moral sense, but quite separate from it.[116] In *Observations on the Feeling of the Beautiful and Sublime*, Kant outlines the process of transformation: "what a large part of mankind would neither have done out of an immediately arising impulse of goodheartedness, nor out of principles, happens often enough simply on account of external appearance, out of a delusion very useful although in itself very shallow—as if the judgment of others determined the worth of ourselves." Kant is arguing that those engaged in politics do not wish to lose face by violating moral principles, thus achieving the "gloss of virtue," if not virtue itself.[117] In the *Anthropology*, Kant sees this process in terms of a "permissible moral illusion," in which "the virtues, whose illusion they have merely affected for a considerable length of time, will gradually really be aroused and merge into the disposition" of mankind (see chapter 4).[118] Thus, the semblance of morality, which is produced by natural factors, encourages the conditions for the emergence of genuine peace by a process in which nature is preparatory for right and, Kant *hopes* in the end, a measure of virtue.

Without a measure of virtue, peace understood simply as the absence of war is problematic in terms of its effects on mankind in that it fosters cravenness and greed in a population that lacks the capacity to seek genuine peace. In addition to fear of death in war and the jeopardization of interests as a result of conflict, acquisitiveness plays an important role in dissuading human beings from war as profits would be badly affected by disturbances to international trade: as Kant insists, the spirit of commerce "cannot coexist with war." The desire for global trade compels states to "promote honourable peace" and prevent war on a global basis—once again, though, Kant admits that the motivation is not "through incentives of morality."[119] This peace is simply the absence of war rather than the institution of a positive, moral order, thus the elimination of war does not *necessarily* lead to the moralization of political behavior, but rather to the continuation of politics and conflict by other means.[120] It is important to bear in mind in this context that Kant is *not* in favor of all kinds of peace: only peace in its *final* form is genuinely admirable.

The clearest expression of Kant's distrust of peace emerging purely as a consequence of natural instincts of self-preservation and avarice is to be found in the *Critique of the Power of Judgment,* in which he contrasts the sublime mentality of people who wage war properly ("if it is conducted with order and reverence for the rights of civilians") against the degenerate mentality that pertains "within a long peace," which causes "the spirit of mere commerce to predominate, along with base selfishness, cowardice and weakness, and usually debases the mentality of the populace."[121] A peace based solely on self-interest and expressed in terms of formal right would not be sufficient to avoid Mendelssohn's cycle of decline: the road to corruption would seem to be the inevitable pathway for a merely negative peace. Such a peace would be the replacement of one form of insufficiency rooted in violent disregard for the moral law with another rooted in the mean-spirited, cowardly desire for self-preservation and acquisition. Kant seems to hint as much in his condemnation of the treatment meted out to the natives by "commercial states" like the Dutch in their exploitation of the Sugar Islands, described as "that place of the cruelest and most calculated slavery."[122] Kant also condemns the eudemonistic lassitude that underlies the happy (but ultimately animalistic and, to him, worthless) peace of the Tahitians.[123] The particular kind of peace that Kant proposes as the ultimate form of human society is of a different kind, which, if it is to be achieved, will require the transformation of the political realm itself through the incorporation of Kantian morality. The difficulty remains, however, of how to incorporate Kantian morality in the absence of a world state. What can serve as an alternative to reason's identification of the world republic as the only way to peace?

The End of Politics? The Moral Politician and the Political Moralist

Perhaps the most important text in our understanding of the relationship between politics and morality in Kant's corpus is the appendix to *Toward Perpetual Peace* entitled *On the Disagreement between Morals and Politics with a View to Perpetual Peace*. The appendix makes clear the limits of practical man for whom morals are "mere theory." In Kant's conception, practical man bases his behavior on prudence; hence the pursuit of interest, or even simple inclination, not right and reason, are the lodestars of practical man's political choices. Practical man is characterized in this text as professing a "despairing denial" of Kant's "benign hope" in the future condition of mankind.[124] For politics as constituted under the logic of practical man, "all the plans of theory for the right of a state, the right of nations, and cosmopolitan right dissolve into ineffectual, impracticable ideals."[125] The logical conclusion is that in the political sphere only a practice that is based on "empirical principles of human nature . . . can alone hope to find a sure ground for its edifice of political prudence."[126] As long as the human being remains a political animal ("a living machine") he cannot escape the logic of power politics, which, when he becomes aware of this fate, renders him "unfree" and "the most miserable of all beings in the world."[127] The nature of the human being calls into question the very foundation of a cosmopolitan international society as "the obstacles that ambition, love of power, and greed, especially on the part of those who are in power, oppose to even the possibility of such a design."[128] Practical man abases himself before power in the name of prudence, locked into a perspective that allows knowledge of human beings solely as political agents. For Kant, practical man can only act in a prudentially adept manner; he cannot conceive of a moral politics, only his own political advantage.

The agent charged with melding technical, prudential reasoning with pure practical reason is the moral politician. The moral politician has the most difficult task in all of political theory in that he must succeed politically while acting morally, very much in the spirit of the biblical invocation to the followers of Christ: "Behold, I send you forth as sheep in the midst of wolves: so be ye therefore wise as serpents, and harmless as doves" (Matthew 10:16). Paul Guyer makes the case that the moral politician ought and therefore *can* play a special role in the reform of politics, but fails to account for *how* the moral politician is to achieve this when confronted with the nature of an international society in which his opponents are *not* bound by Kantian morality.[129] The anticipated role of the moral politician is described well by Howard Williams, who argues that once the *telos* of human destiny becomes clear, the moral politician can actively seek to move toward that *telos* because "[b]y seeing history as embodying purpose the ethical person can enter the seemingly amoral quagmire of politics, and take advantage of its arbitrariness and unpredictability, to bring about a moral end."[130] The moral politician, envisaged as a catalyst, has the task of avoiding "all unnecessary hardship by trying to bring about, through skill and diplomacy, aims which the natural progress of history will only realize very slowly and with great suffering."[131] The moral politician, then, performs the duty of turning "the evil circle into an ascending spiral."[132]

Even a sympathetic scholar like Williams, however, points to a significant problem for the moral politician: "Politicians following the path that Kant recommends would be predictable in their actions, and would therefore be more vulnerable to calculated intervention than the unprincipled politician."[133] Niccolò Machiavelli, through the figure of Girolamo Savonarola, describes the fate of those who mistake moral virtue for political logic and who cannot force a fickle public to remain committed to the "moral" course.[134] That politicians may continue to remain wedded to the political arts of technical practical reason without a genuine commitment to pure practical reason remains a serious problem, not only for Kant but also for his contemporary followers—the wolves and serpents are prepared to do that which the sheep and doves are not permitted to do, at least not if they want to remain sheep or doves. Kant recognizes the problem of the psychology of the politician in the *Anthropology* where he claims that it is politicians who condemn the majority to live in immaturity because it

suits their prudential, technical practical ends to promote and to use "this docility of the masses."[135]

Due to the manifest shortcomings of human beings, and especially politicians, the only position for Kant to take is "benign hope" in the eventual overcoming of politics by morality.[136] This overcoming requires a final revolutionary period of consciousness alteration, Enlightenment, before mankind can be
considered capable of living according to pure practical reason.[137] This possible victory of rational morality is rooted in the recognition of the existence
and (putative) superiority of pure practical reason. Whereas for technical
practical human beings the limits of morality are set by prudence, for pure
practical humanity a different relationship applies: "if one finds it indispens-
ably necessary to join the concept of right with politics, and even to raise it to
the limiting condition of politics, it must be granted that the two can be
united."[138] This unity can only be achieved through the superiority of the
moral; as Kant claims, "I can indeed think of a *moral politician* . . . but not of a
political moralist."[139] This is an interesting proposition, but Kant never really
illustrates *how* and *why* the human being (and it must be assumed that
politicians—who are at the core of the problem of politics—will retain the self-
perception of human beings) should dispense with technical practical reason
and replace it with pure practical reason from a perspective rooted *within*
technical practical reason, i.e., he does not provide a politically viable reason
for the human being to renounce the political in its own terms. Rather, he insists on categories outside politics, pure practical reason and morality, which
are subordinate within the political sphere to technical practical reason.[140] The
best that he can offer is the possibility that evil actors will oppose and cancel
each other out by nefarious means and in doing so leave the field to the moral
politician. Kant's argument here relies on two factors: "benign hope" and faith
in the purposive arrangements of nature (as arranged by providence), which
are inimical to the political understanding of the world of those operating under the lower anthropological perspective.

The problem then is that Kant still offers no incentive for technical practical
human beings to attain pure practical humanity: even if human beings achieve
peace through political means it will not be the peace prescribed by reason, but
rather a poor imitation thereof that reflects the limits of the lower anthropological perspective. The best Kant can do is to frame this in terms of *hope*—that
the semblance of morality will become morality. Logically, however, there is no
reason to think that the pretense of morality will necessarily become genuine

morality. It is equally likely that the pretense of morality will remain just that and perhaps degenerate further into being a cynical fig leaf used to cover immoral intentions and justify immoral actions. At this point Kant encounters Hume's is/ought problem, i.e., Kant begins by recognizing how human beings "are," but concludes with how humanity ought to be, without offering a convincing account of how the chasm separating these positions could be bridged from a position *inside* the natural, political realm of how the human being *is* (or, more accurately, appears to be) when viewed from the lower anthropological perspective.[141] Even the prospect of annihilation in war is conceived and resolved in the calculation of interests (i.e., a political calculation) rather than in the "positive" sense of transcending the political by becoming moral. Kant's "natural" peace does not transcend the condition of war because it remains a relationship based on power and fear of the other, "even if it is not a condition of actual war and actual attacks being constantly made." In such a scenario Kant recognizes that the Mendelssohnian possibility always remains, i.e., that regression might occur.[142] As Kim Hutchings perceptively notes: "The kingdom of devils remains a kingdom of devils, for whom peace is simply a more secure and profitable alternative than war."[143] If it were the case that war became the profitable option, the devils would return to it without hesitation. Human beings, less adept at technical practical calculation of interests, and far more susceptible to factors such as emotion, are even more likely than rationally self-interested devils to deviate from optimal decision making and hence to return to the state of war. In response to the is/ought relationship, Kant therefore can only invoke hope and faith that "ought" can become "is" and that perception be altered across the species from the lower anthropological perspective to the higher. It must also be borne in mind that Kant's position is *practical*. A definitive conclusion on this possibility cannot be reached via any empirical or synthetic a priori grounds, which may explain why, in Kant's memorable formulation, knowledge must be sacrificed for faith.[144]

The political tendencies of human beings exhaust Kant's attempts to point a route beyond Mendelssohn's cyclical reading of history and the relatively unchanging ratio of moral and immoral behavior. As will be explored in greater detail in the conclusion, only *belief* in providence, distinct from nature's guarantee, can assure mankind of achieving or even approximating perpetual peace in its final form—but this belief is only possible in the wake of the reorientation from technical practical reason to pure practical reason, in essence in the aftermath of a perceptual revolution that permits the higher perspective on mankind to be taken. The following chapter investigates the possibility of such a revolution in species perception.

Conclusion

Kant attributes the failure of mankind to achieve genuine peace to human beings themselves. Human beings are the primary impediment to the achievement of perpetual peace because they create a political sphere in accordance with their perceived natures, which it must be remembered are, at base, those of animals. As purely *natural* entities human beings must follow a logic predicated on the desire for power, security, and the satisfaction of self-interest, either for the individual at the level of domestic society or the state at the level of international society. To have any hope of escaping from this condition, the human being must achieve independence from nature, or, at least, suppress nature's dominance by the elevation over it of rationality, a condition Kant refers to as *personality*, "that is freedom and independence from the mechanism of the whole of nature."[145] As Flikschuh notes, however, "we cannot know that the will is independent of the causality of nature," but "we must assume the possibility of such independence for practical purposes."[146]

Kant's ultimate formulation of a solution to the problem of human political life is problematic to contemporary eyes because it depends ultimately on an understanding of the cosmos and of mankind's role within it that is predicated on a *concursus* between mankind and God. Mankind can achieve perpetual peace but only on the condition that it lives *as if* there were a rational plan of nature initiated by God. Without belief in God human beings remain insufficient entities and are condemned to remain inadequate in perpetuity. With belief in God, the human being attains a different significance as an intermediary entity en route to something greater—membership in the moral species humanity. Viewing mankind in this manner allows Kant to infer meaning into events that could be read in a completely different manner. Without belief in God, violence and conflict are merely violence and conflict—and are not part of a wider plan for the ultimate transcendence of the natural mode of being. Unsocial sociability and antagonism from this perspective would be merely "natural" facets of human life, with no meaning beyond that point, as opposed to motors of social progress toward the eventual transcendence of nature. The best that could be said of unsocial sociability in this case is that it contributes to culture, which, it must be recognized, fosters the worst vices of all (for elaboration, see chapter 5). Such an understanding undermines instead of underpins hope of progress toward true perpetual peace. From Kant's perspective if human beings do not read a plan into nature, then there is no hope for the achievement of a genuine perpetual peace, hence the necessity to *believe* in a plan of nature and by extension an author of that plan sufficient to compensate for the insufficiency of human beings and *through belief* begin the process of overcoming that insufficiency.

Toward Perpetual Peace is itself a testament to the *limits* of human beings to achieve positive peace through their own powers. The peace that human beings can achieve of their own volition is a weak and imperiled thing: it is at best a basis for a "benign hope" that genuine peace might emerge from it—it is not peace in a truly positive sense.[147] Kant is quite clear that the human impulse for peace in the first instance in *Toward Perpetual Peace* is fear of death and the pursuit of wealth, i.e., the rational calculations of survival, self-interest, and acquisition. This is precisely the kind of peace that he warns against in the *Critique of the Power of Judgment*, i.e., the peace that debases the population. If the ultimate product of this kind of peace is mental degradation, this would imply either the possibility of regression toward war or a global society lacking anything other than a mean-spirited selfishness, cowardice, and a lack of commitment on behalf of its constituent members to peace in the positive sense. Such a peace, forged in the name of fear and greed rather than rational morality, would be a "peace" teetering forever on the edge of regression or entropy. In a Godless universe, the human being can at best achieve a poor imitation of genuine, positive peace. It is for this reason that Kant insists that this is merely a preparatory phase in which it is his "benign hope" that the moral politician can effect positive peace in accordance with "the profound wisdom of a higher cause which predetermines the course of nature and directs it to the objective final end of the human race."[148] The culmination of the project of perpetual peace reduces to the two most Kantian concepts of international politics—*hope* and *faith* that human beings can become sufficiently independent from nature to act as rational moral beings. Hope and faith in turn are dependent upon mankind taking "a higher standpoint of anthropological observation" upon its own activities.[149] It is Kant's *hope* that human beings can eventually reorient their self-understanding and identify themselves as the moral species of humanity, and it is his *faith* that God has made this process possible. These two subjects, hope in the eventual reorientation of mankind from the mere aggregate of human beings to a coherent moral species and the special role of faith in God in relation to the eventual resolution of human existence, are the themes of the final two chapters. It is only after delving into the depths of Kant's anthropological and theological commitments that a full appreciation of his final position in *Toward Perpetual Peace* may be attained.

CHAPTER 4

The Instruction of Suffering

Kant's Theological Anthropology

The resolution of human political history in the form identified in *Toward Perpetual Peace* requires the thorough reorientation of mankind to a position where pure practical reason, morality, and law direct the behavior of mankind. As seen in chapter 3, Kant refers to the theorization of this alternative orientation as the product of a "higher anthropological vantage point." This chapter investigates Kant's anthropology in the light of this fundamental distinction between lower and higher anthropological vantage points, seeking to discover the extent to which Kant thought it was possible for the vision embodied in the higher vantage point to become the primary means by which mankind comprehends itself. Kant's political and IR theory reduces to the fundamental question: Can human beings shift perceptions of themselves and their environment to such an extent that they are closer to the ideal represented by humanity?

Human moral and political progress is for Kant a deeply *unnatural* process. In the *Conjectural Beginning of Human History* Kant makes it clear that the defining characteristic of human beings, their quest for freedom, is in defiance of nature and has exacted a terrible cost on human beings, resulting in "on the moral side a fall; on the physical side a multitude of ills. . . . The history of nature thus begins from good, for that is the work of God; the history of freedom from evil, for it is the work of the human being."[1] This theme of the *unnaturalness* of human development is already present in Kant's review of Pietro Moscati's *Of the Corporeal Essential Differences Between the Structure of Animals and Humans*.[2] In this review the most distinctive aspect of human physiology, bipedal uprightness, is described as "contrived and against nature."[3] Kant is clear that the human being must suffer for his unnaturalness, condemned to endure pain, discomfort, and unease as the price for sacrificing natural animal contentedness in favor of developing his or her cognitive faculties as a rational entity. Kant's anthropological works are in large part concerned with theorizing the consequence of human beings' embrace of the evil of the pursuit of freedom but also the means by which human reason may be rehabilitated with the will of God—anthropology as the process of the redemption of human reason and freedom. Kant's task is to argue that although freedom begins as a consequence of human evil, it does not have to remain tied to this origin; rather, human freedom can be transformed into the means by which mankind can best understand its role within and *beyond* nature. The irony of Kant's anthropology is that it is the bitter fruits of the human being's repudiation of nature—pain and discomfort—together with the operation of human beings' various cognitive faculties, that prompt mankind to act in accordance with the designs of providence.

Kant's anthropological works are significant, then, because they examine the capacity of human beings to evolve as moral and political entities. If human beings are not capable of moving beyond their current status, then Kant's vision of redemption through a reformed reason cannot occur. A related question presents itself: Exactly *how* are human beings to be redeemed? I propose that, at root, the answer to this problem is not found in human beings or nature, but rather in the supernatural—in the *idea* of God. The chapter begins with a consideration of Kant's theory of human beings as they exist within nature, typified by their "deep abasement" as moral and political entities. The second part of the chapter examines Kant's attempts to draw an escape route from this condition through the operation of the faculties of cognition and the emergence of permissible and useful illusions of morality, which according to Kant will serve as the foundation for the gradual grafting of genuine morality onto the body politic. The third part investigates the role that education ought to play in human progress. The final section considers Kant's idea of the "education from above" of human beings—the role that belief in God plays in the disciplining of human beings as they move toward the redeemed status of "humanity" and beyond nature.

The "Deep Abasement" of Human Nature

The primary impediment to the development of human beings is their material nature. The precritical Kant explored this condition in his *Universal Natural*

History, in which any given man or woman is typified by "the crudeness of matter into which his spiritual part is sunk." The very fabric of the human body is at fault for human beings' inability to secure progress in that every human being acts under severe limitations due to the fact that "the nerves and fluids of his brain deliver to him only gross and unclear concepts," and thus cannot provide ideas sufficient to act as a counterforce to the passions. As a result human beings end up "overwhelmed by the turmoil" that maintains their bodily machines.[4] Human beings' reliance on the parts of their bodies ("gross and rigid matter") account for the sluggishness of their ability to think properly, which is the source not only of human "depravity, but also of error."[5] Yet despite the miserable nature of human beings, "a road is open for them under most desirable conditions to reach a happiness and nobility which are infinitely far above those advantages which nature's most exceptional dispositions can achieve."[6] This passage is significant in that it establishes a distinction between a natural order and another higher order of which human beings could become a part and thereby share in much greater happiness than any achievable through nature. It is access to this higher order that constitutes the potential reward for mankind for breaking with nature. Kant's anthropological work is concerned with whether or not human beings are capable of achieving this "happiness and nobility" from the lowly position in which they find themselves, or, if once undertaken, such a journey into self-cognition leads "to an unfathomable depth, to an abyss" in the exploration of their being.[7] Kant then presents human destiny in stark terms—either human beings will achieve moral and political evolution or they will remain unsatisfactory entities deprived equally of the comforts of animal contentedness or the full benefits of being a part of the community of rational beings. In this latter scenario, the human being is reduced to a botched freak of nature in a meaningless universe.

From Human Beings to Humanity?

Kant's task as an anthropologist is twofold: first, to acknowledge the difficulty inherent in the transition from human beings as they appear to themselves to approximating humanity as it ought to be; and, second, to demonstrate how this transition may occur. This distinction can be seen as symptomatic of a fundamental division in Kant's understanding of what is cognizable:

> We can cognize either (1) what there is, or (2) what there should be. The former belongs to nature, the latter to freedom. Nature is the summation of what there

is, and the summation of what there should be is morals. We have thus two parts of philosophy. The philosophy of nature considers things that are there. Philosophy of morals concerns free actions that ought to happen.[8]

Anthropology occupies a middle ground between the philosophies of morals and nature. It may struggle to qualify as a "formal" science, but it is nonetheless important as an attempt to understand the space between these philosophies and how it may be crossed.[9] One of Kant's most important attempts to get to grips with addressing the issue of human destiny is the precritical *Observations on the Feeling of the Beautiful and the Sublime*. The *Observations on the Feeling of the Beautiful and the Sublime* expresses themes that would become typical in that the book holds out the possibility of true virtue being grafted onto the "feeling of the beauty and the dignity of human nature," while also stressing that the majority of the human race is not susceptible to the "universal moral feeling" that is necessary for true virtue. Because of this "weakness," through divine dispensation providence "has placed in us as supplements to virtue assisting drives" that can direct even those without principles toward "beautiful actions."[10] In addition, providence has also introduced honor and shame into "inert" human nature, which motivates human action and also counteracts "coarser selfishness and common sensuality."[11] This is an early instance of one of the key themes of Kant's anthropology—that providence, while not necessarily performing an interventionist role in human history, has played an important part in that belief in providence supplies the means and capacity for human progress.

In the main, however, Kant recognizes that among human beings as they currently understand themselves and appear to each other, "there are but few who behave according to principles—which is extremely good" as it is easy to err in relation to these principles with the effect that the error is easily spread by the resolute. The majority, however, act according to self-interest: "most men are among those who have their best-loved selves fixed before their eyes as the only point of reference for their exertions, and who seek to turn everything around self-interest as around the great axis." Anticipating the concept of unsocial sociability in his later political works, Kant argues that this is a positive state of affairs as "[n]othing can be more advantageous than this, for these are the most diligent, orderly, and prudent: they give support and solidity to the whole, while without intending to they serve the common good," and create the conditions for "finer souls" to "spread beauty and harmony."[12]

The first strand of human progress is based on the competition between human beings, which produces an order of sorts that in turn allows for the dissemination of ideas relating to beauty, harmony, and eventually morality as the social expression of these virtues.

This vision of an eventual convergence of aesthetics and morality does not change the fundamental fact for Kant that from birth to old age the "proportion of cunning, deception, and evil is always the same" in human beings in general, and until that point of convergence between aesthetics, morality, and reason in the distant future, this is likely to remain the case.[13] In an essay ostensibly about mental illness Kant explores why, even though art advances, reason and virtue are merely fig leafs and shibboleths for a species in which "everyone is far more jealous of the advantages of the understanding than of the good properties of the will."[14] The first casualty of a society of such beings, who predicate their existence on "art" and "fine cleverness," is sincerity, "which in such relations is only obstructive [and] can well be done without."[15] As a consequence of the dismissal of sincerity, "intrigue and false devices have gradually become customary maxims in civil society and have very much complicated the play of human actions." In such a world, a good man is a simpleton.[16] Kant provides in this essay a valuable typography of men involved in public life: the fool, the foolish person, the shrewd man, and the wise man. The fool is unredeemable, and cannot attain prudence as his passions overwhelm him—the examples Kant provides are Pyrrhus and Nero. The foolish person is not without wit and intelligence, but is prone to mistakes. The shrewd man is a man of prudence, capable of controlling his passions and achieving his aims. The foolish person may become shrewd over time if he learns from experience. Finally, the wise man is "he who is without folly. . . . This *wise man* can perhaps be sought for on the moon; possibly there one is without passion and has infinitely much reason." Clearly, this entity cannot be found on earth.[17] The best hope for the foolish person is that he become shrewd through age or hard experience, i.e., that he learn from his experiences and by doing so achieve the first stage of wisdom, prudence. Political life then is at best severely compromised, and at worst mired in evil, because of the overdependence of human beings on the "lower" cognitive faculties of the understanding and technical practical reason.[18] The task that Kant sets himself is the reformation of human beings sufficient to effect a switch in the cognitive foundations upon which they form their maxims. It is only by means of such a reformation that genuine peace can be achieved on a lasting basis.

Cognition and Experience: The (Re)Formation of the Self

Kant's initial starting point regarding human beings is the primacy of egoism. Once the human becomes aware of himself as "I," he brings the "beloved self" to the fore in all his dealings with others.[19] It is this "egoism" that institutes the "complex dynamics of human social interaction."[20] Any given human being's actions, claims Kant, are designed to achieve gratification of the beloved self by gaining "a superior worth in the judgment of others."[21] Logical and aesthetic egoism are fairly harmless in that they merely attest to the expression of intellectual opinion and preferences in taste. The moral egoist, however, is of political significance in that he "limits all ends to himself, sees no use in anything except that which is useful to himself, and as a eudaemonist puts the supreme determining ground of his will simply in utility and his own happiness, not in the thought of duty."[22] It is this eudaemonism that Kant sees as a primary obstacle in terms of the development of a pluralistic, cosmopolitan alternative to existing world order, as the eudaemonistic mode of thought leads to an unmanageable chaos of competing concepts of happiness, leading to a situation where "it is precisely egoism which drives him to have no touchstone at all of the genuine concept of duty, which absolutely must be a universally valid principle."[23] The problem lies in the fact that human beings pay more attention to their faculty of representing objects than their faculty of abstracting from objects to higher, more universal concepts. Kant maintains that "this faculty of abstraction is a strength of mind that can only be acquired through practice."[24]

The importance of the faculty of abstraction only becomes apparent over time. In the interim, mankind grows to self-knowledge through experience. Experience is processed either through the *sensus communis* or through science. The combination of both in sound human understanding is important:

> Sound understanding can demonstrate its superiority only in regard to an object of experience, which consists not only in increasing knowledge through experience but also in enlarging experience itself; not, however, in a speculative, but merely in an empirical-practical respect. For in the speculative employment of the understanding, scientific principles a priori are required; however, in the empirical-practical employment of understanding there can also be experiences, that is, judgments which are continually confirmed by trial and outcome.[25]

This is preparatory to Kant's wider argument, that human beings will use the *sensus communis* until such time as its operation creates the required collective intellectual conditions in which science can finally supplant it as the predominant mode of human cognition. This is also linked to Kant's theory of the mind as being active while also being passive in terms of receptivity: "Cognition requires both an active and a passive element, both concepts and intuitions. Intuitions arise from sensations represented in a spatial and temporal order. Concepts allow the understanding to subsume intuitions under kinds (e.g., chair, dog)."[26] The cognitive faculty can be subdivided into the sensuous (lower) faculty of cognition and the intellectual (higher) faculty of cognition. The former deals with representations "in regard to which the mind behaves passively, and by means of which the subject is therefore *affected*." The latter deals with ideas "that comprise a sheer activity (thinking)."[27] The mind therefore makes sense of both the self and the external environment, including all levels of society, in that experience is "empirical cognition, but cognition (since it rests on judgments) requires reflection."[28] The mind in effect creates merely the appearance of the self as an empirical intuition ("I nevertheless cognize myself only as I appear to myself, not as a thing in itself"), but this appearance is nonetheless important as "through reflection and the concept of understanding arising from it, [it] becomes inner experience and consequently truth."[29] The understanding plays the important role of connecting and bringing order to the manifold of appearances by making appearances into experiences. The important thing is that human beings in this respect are malleable and unfixed—"custom is a subjective necessity, not an objective one, based upon the workings of the reproductive imagination."[30] The human mind is populated by illusions both of itself and its relationship with others, but these illusions are of enormous social benefit and constitute a means by which human beings may realize that an escape from their mistaken notions about themselves is possible. Kant's point here is that how human beings appear to themselves and to each other may be reformed and that the very foundations of human life as they appear to exist are merely contingent.

Permissible Illusions of Morality

The play of illusions is crucial to the success of human civilization as "the more civilized human beings are, the more they are actors. They adopt the illusion of

affection, of respect for others, of modesty, and of unselfishness without deceiving anyone at all, because it is understood by everyone that nothing is meant
sincerely by this." Thus insincerity, which for Kant is such a moral and theological problem, is in political and social terms an enormous asset. According
to Günter Zöller, "In Kant's bleak picture of the origin and development of human social life social mores are essentially marked by dissimulation, conceit
and hypocrisy, not to mention the violent alternatives to the failures of these
measures."[31] Kant furthermore states that the condition of insincerity is a social
good in that "when human beings play these roles, eventually the virtues, whose
illusion they have merely affected for a considerable length of time, will gradually really be aroused and merge into the disposition."[32] The illusions that promote civility, propriety, and politeness are all the more useful given the paucity
of genuine human virtue, the quantity of which Kant claims "is small change—it
is a child who takes it for real gold.—But it is still better to have small change in
circulation than no funds at all, and eventually they can be converted into genuine gold, though at considerable loss." It is the use of illusions that acts as the
means by which insincerity can be replaced with sincerity, "for out of this play
with pretenses, which acquires respect without perhaps earning it, something
quite serious can finally develop."[33]

The idea that pretenses could become reality is one of Kant's most important, but also one of his most perplexing, anthropological claims. The difficulty
is twofold: first, how can the illusion become a social reality? Second, is Kant,
who rejects immoral means to achieve ends, contradicting one of his most essential principles? For Alix Cohen, the illusion becomes reality through deceit
of the self and others: "By deceiving others through politeness and social pretence, we in fact deceive ourselves into virtuous behaviour. . . . By deceiving
others through the pretence of virtue, we foster civil society; and in doing so,
we deceive ourselves by transforming our pretence of virtue into a disposition
for virtue itself."[34] Patrick Frierson offers an interpretation of this issue that
denies that Kant promotes deceit; instead, Frierson introduces a distinction between illusion and deception, claiming that illusion merely "clothes the truth"
while a deception excludes it. Importantly, "illusion does not depend on making another believe a falsehood," and as such is not morally wrong.[35] This remarkable contortion, however, depends upon the assumption that everybody
else knows that each of his fellows is insincere, which rather militates against
the idea that these are conditions in which the illusion of morality may become

genuine—a prudent entity will hardly embrace Kant's rational morality in an environment where he suspects that he would be alone in this conversion.

The importance of illusion is further extended to the realm of political institutions. Kant maintains that "a political artist . . . can guide and rule the world . . . by deluding it through images in place of reality; for example the *freedom* of the people (as in the English Parliament), or their rank and *equality* (as in the French Assembly), which consist of mere formalities." Freedom and equality as expressed in these polities are illusions, but important in that "it is still better to have only the illusion of possessing this good that ennobles humanity than to feel manifestly deprived of it."[36] Most people are docile and politically immature, living in a degraded but reasonably comfortable condition. Politicians exploit this docility and keep their subjects happy, but complacent, "condemned to permanent immaturity with regard to their own best interest."[37] This cynical handling of human beings may have its drawbacks, but Kant maintains that it is the surest means of maintaining a legal order.

The dependence of the majority on the leadership of politicians is a significant problem in terms of the achievement of freedom and the development of the human species, in that the rule of leaders is limiting, but these limits are politically desirable in terms of maintaining political order. Kant's hope is that over time a larger proportion of people in successive generations will embrace rational morality in a process of evolution via the institution of a lawful society. This hope, however, is quite possibly misplaced as "a lawful order forces the individual merely to hide his evil motives, not to abandon them, causing him to add hypocrisy to his other vices . . . no society can legislate a good will."[38] Kant fails to provide a convincing account of how his envisaged transvaluation should take place—his hope that this *might* occur has to be weighed against the strong possibility that human beings will remain venal, insincere creatures. Rather than engage with this idea, Kant dismisses it out of hand as resulting either in the "moral terrorism" of human destruction or the hapless folly of an abderite species shuffling between better and worse periods of human history.[39]

The Instruction of Suffering

Kant's hope that human beings will evolve is based on a foundation of pain—"pain is always first."[40] Although the opposition between pain and pleasure is the basis for life, "[p]ain is the incentive of activity, and in this above all we feel our life; without pain lifelessness would set in."[41] Pain is the spur to improvement, but the improvement does not entail contentment.[42] This idea of human beings suffering constant pain has been interpreted as Kant's challenge to philosophers such as Aristotle who argued that happiness was possible in this life. For Kant, if happiness is achievable, it can only be in a future life.[43] This concept of pain is extended to the nature of human interaction. Kant maintains that human beings' "enjoyment increases through comparison with others' pain, while their own pain is diminished through comparison with similar or even greater sufferings of others."[44] Even in the discussion of matters of taste, there is "a *social condition* (talking with others) which is not always sociable (sharing in the pleasure of others), but at the beginning is usually barbaric, unsociable, and purely competitive"; the individual only acts "in order to show himself to advantage."[45] Despite the egoistic aspect underpinning discussions of taste, such dialogues contribute to the advancement of morality, because well-mannered human beings, with agreed rules for tasteful behavior, are human beings in preparation for genuine morality. People imitate those "higher" than themselves in an attempt not to appear "lower" than others. The socialization of taste is a competitive process that has self-interest at its core, but order and harmony as its products. This is a prime example of how nature produces moral development as a by-product of its operation in that there is a "natural tendency" to express superiority, which engenders a pressure to act according to the mores of superior taste, which can be described, according to Kant, as "morality in external appearance."[46]

Desire, Inclination, and Passions

The desire for power is indicative of desire in general, "the self-determination of a subject's power through the representation of something in the future as an effect of this representation."[47] This is desire understood as the lower faculty of desire, wherein the inclinations and the passions determine the choices, means, and ends of human beings. The passions play an important and particular role in that unlike the inclinations they "can be conquered only with difficulty or not at all by the subject's reason." Passions and affects (feelings of pleasure or displeasure) are a threat because they "shut out the sovereignty of reason."[48] The strength of the passions is so great that the "physician of the soul" recognizes that the treatments he provides against their influence are "for the most part not radical, but almost always merely palliative."[49]

Kant's attitude toward the passions is best encapsulated in the passage "no human being wishes to have passion. For who wants to have himself put in chains when he can be free?" The problem that Kant faces is, as he recognizes, that the passions are "cancerous sores for pure practical reason, and for the most part they are incurable because the sick person does not want to be cured and flees from the dominion of principles."[50] Politics is the product of passion, which makes it resistant to rational morality—hence Kant's insistence that the passions admit only a palliative remedy.

The linkage between politics and passion is clear in that both kinds of passion, the (inflamed) passions based on the inclinations of freedom and sex and those (cold) passions based on "the persistence of a maxim established for certain ends," i.e., the manias for honor, dominance, and possession, are intensely political in that they are "desires, directed by human beings to human beings."[51] The specifically human dimension is important in that the passions are directed "to ends that harmonize or conflict with one another, that is in so far as they are love or hatred."[52] Although Kant highlights the power of these passions, and the extent to which they make progress difficult, he is vague as to how they may be overcome.

Prudence

As there is no final cure for the passions, and as the social and political worlds that they engender are characterized by their influence, human beings require a means by which to negotiate the dangers inherent in political and social life. Kant argues that it is this insecurity that fosters the inclination to have influence in general over other human beings, to better control the social environment. This inclination "comes closest to technically practical reason, that is, to the maxim of prudence." The mechanics of this inclination are important in that it promotes a lust for power, "getting other human being's inclinations into one's power, so that one can direct and determine them according to one's intentions, is almost the same as *possessing* others as mere tools of one's will. No wonder that the striving after such a *capacity* becomes a passion."[53] According to Kant, if one possesses "honor, authority, and money . . . one can get to every human being and use him according to his purposes, if not by means of one of these influences, then by means of another." It is important to note that Kant here is not discussing "*wisdom*, which admits of no passions at all, but only of *prudence*, by which one can manage fools."[54] The mania for honor, or rather the semblance of honor, allows the human being to be manipulated by flattery in relation to her reputation. The mania for domination develops from fear of oppression, which results in one being "soon intent on placing the advantage of force over" other members of society. This mania, however, is imprudent as well as unjust in that it arouses opposition and is contrary to freedom under law.[55] The mania for possession develops a hold over human beings in that it convinces those who fall under its spell that it contains such power that it compensates for the lack of every other power.[56] Despite being nonprovidential, "from time to time nature wants the stronger stimulations of passion in order to regenerate the activity of the human being, so that he does not lose the feeling of life in mere *enjoyment*."[57] Nature, therefore, uses the passions to stir the naturally lazy human being into action. Despite this, laziness and other vices have their positive attributes and play an important natural role as well as otherwise:

> If *laziness* did not intervene, *indefatigable* malice would commit far more ill in the world than it does now; if *cowardice* did not take pity on human beings, militant blood-thirst would soon wipe them out; and if there were no *duplicity*, then, because of the innate malice of human nature, entire states would soon be overthrown [for among the many scoundrels united in conspiracy in great number (for example, in a regiment), there will always be one who will betray it].[58]

In addition to these vices, "the invisible reason (of the ruler of the world)," through love of life and sexual love, provides for the highest physical good of the world, i.e., "by means of the general mixing of the sexes, the life of our species endowed with reason is *progressively* maintained, despite the fact that this species intentionally works toward its own destruction (by war)."[59] The preservation of the species allows for the growth of culture, even in the midst of war, which permits "the prospect of a state of happiness for the human race in future centuries, a state which will never again regress."[60] It is telling that the basis of this position that human beings will not regress is based in faith and hope derived from Kant's assumptions about human history expressing a rationality greater than human beings' own apparent rational capacity.

Civilization and Cosmopolitanism

The one advantage of the human being is that in the absence of any nonterrestrial rational species against which to compare himself, "nothing remains for us than to say that he has a character, which he himself creates, in so far as he is capable of perfecting himself according to ends that he himself adopts."[61] Human beings, therefore, have the freedom to set their own ends, and because of this any human being, "as an animal endowed with the *capacity of reason (animal rationabile)*, can make out of himself a *rational animal (animal rationale)*."[62] The problem, however, is that "the characteristic of the human species is this: that nature has planted in it the seed of *discord*, and has willed that its own reason bring *concord* out of this, or at least the constant approximation to it." One of the most important aspects of Kant's teleology is that it is God (the "supreme and, to us, inscrutable wisdom") that has ordained this state of affairs, with the conclusion of this process resulting in the "perfection of the human being through progressive culture, although with some sacrifice of his pleasures of life."[63]

Kant identifies the existence of several predispositions as evidence of the capacity of human beings to achieve progress: the technical predisposition toward skill, the pragmatic predisposition toward prudence, and the moral disposition to bring good out of evil. In terms of human beings' political and moral development, the latter predispositions are crucial. The pragmatic predisposition underpins the political evolution of mankind from the "crudity of mere personal force" to becoming "a well-mannered (if not yet moral) being destined for concord." It is important to note that the individual cannot achieve the "complete vocation" of humanity, only the species, and then only "through progress in a series of innumerably many generations." Kant is cautiously optimistic in his faith in the political future in that "while the tendency to this final end can often be hindered, it can never be completely reversed."[64] The moral predisposition is more complicated in that mankind is innately good according to its predispositions and in terms of each person as an intelligible character, yet experience demonstrates the tendency of human beings to desire what is unlawful and hence evil: "Thus according to his sensible character the human being must also be judged as evil (by nature)."[65] There is certainly no comfort in the historical record as "the experience of ancient and modern times must disconcert every thinking person and make him doubt whether our species will ever fare better."[66] Even in the civil constitution, "the highest degree of artificial improvement of the human species' good predisposition to the final end of its vocation, animality still manifests itself earlier and, at bottom, more powerfully than pure humanity."[67] This animality expresses itself in conflict as "the human being's self-will is always ready to break out in aversion toward his neighbor," and to compound this ever present threat of violence, the human being's lust for freedom blends into a desire for mastery such that he is not content to be merely independent, but he wishes to be master over "other beings who by nature are equal to him."[68] The tragedy of human insufficiency is that despite numerous sharp lessons administered to the human species, the instruction of suffering has *not* effected the necessary change in mentality required for human beings to reformulate the bases of their social interaction. Human beings have proven to be remarkably slow learners—it is Kant's *hope* that they will eventually become capable of recognizing their true interests.

Pedagogy and the Supplementary Civilizing Impetus of Education

If the examination of human history leads to despair, does the future offer a more optimistic prospect? Can human beings play a positive role in their development? Kant makes an interesting claim in the *Idea for a Universal History* when he argues that "we could, through our own rational contrivance, bring about faster" a society in which rational behavior would be the norm. This "rational contrivance" would be the process of enlightenment through education.[69] Kant's education is future oriented, with its guiding principle being that it should be based on the ideal of "a future possible improved human condition, in accordance with the idea of humanity and its entire destiny."[70] The linkage between education and cosmopolitanism (a major element of what Kant argues should be the future destiny of humanity) is evident in his advocacy of financial support for Johan Bernhard Basedow's philanthropium, "which is dedicated to humanity and therefore to the participation of every cosmopolitan."[71]

The great dilemma of education for Kant is that the training and instruction of human beings is provided by other beings, who by virtue (or vice) of being human are consequently compromised in terms of providing an increase in edification. If education were provided by a higher being, then we would have a better idea of "what the human being could become." In the absence of such an education, "one can never know how far his natural predispositions reach." Kant's response to this dilemma is to project a possible future resolution:

> Perhaps education will get better and better and each generation will move one
> step closer to the perfection of humanity; for behind education lies the great

secret of the perfection of humanity. Henceforth this may happen. . . . It is delightful to imagine that human nature will be developed better and better by means of education.[72]

By orienting education to the future, Kant believes it is possible to avoid the narrowing of human vision that limits politics to domestic advantage and the furtherance of princely ambition.[73] By instituting such an educational philosophy, one promotes the natural predisposition to the good in human beings: "One does not find grounds of evil in the natural predisposition of the human being. The only cause of evil is that nature is not brought under rules. In the human being lie only germs for the good."[74] Kant complicates this matter in *Religion within the Boundaries of Reason Alone* by introducing the universally acquired propensity to evil ("radical evil"). Kant claims that the predisposition to the good is the original moral setting of human beings, and that the task of moral reform is in large part a process of removing the propensity to evil.[75] The problem for Kant is that the propensity for depravity in the human being is "inextirpable," albeit with there being an unremitting counteraction against it leading to "a progression from bad to better extending to infinity . . . he must be able to *hope* that, by the exertion of *his own* power, he will attain to the road that leads in that direction."[76]

The means of bringing forth the good lies in the improvement of human beings through discipline, cultivation, and the teaching of prudence and moralization. The last quality is the most important for Kant as "a human being can be highly cultivated in physical terms, he can have a well-formed mind, but still be poorly cultivated in moral terms, and thus be an evil creature."[77] A practical education is dedicated to improving the skill, the prudence, and morality of a child. The latter two qualities are the most important, with prudence, "how to use human beings for one's purposes," occupying the second rank and morality the first rank. "If the child is to be given over to worldly prudence," writes Kant, "it must be able to conceal itself and make itself impenetrable, but at the same time be able to scrutinize the other person." The child must learn to dissimulate and to hide its character behind a screen of propriety. Yet at all times the child must, despite sailing close to the wind of dishonesty, remain "upright."[78] If the moral politician of *Toward Perpetual Peace* can be created by means of a program of education this would seem to be the method. Morality is a matter of instilling character in a child; this is done by stressing the importance of duty, essentially duties to oneself that revolve around the ennoblement of the self and duties to others, which are based on respect for the rights of other human be-ings.[79] The idea of "humanity" as it should, and possibly will be, is a constant spur to the child: "The human being reprimands himself when he has the idea of humanity before his eyes."[80] The concepts of duty and of God complete the foundations of Kant's pedagogy. The idea of God is necessary because the idea of divine provision inculcates a respect for creation and because it protects from "the propensity toward destruction and cruelty." The idea of God is also tied to God's role as universal lawgiver, and as the guarantor of humanity's pro-gressive destiny. The concept of duty has the positive effect of fostering respect for the self and others and acts against the deleterious effects of the inclinations and the passions.

All the potential benefits for human beings from education, however, have to be seen in the light of the fundamental paradox facing all human attempts to educate any given youth: "He who is to educate him is on the other hand a hu-man being who still lies in the crudity of nature. . . . Hence the continuous de-viation from his vocation with the always-repeated returns to it."[81] This piece-meal nature of human progress is for Kant a serious problem, as he notes (echoing Mendelssohn) that there is "no guarantee against regression." To es-cape the crudity of nature and to create at least the possibility of escaping re-gression, it is necessary to look *outside* nature.

The Importance of "Education from Above"

Ultimately, Kant devolves responsibility for mankind's education as a species to God. This "education from above" is to be "harsh and stern in the cultivation of nature, which extends through great hardship and almost to the extinction of the entire race." The role of human beings is to promote the approach of "this goal with all prudence and moral illumination (each to the best of his ability)."[82] Kant's hope is that with the advance of culture human beings will "feel ever more strongly the ill which they selfishly inflict on one another," and will unite in subjugating themselves to self-prescribed laws. Thus pain and suffering are the educational means that providence employs to teach human beings, with war being "a mechanical device of Providence," used to coerce them to pass from the crude state of nature to the civil state at both the domestic and the international level.[83] The final result of unsocial sociability, according to Kant, is that human beings feel "destined by nature to [develop], through mutual compulsion under laws that come from themselves, into a cosmopolitan society."[84] Kant admits, however, that this idea is "unattainable" and is to serve not as a constitutive principle, but rather as a regulative principle, i.e., something to be strived for rather than something likely to be instituted, although Kant hedges this position by arguing that the projection of a cosmopolitan society is "not without grounded supposition of a natural tendency toward it," despite "the propensity of our species to be evil-minded toward one another."[85]

For Kant, it is the capacity of human beings to recognize and condemn their moral failings that reveals a moral predisposition and the propensity to work against these failings. Progress toward the ultimate end of nature, the cultivation of morality and reason, cannot be reached by conscious effort or free agreement of individuals but only by "progressive organization of citizens of the earth into and toward the species as a system that is cosmopolitically united."[86] Kant is clear, however, that the education of the human species, the cosmopolitan order, and civil constitution are to be thought of by the human being as benefits only achievable through providence: "that is, from a wisdom that is not *his*."[87] The human being, according to Kant, "through his own fault" has only "an impotent idea" of the ends to which she or he is progressing as a result of the design, if not the intervention, of the divine. Despite the autonomy and volition afforded to human beings it has to be believed that it is providence that "will provide an outcome for the end of humanity as a whole species to reach its final destination."[88] The point here is not that human beings do not have a moral incentive to improve as moral agents, but rather that without the painful "education from above" they will not come to realize that this is a political and social requirement and not merely an abstract moral one. The idea of God is essential as "the unconditioned ground of the hope binding the moral community."[89] As seen in earlier chapters, in the *Idea for a Universal History with a Cosmopolitan Intent, The Critique of the Power of Judgment*, and his other works on teleology, Kant seeks to develop this "impotent idea" as far as possible in order to trace a developmental trajectory from the aggregate of human beings toward the ideal of humanity.[90] The theological dimension of Kant's position is explored in more detail in the final chapter of this book.

Conclusion

Kant's anthropology leads to extraordinary conclusions. Human life as we understand it, and ourselves, is based on the operation of illusions. Kant offers only the *hope* that a means of liberation from these illusions is possible and then only if mankind believes in a hidden plan of nature concealed within the fabric of the human mind. Such is Kant's skepticism in relation to the intellectual ability and moral capacity of human beings that he is compelled to argue that they cannot be guaranteed to secure their own future progress—any purposiveness that may be inferred in nature is attributed by Kant to "the profound wisdom of a higher cause directed to the objective final end of the human race and predetermining this course of the world, it is called *providence.*"[91] Human salvation is not in the gift of human beings; rather, it is the product of the successful culmination of the relationship Kant insists we must believe to exist between mankind and God. Kant's philosophical anthropology—a key component of his international political theory—is revealed to be a soteriological theory that posits the redemption not of blessed individuals but of the species as a whole.

CHAPTER 5

An "All-Unifying Church *Triumphant!*"

Thus I had to deny knowledge in order to make room for faith.[1]

This study has encompassed Kant's representation of mankind and the developmental paths open to human beings and humanity in the critical, political, and anthropological works of Kant. In each case the nature of the relationship between man and God has emerged as a major theme, with mankind presented as working its way toward conformity with the divine will. Kant's aim therefore is both political in the sense that it is concerned with political reform culminating in the establishment of perpetual peace, and theological in that it revolves around the complex relationship between an entity defined by its moral insufficiency and a Creator who is determined not to interfere in the process by which human beings become worthy of entry into the community of truly rational beings. This chapter engages directly with the theological concepts that appear within Kant's other projects and are revealed here as the essential buttresses that maintain the structural integrity of the vast cathedral constituted by Kant's thought.

In this chapter, the "deep abasement" of human nature, the defining characteristic of human beings, that which explains the persistent conflict that permeates existing political systems, is revealed to have its origins in a theological concept—radical evil. Yet Kant's political theology does not leave us mired in his equivalent of original sin. Kant offers a way out of evil by means of both perceptual shifts within mankind and a reformation of human society by means of the influence of rational religion and what he sees as an essential part of cosmopolitanism: the all-unifying church triumphant.

The Human Being in Kant's Theology

In the precritical piece *On the Miscarriage of all Philosophical Trials in Theodicy*, Kant characterizes "the propensity to falsehood and impurity" as "the principal affliction of human nature" in contrast to sincerity. Sincerity is the very basis of a good character and yet, according to Kant, it is "the property farthest removed from human nature—a sad comment, since all the remaining properties, to the extent that they rest on principles, can have true value only through that one." Such is the condition of the human being as he currently understands himself that, according to Kant, "[n]one but a contemplative misanthrope (who wishes evil to nobody, yet is inclined to believe evil of all) can hesitate whether to find human beings to *deserve hatred* or rather *contempt*." The human being deserves hatred when he does harm, but insofar as he has a propensity to evil itself, even when he does no harm he is still contemptible. This contempt is directed at the human being's mendacity, "the impurity that lies deep in what is hidden, where the human being knows how to distort even inner declarations before his own conscience."[2] This tendency of mendacity to distort the conscience is linked to the abuse of reason for Kant, with inner evil in effect being the product of self-serving maxims supplanting the proper role of the moral law.[3] Kant's moral standard is particularly exacting in that "any person who does not *always* make the moral law their sole and supreme incentive for adopting a maxim has an evil disposition."[4]

Kant expands on these themes in *Religion Within the Boundaries of Mere Reason*, in which he attempts to get to grips with the origin and nature of evil as an innate element of human character. Kant ascribes to human beings a "propensity" toward evil. The term propensity is important in that a "propensity can indeed be innate *yet* may be represented as not being such: it can rather be thought of (if it is good) as *acquired*, or (if evil) as *brought* by the human *upon* himself."[5] Kant insists that this evil should be viewed as a universal propensity and hence *natural*: "It will be noted that the propensity to evil is here established (as regards actions) in the human being, even the best; and so it also must be if it is to be proved that the propensity to evil among humans is universal, or, which here amounts to the same thing, that it is woven into human nature."[6]

The human being is "only evil because he reverses the moral order of his incentives in incorporating them into his maxims," i.e., he subordinates morality to self-love and other incentives rooted in our natural inclinations. Despite the radical nature of evil within human beings it may be overcome as they are not *absolutely* evil in the sense of malice, merely perverse in the sense that they do not prioritize the moral law. This perversity operates within the moral faculty wherein free choice, informed by reason, allows the moral subject to reject evil.[7] Reason, however, is often led astray by perfidy on the part of the human heart, which deceives itself and others with the important result that

> if this dishonesty is not to be called malice, it nonetheless deserves at least the name of unworthiness. It rests on the radical evil of human nature which (inasmuch as it puts out of tune the moral ability to judge what to think of a human being, and renders any imputability entirely uncertain, whether internal or external) constitutes the foul stain of our species—and so long as we do not remove it, it hinders the germ of the good from developing as it otherwise would.[8]

This "germ of the good" is important in that it reflects Kant's belief that human beings were originally predisposed to goodness but have developed over time a propensity to innate depravity.[9] In fundamental terms, human beings were created good, but are not good as such because of the universal acquisition of innate evil. Human beings remain redeemable, however, because they have the capacity to *choose* to be good. Kant proposes the reformation of human beings through virtue, as the virtuous human being is "in need of no other incentive to recognize a duty except the representation of duty itself." In contrast to merely legal virtue, this reformation of the human being "must be effected through a revolution in the disposition of the human being."[10] From Kant's perspective the onus is on human beings to curb their natural inclinations and to develop rational morality as the basis of their maxims.

The problem with this revolution in human moral consciousness is that Kant "candidly admits that such a revolution is inexplicable," in the context of what human beings take to be their own natures and the attendant society that is the product of those natures, "while also insisting that it must be possible, since we ought to undertake it."[11] The propensity to evil and the predisposition to good are competing elements of human existence. The problem for Kant is that the propensity for depravity in the human being is "inextirpable."[12] Kant makes the claim that approximating an impossible ideal is the means by which to secure human improvement in the species by "an ever-continuing striving for the better, hence as a gradual reformation of the propensity to evil, of the perverted attitude of mind," and by doing so affirms the possibility of reattaining (at least in an approximate sense) the original predisposition to good in humanity. This predisposition is astonishing for Kant in that it places mankind in conflict with the incentives of nature, yet human beings generally are capable of seeking to obey its strictures.[13]

If human beings achieve this transcendence of nature by the observance of a duty derived from rational morality, they will succeed in becoming the final end of creation, from which "happiness follows in the will of the Highest Being directly as from its supreme condition."[14] As a means to this end Kant selects faith in Jesus as a moral prototype to whom the rest of mankind should aspire (while acknowledging that mankind cannot attain the moral perfection of Christ); only a human being that attempts to live in such a manner "is entitled to consider himself not an unworthy object of divine pleasure."[15] From Kant's point of view, because we "*ought* to conform to it . . . therefore we must also *be able* to" conform to such a moral standard because it is a duty to do so.[16] The distance between where the human being starts, mired in evil, to the end of goodness is in fact infinite, and conformity of behavior with the moral law "is not exhaustible in any time."[17] According to Kant evil as transgression of the moral law is infinite, and results in an "*infinity* of guilt . . . consequently, every human being has to expect infinite punishment and exclusion from the Kingdom of God." It is only when human beings leave their condition of sin and the reformed good disposition has the upper hand over his propensity to evil that the punishment of God is suspended as the "new man" he has become cannot reasonably be punished for crimes committed before his "rebirth."[18] Even after his conversion, however, at any given time in relation to the moral law the human being is deficient, but has the consolation that insofar as he or she approximates the moral law "a human being can still expect to be generally well pleasing to God, at whatever point in time his existence be cut short."[19] The level of separation between the observance of the moral law and politics is made clear by Kant's statement that "the evil principle is still called the prince of this world, and those in this world who adhere to the good principle should always be prepared for physical sufferings, sacrifices, and mortifications of self-love, all of which are portrayed in this world by the evil principle as persecutions, since in his kingdom he has rewards only for those who have made earthly goods their ultimate aim."[20] The earthly goods of power, wealth, and influence then would seem to belong to those aligned with the evil principle.

The Problem of Politics: Immoral Society

The highest achievement for an individual person is to secure freedom from the evil principle. The human being living in isolation is more likely to succeed as a moral entity than one living in society.[21] In society, the human being becomes anxious about his place relative to others. This insecurity leads to "[e]nvy, addiction to power, avarice, and the malignant inclinations associated with these assail his nature, which on its own is undemanding, as soon as he is among human beings." The mere presence of other human beings is sufficient to "corrupt each other's moral disposition and make one another evil."[22] The international political environment in particular is a "state wondrously compounded" of the vices of civilization and savagery, "where civilized peoples stand vis-à-vis one another in the relation of raw nature (the state of constant war) and have also firmly taken it into their heads not to get out of it."[23] The international environment is further complicated by the apparent operation of a "propensity in human nature (perhaps put there on purpose) that makes each and every state strive, when things go its way, to subjugate all others to itself and achieve a universal monarchy but, whenever it has reached a certain size, to split up from within into smaller states."[24] As the culmination of a cosmopolitan project that also encompasses reform of the individual and the state (through the adoption of a republican constitution) and the development of a federation of republics, Kant proposes to institute an association of all mankind under the laws of virtue, i.e., an ethical, or ethico-civil, society or an ethical community:

> an enduring and ever expanding society, solely designed for the preservation of morality by counteracting evil with united forces . . . the dominion of the good principle is not otherwise attainable, so far as human beings can work toward it, than through the setting up and the diffusion of a society in accordance with, and for the sake of, the laws of virtues—a society which reason makes it a task and a duty of the entire human race to establish in its full scope.—For only in this way can we hope for a victory of the good principle over the evil one. . . . morally legislative reason unfurls a banner of virtue as a rallying point for all those who love the good.[25]

The scale of this project is, in principle, universal, "since the duties of virtue concern the entire human race, the concept of an ethical community always refers to the ideal of a totality of human beings."[26] This state of affairs is, however, beyond our hopes because although the "idea of such a state has an entirely well grounded, objective reality in human reason (in the duty to join such a state) . . . we cannot subjectively ever hope of the good will of human beings that these will work harmoniously toward this end." The existing political scenario is that of the juridico-civil state, which is a political community in which the citizens are "still in the *ethical state of nature*."[27] In an ethical state of nature, mutual corruption leads to evil, "a public feuding between the principles of virtue and a state of immorality which the natural human being ought to endeavor to leave behind as soon as possible." The means to achieve this is to institute an ethical community composed of well-disposed human beings working toward "a universal republic based on the laws of virtue," despite the problem that mankind cannot know whether such an achievement is possible.[28] An ethical community begins in the establishment of a juridical community in the subjection of the citizenry to public legislation and the recognition of the laws of a universal lawgiver, which in a republic would be the population establishing an external legal constraint, but an ethical community requires *moral* as opposed to merely legal legitimacy, which is related to inner morality as opposed to public observance of the law. In short, the legislator/ruler of the ethical community is God. Human individuals can and should aim to bring about the ethical community but without belief in God there is no *political* reason for them to do so because, despite having both the potential and the onus to reform, they could simply choose to ignore the demands of rational morality. Without belief in God as ruler and, perhaps more important, as judge, there are no *extra-moral* incentives for human beings to act as moral agents.

Kant is quite adamant that human beings are incapable on their own of achieving a genuine ethical community, but can only imitate the idea of it according to their capabilities: "The sublime, never fully attainable idea of an ethical community is greatly scaled down under human hands. . . . But how could one expect to construct something completely straight from such crooked wood?"[29] Such is the inadequacy of the human species in relation to the task of achieving an ethical community that "[t]o found a moral people of God is, therefore, a work whose execution cannot be hoped for from human beings but only from God himself."[30] Kant conceives of this society as a church, the *church invisible*, which is the "idea of the union of all upright human beings under direct yet moral divine world-governance, as serves for the archetype of any such governance to be founded by human beings," and the *church visible*, which is the "actual union of human beings into a whole that accords with this ideal."[31] The characteristics of a true church are universality, purity of moral intent, relation under freedom, and unchangeableness of constitution.

Kant admits the failure of attempts to create an ethical community or church in the past, but insists it is a duty for human beings to follow until the ideal is achieved or approximated. The ecclesiastical churches precede the establishment of rational religion and can serve as the vehicle for the promotion of a rational religious agenda.[32] Kant maintains that there is one true religion that is approximated in the various faiths.[33] Historical faith and rational religion are conjoined, yet historical faiths are often in conflict, a situation Kant argues will eventually resolve itself by historical faith "flowering into the unchanging and all-unifying church *triumphant!*"[34] This will be achieved by gradually shedding the ecclesiastical elements of religion and instead embracing a universal religion directed by reason, a process described by Kant as "a continual approximation to the ultimate perfection . . . the whole that will one day enlighten the world and rule over it."[35] The universal church is evidence of "the work of the good principle—unnoticed to human eye [*sic*] yet constantly advancing—in erecting a power and a kingdom for itself within the human race, in the form of a community according to the laws of virtue that proclaims the victory over evil and, under its dominion, assures the world of an eternal peace."[36] This process of religious reform therefore runs parallel to and reinforces the processes of technical practical reason that underpin the political project of perpetual peace and also mirrors the pure practical ideal of the Kingdom of Ends. These parallels suggest that the cosmopolitan vision is not complete without a theological component.

Kant raises the question of human progress again in the *Conflict of the Faculties* (1798). In the second essay, "An Old Question Raised Again: Is the Human Race Constantly Progressing?" he claims that it is to the idea of a speculative moral history of human beings, as opposed to the actual historical record, to which we should look for evidence of human progress. Kant makes the case that this moral history is best understood displaced to the future, as "a divinatory historical narrative of things imminent in future time," i.e., a time susceptible to rational, as opposed to historical, analysis—a task made possible if one accepts that the "diviner himself makes and contrives the events which he announces in advance."[37] This, according to Ferenc Fehér, is Kant's great contribution to political thought, that he did not "design political-philosophical blueprints for future action from past models. Rather . . . Kant transformed the present process understood as history into the raw material as well as a treasure trove of unresolved dilemmas for political philosophy."[38]

Returning to the conceptual terrain of the *Groundwork*, Kant makes the possession of a good will his lodestar for future moral development. The action of good will is important because if the historian of future humanity would be able "to attribute to the human being an inherent and unalterably good, albeit limited, will, he would be able to predict with certainty the progress of his species toward the better."[39] In this light Kant argues that

> [t]here must be some experience in the human race which, as an event, points to the disposition and capacity of the human race to be the cause of its own advance toward the better. . . . This conclusion then could also be extended to the history of the past (that it has always been in progress) in such a way that that occurrence would have to be considered not itself as the cause of history, but only as an intimation, a historical sign.[40]

Kant finds this experience in his own time in the reaction of disinterested observers in relation to the French Revolution. The revolution itself is not as important as the "mode of thinking of the spectators which reveals itself *publicly*" in "a universal yet disinterested sympathy for the players on one side against those on the other, even at the risk that this partiality could become very disadvantageous for them if discovered . . . this sympathy can have no other cause than a moral predisposition in the human race."[41] This sympathy is read by Kant as evidence of a moral impetus toward establishing the right to a popular civil constitution in the form of a republican state that will have the effect of promoting progress and eventually removing war as an instrument of policy.[42] The significance of the "aspects and omens" of Kant's era is that he can predict mankind's "progress toward the better" because of the example of the French Revolution in providing an alternative form of existence to the old regime, because "such a phenomenon in human history will not be forgotten."[43] Kant's prophetic history is, however, to be thought of as being indefinite and as a contingent process, albeit one in which "the human race has always been in progress toward the better and will continue to be so henceforth," and which viewed from a universalistic perspective applies to "the whole scope of all the peoples on earth who will gradually come to participate in progress, this reveals the prospect of an immeasurable time" in which reason can act on stubbornly recidivist human beings.[44] Kant's thesis of gradual moral progress uniting all the peoples on earth in an unfathomably distant future is akin to his argument in *Toward Perpetual Peace* that gradual political progress will eventually lead to a peace confederation. Giving history a final moral aim is what enables Kant to support the goals, if not the means, of the French Revolution, "a moral enthusiasm for the Revolution which his formalistic moral system does not justify."[45]

Like *Toward Perpetual Peace*, in *Religion* Kant makes an argument outside of any given time and therefore out of any possible scrutiny on a historical or experiential basis as any such criticism may be dismissed by reference to the countless generations that have to pass before the conditions are ripe for Kant's millenarian resolution of history itself. Kant is forced to go outside known history to an abstract future history in order to argue the case for a progressive interpretation of history that he can then read back into known history. Kant does this by interpreting the course of future history according to the assumption of rational morality, while recognizing that human actions are unpredictable—"we are dealing with beings that act freely, to whom, it is true, what they *ought* to do may be *dictated* in advance, but of whom it may not be *predicted* what they will do."[46]

Kant seeks to reconcile is and ought in the process of human progress. Kant works forwards from what is the case and backwards from what ought to be the case in order to argue the eventual achievement of a peaceful world. The process itself is an incremental one:

Gradually violence on the part of the powers will diminish and obedience to the laws will increase. There will arise in the body politic perhaps more charity and less strife in lawsuits, more reliability in keeping one's word, etc., partly out of love of honor, partly out of well-understood self-interest. And eventually this will also extend to nations in their external relations toward one another up to the realization of the cosmopolitan society.[47]

Kant is careful, however, to stress that "we must also not hope for too much from human beings in their progress toward the better lest we fall prey with good reason to the mockery of the politician who would willingly take the hope of the human being as the dreaming of an overstressed mind."[48] For Kant the best *hope* for human beings lies in education toward the good, but Kant is quite explicit that this initiative is insufficient because the "hope for its progress is to be expected only on the condition of a wisdom from above (which bears the name of providence if it is invisible to us)."[49] It is telling that even hope itself is to be expected on condition of wisdom from above, not wisdom from within.

The problem with Kant's argument is that if one were to use Kant's technique of projecting human destiny into an unimaginably distant future, one could not guarantee his vision of the achievement of "the highest good" over either the absolute destruction of humanity (a more likely scenario now than in Kant's era, given the advent of nuclear weapons) or what he took to be Mendelssohn's projection of a series of abderite progressions and regressions ad infinitum. There can be no guarantee against regression or destruction in the future. Ought might imply what *can* happen, but does not ensure what *will* happen—human beings have the capacity to reject Kant's idea of rational morality and prioritize other aspects of being if they so wish. The faculty of choice is not determined by moral incentives due to the influence of radical evil. Incentives to self-love may trump morality in perpetuity as moral imperatives are not *necessarily* political determinants.[50] Kant's projection is once again based on hope and faith, hope in the redemption of human beings by reason and faith in the idea that God has arranged and guaranteed this outcome. God, as the source of hope and faith, becomes, therefore, an essential component in Kant's argument for human progress.

The Role of God in Kant's Reading of Human Destiny

Kant's concept of God's role evolves over time, but the essence remains remarkably stable, i.e., that human beings on their own are incapable of salvation and require God, or at least the idea of God, in order to achieve a higher state of being. The most important of Kant's precritical writings about God is the essay, *The Only Possible Argument in Support of a Demonstration of the Existence of God*, in which Kant makes the case that God is the "necessary being" and the ultimate real ground of all things. God is referred to as a "mind" and linked to the concepts of truth, beauty, and order. Nature is to be understood as being subsumed under God. The harmony and order of existence is inferred a posteriori to God's design, although this does not constitute proof of his existence as such. Kant's proof of God's existence is that the existence of contingent beings presupposes a being who is not contingent. Kant concludes the essay with an important idea that was to influence most of his subsequent works, i.e., that it is "absolutely necessary that one should convince oneself that God exists; that His existence should be demonstrated, however, is not so necessary."[51]

In the *Critique of Pure Reason* Kant incorporates the concept of God into the wider critical project in the formula "the ideal of pure reason . . . is the object of a transcendental *theology*."[52] There is no way of knowing whether God is an actual or merely possible being—if God does exist, a proposition that Kant insists we must believe, then he is a being of pure thought, which is a problem for Kant in that "for objects of pure thought there is no means whatsoever of cognizing their existence."[53] God, therefore, although a necessary being, can in terms of speculative reason only be known as an idea, and hence cannot be proven or cognized beyond this insight. Kant's preferred means of conceptualizing God is to stress the importance of God as a practical entity in that "moral laws not only presuppose the existence of a supreme being . . . they rightly postulate this existence, although indeed only practically."[54] God in the first *Critique* is "for the merely speculative use of reason a mere *ideal*—but yet a *faultless* ideal, a concept that concludes and crowns the whole of human cognition."[55]

In Kant's later work the permanent deficiency of human beings as they appear to exist plays havoc with the projected resolution of rationally and morally imperfect human beings into the moral species of humanity. The distance between how human beings appear to themselves and each other, and the projected end point of an ethical community, is so great that Kant admits human beings cannot accomplish this transition on their own.[56] As a consequence of this deficiency Kant claims that a supernatural being, God, must be believed to act as the means by which human beings will at least get closer to approximating the ideal. Each person must "so conduct himself as if everything depended on him . . . Only on this condition may he hope that a higher wisdom will provide the fulfillment of his well-intentioned effort," but it must be remembered that the prior condition is that "[t]o found a moral people of God is . . . a work whose execution cannot be hoped for from human beings but only from God himself."[57] It is through God's will and "universal organization [that] the forces of single individuals, insufficient on their own, are united for a common effort."[58] A fundamental assumption of Kant's IR that is absent from present-day cosmopolitan accounts is the extent to which for Kant God is the "omnipotent moral being [that] must be assumed as ruler of the world," under whose care mankind becomes capable of ushering in the highest good. As a consequence, claims Kant, "morality leads inevitably to religion."[59] God, not the people, is the "public lawgiver of an ethical community," and it is the idea of God as a "moral ruler of the world" that allows the representation of an ethical community, "conceivable only as a people of God, and indeed in accordance with the laws of virtue."[60]

Kant's status as a political theologian finds no better expression than his observation that practical reason requires *faith* that God is "(1) the almighty creator of heaven and earth, i.e. morally as *holy* lawgiver; (2) as the preserver of the human race, as its *benevolent* ruler and moral guardian; (3) as the administrator of his own holy laws, i.e. as *just* judge."[61] Practical reason requires this faith in order to point the way toward mankind's moral salvation.[62] This salvation is linked to human beings moving away from a natural mode of being toward a rational and moral mode of being—humanity. It is impossible to discern a direct influence of God on mankind's transition from natural to rational being, beyond a vague sense of the operation of grace. Kant is anxious instead to insist on the human being's duty through "the earnest endeavor to improve his moral nature in all possible ways, thereby making himself capable of receiving a nature fully fit—as is not in his power—for divine approval."[63] By becoming fit for God's approval, mankind demonstrates its superiority over nature and finally affirms its affiliation to reason and morality.

The Importance of Belief in God

Although there are important differences in Kant's approach to belief in God in both his precritical and critical works, the question of God's role in the universe and the importance attached to it is a key theme throughout his career.[64] Belief in God underpins and guarantees both the physical universe and the moral law. It is important to recognize that God does not have to exist in an *actual* sense within Kant's theory scheme. In effect, God is an inscrutable figure who can only be postulated by reference to the moral law and the necessity for the moral law to be rooted in a noncontingent and perfect source.[65] As a practical postulate of reason God is indispensable to Kant's project because, without belief in God, "we have precisely no ground to suppose that the world dances to the tune of human needs."[66] Without this ground, the edifice of pure practical reason and the hope for human reform that it represents becomes contingent at best and at worst crumbles under the weight of its concepts.

Kant's *Lectures on the Philosophical Doctrine of Religion* (the published version of which were delivered in the 1780s) are perhaps the most clear and coherent expression of his arguments in favor of belief in God. Kant builds his "fortress"-like proof for belief in God on morality because "the whole system of duties, which is cognized a priori with apodictic certainty through pure reason," is hence "as certain as a mathematical demonstration."[67] The foundation for belief is the "absolutely necessary morality of actions" flowing from "the idea of a freely acting rational being and from the nature of the actions themselves . . . nothing firmer or more certain can be thought in any science than our obligation to moral actions. Reason would have to cease to be if it could in any way deny this obligation." The certainty underpinning Kant's belief is that "these actions do not depend on their consequences or circumstances; they are determined for the human being once and for all simply through their own nature. It is only through setting his end in them that he becomes a human being, and without them he would be an animal or a monster." Consciousness of the binding nature of these rules of action enables the human being to recognize with certainty that "he is also a member of the chain of the realm of ends," and it is this membership in the realm of ends that "makes him most inwardly noble and worthy of happiness, raising him to the hope of constituting a whole with all rational beings in the realm of morality." Kant regards membership in the realm of ends as a "secure foundation" for belief in God because the realm of ends, under God's direction, is evidence within mankind of "a drive to hope for a lasting happiness." The human being seeks to resolve the tension between the inner commands of duty and the demands of his other incentives in the concept "of a being whose will is those very commands which he recognizes to be given by themselves a priori with apodictic certainty." The "moral" argument leads to Kant's conception of God:

> This being he will have to think of as the most perfect, for otherwise his morality would not obtain reality through it. It must be *omniscient* of [*sic*] it is to know the smallest stirrings of his innermost heart and all the motives and intentions of his actions. And for this merely much knowledge will not suffice, but only omniscience.—It must be *omnipotent*, so that it can arrange the whole of nature to accord with the way I act regarding my morality. It must even be *holy* and *just*; for otherwise I would have no hope that the fulfillment of my duties would be well-pleasing to it.[68]

Kant claims that the moral theist must believe in God with certainty, "because otherwise he would have to reject the necessary laws of morality which are grounded in the nature of his being. Thus he derives theology from morality, yet not from speculative but from practical evidence; i.e. not through knowledge but from faith." The linkage between the necessity of belief in God and the requirement to be moral for Kant is manifest in his finding that "the existence of a wise governor of the world is a necessary *postulate of practical reason.*"[69]

Moral Theology

The purpose of moral theology is to bring to the fore God as a *practically* necessary being. God as a practically necessary being plays a crucial role in the culmination of moral and political life in that belief in God ensures the eventual triumph of moral behavior in his role as ruler of the universe:

> There must exist a being *who rules the world according to reason and moral laws,* and who has established, in the course of things to come, a state where the creature who has remained true to his nature and who has made himself worthy of happiness through morality will actually participate in this happiness; *for otherwise all subjectively necessary duties which I as a rational being am responsible for performing will lose their objective reality.* Why should I make myself worthy of happiness through morality if there is no being who can give me this happiness.[70]

Belief in God and his provision of a future in which human beings ultimately achieve moral worthiness and happiness as the redeemed-by-reason species of humanity is therefore "a *necessary postulate for the incontrovertible laws of my own nature.*"[71] Thus, although human duties and obligations are apodictically certain, "there would be no incentives to act in accord with these duties as a rational human being if there were no God and no future world."[72] For Allen Wood, "morally disposed people are involved in a kind of practical irrationality unless they believe in the future life and a providential and gracious Deity." Kant's arguments in favor of belief in God therefore "rescue such an agent from a practical paradox."[73] Belief in God's divine rule is crucial to the success of moral life for humans as otherwise there is no reason to obey the moral law— even if I recognize the apodictic certainty of the moral law, I could choose to live *as if* God does not exist, and there would be no disincentive, divine or otherwise, to prevent me from living solely for my own gratification. Reason, informed by this fear of the alternative, leads Kant to conceive of God as a "holy legislator," while the inclination for happiness "wishes" God to be a "benevolent governor of the world" and conscience "represents" God as a "just judge."[74] Reason in itself is not enough to compel an actor to morality—there must be a God to reward the actor's attempts to make himself worthy of happiness; otherwise the actor is simply tying his hands and restricting his activities unnecessarily. This is not to state that one is acting morally if one acts in a moral fashion out of fear of coercion or out of a wish for reward. Rather, what is at stake here is the very issue of why one would choose to follow the moral law and not other incentives. Without an apparatus of incentives and disincentives there is nothing to prevent agents from disavowing the moral law. God is a necessary postulate of practical reason precisely because it is only God who can provide a horizon beyond death in which the actions of this life have meaning. Thus, although separate from the moral law, the apparatus of incentives and disincentives helps to maintain its structure in addition to the good will that is supposed to be its foundation (and which Kant recognizes is not the most reliable of qualities in human beings).

Moral theology serves as a basis for thinking beyond the appearance of human beings to the ideal state of humanity. Kant projects a vision of God, freedom of the human will, and the possibility of a moral world allowing human beings "to transport ourselves in thought beyond all possible experience and out of the sensible world; only here may we assume and believe something from a practical point of view for which we otherwise have no adequate speculative grounds," although Kant is anxious to stress that this applies only "on behalf of our morality, we are in no way justified in admitting ourselves further into this idea. . . . For here the limits of our reason are distinctly indicated, and whoever dares to transcend them will be punished by reason itself for his boldness with both pain and error." Kant seeks to hermetically seal a pure morality from other aspects of human existence, to insist on a "pure" morality that has to be distinct from incentives not rooted in pure practical rationality. In political terms, however, such a morality is impossible or an irrelevance. Kant affixes limits to his moral theory that preclude political calculation; it is only "if we remain within these boundaries, then our reward will be to become wise and good human beings."[75] These boundaries, however, can only result in either withdrawal from political life, as in Kant's ideal of the hermit as expressed in *The Critique of the Power of Judgment*, or political paralysis in that to pursue such a morality would likely exclude any given human being from participating effectively in a political setting where the pursuit of interests is the principal objective.

Kant avoids the problem of the imperfect nature of human life by insisting in the manner of Dr. Pangloss that the existing world is the best of all currently possible worlds and that it should be believed that it has been arranged just so by God, albeit with a prospect of improvement.[76] At the center of Kant's "best of all possible worlds" lie human beings, the earth's representative rational species, and as such the "true perfection of the world-whole has to lie in the use rational creatures make of their reason and freedom."[77] Despite, or perhaps because of, his reservations about the ability of human beings to even approximate this true perfection, Kant expresses the future state of human beings in terms of faith: "However disordered and purposeless as history may describe human conduct, yet we should not let this drive us crazy, but should rather believe nevertheless that the human race is grounded on *a universal plan* according to which it will in the end *attain to its highest possible perfection*. For up to now we have surveyed the plan *only in its individual parts and fragments*."[78] This requires a leap of faith that the historical evidence, as Kant admits, does not support. Human beings are asked to sacrifice the knowledge they have gained from experience on the altar of Kant's "hope," "faith," and "belief."

God's government is the capstone of Kant's philosophical doctrine of religion and is extremely important in relation to his moral theory, IR theory, and the resolution of the question of human destiny. The linkage between Kant's theological project and his moral project is clear in the *Opus Postumum*, in that God is presented as a "being, who is capable of and entitled to command all rational beings according to laws of duty (the categorical imperative) of moral-practical reason."[79] Kant argues that "God's government of the world in accordance with moral principles is an assumption without which all morality would have to break down. For if morality cannot provide me with the prospect of satisfying my needs, then it cannot command anything of me either." In lieu of knowledge of the mind of God, human beings have the principles of morality to guide their actions, but these actions only have power over them through belief in a God-based set of inducements and punishments to act as incentives to act in conformity with the law—hence, in this sense, "cognition of God must therefore complete morality."[80] As the moral project is one of the bases of Kant's IR theory and, at least in part, the foundation for perpetual peace and cosmopolitanism, Kant's linkage of God and morality is significant from a disciplinary perspective. The cement that binds the concepts of Kant's IR together is theological: even when not immediately apparent, it nonetheless runs through and under what are understood to be more prominent aspects of Kant's project. Both the *telos* and the blueprint of Kant's vision of world order are in effect theological.

Conclusion

Kant is forced into *faith* in God as otherwise hope exits and meaninglessness enters existence. Kant admits that the concept of God is one "which we ourselves have created," but this is not a denial of God's existence, merely an admission that our concept of God is a human creation, which may or may not reflect the nature of God.[81] Viewed from outside Kant's system, however, God is nothing more than the material with which Kant plugs the gaps of his philosophy and by which he achieves his desire for unity: as Allen Wood recognizes, there "can be no doubt, of course, that for Kant faith in God is introduced as a response to the dialectical perplexities which threaten practical reason."[82] From a non-Kantian perspective God is always introduced by Kant on those occasions when Kant's system begins to crack under the weight of unresolved tensions, culminating in a series of stopgap measures designed to shore up the problematic foundations at the heart of Kant's project, i.e., in the absence of any real incentive for human beings to renounce technical practical reason and political life as the expression of self-love and the inclinations, Kant has to posit God as the guarantor of a future in which rational morality prevails.

If the idea of God is too weak to bear the weight that is put upon it, the implications for Kant's project as a whole are profound. The most common understanding of Kant's God is that as an idea of reason it should be treated as a regulative, as opposed to constitutive, concept. Viewing God in this way, it is argued, allows us to comprehend the role of the divine as being merely a hypothesis that plays "a useful role of systematizing scientific data."[83] This position, however, seriously underplays the significance of the role played by belief in Kant. As Allen Wood argues, if there is no God or afterlife, there is only "a painful and feeble striving toward an empty and meaningless goal."[84] Such is the centrality of the concept of God that "it is only through faith in divine grace that it is possible for man to conceive of an appropriation of 'a righteousness not his own.' . . . God's grace must be presupposed if an *absurdum practicum* is to be avoided as regards the unconditioned component of the highest good."[85] *Especially* as a regulative concept God is hugely important to the operation of Kant's system, as God is embedded in the very grammar of his project. In this sense belief in God provides the glue that binds the various elements of Kant's IRrelevant work together.

Conclusion

Believing in the Possibility of Salvation

At first everything must be attributed to nature, but later nature itself must be attributed to God.[1]

I have learned from the critique of pure reason that philosophy is not a science of representations, concepts and ideas, or science of all the sciences, or anything else of this sort. It is rather a science of the human being, of his representations, thoughts and actions: it should present all the components of the human being both as he is and as he should be— that is, in terms both of his natural functions and of his relations of morality and freedom.[2]

The foregoing chapters demonstrate the extent to which political-theological concerns permeate the fabric of Kant's work in the critical philosophy and in those works in which he seeks to get to grips with the peculiar problem posed by human beings. The problem is one of human insufficiency: Can human beings, despite the limitations of their own powers of comprehension and less than perfect moral characters, be saved from political and social systems that are the product of prudential calculation of interest derived from what they know of themselves and each other? Any such salvation would be contrary to the empirical evidence offered by the study of human behavior when it is processed primarily through the faculty of understanding and technical practical reason. Kant's answer to this question is that mankind can be saved, but only by putting the insights derived from the understanding and technical practical reason in a new context, i.e., sacrificing them in order to make room for faith. This sacrificial recontextualization of the knowledge gained from the understanding and technical practical reason does not result in its erasure, but it is rendered secondary to, and preparatory for, the insights of pure practical reason and rational morality. What a human being can *know* as a natural entity is merely a developmental phase that prepares the mind for the more fundamental question of how he ought to act. The division between *knowledge* of human beings and *faith* in humanity also accounts for Kant's lower and higher anthropological vantage points: a thoroughly pessimistic anthropology derived from observation of human beings is consistently contrasted against an anthropodicy rooted in the *idea* of humanity. This division also plays itself out in the termination of Kant's philosophy of history and political theology, with both human beings and humanity having ends (or *eschata*) corresponding, respectively, to their natural fate or redeemed destiny.

Read in this light, *Toward Perpetual Peace* is an eschatological text that presents three possible outcomes for mankind: destruction in an apocalyptic war orchestrated by human beings following their natural instincts for power and subjugation; a precarious and uncertain peace predicated on self-interest developed from technical practical reason; and finally a *genuinely* perpetual peace that proceeds from pure practical reason underwritten by belief in providence. Kant therefore combines both *Weltgeschichte* and *Heilsgeschichte* in a compelling and powerful manner.[3] Kant's eschatological rendering of both the fate of human beings and the destiny of humanity provides a "position and a yardstick" from which to critically assess mankind's progress, which is revealed from this perspective to be "necessarily the history of salvation."[4] Kant's eschatology emerges from his critical engagement with "the eschatology of the eighteenth century as expressed in terms of cosmology and saving history" in *The End of All Things*, and finds a specifically political expression in *Toward Perpetual Peace*.[5] What makes Kant's "*transcendental eschatology*" distinctive is that "it no longer depends on the support [*Krücken*] of scripture, which has long become suspect; nor is it confident of possessing the truth, as generated by the rational arguments of the Enlightenment."[6] Kant's philosophy of history, and by extension his theory of international politics, are products of his post-scriptural, critical theology rooted in a new form of faith indebted to but distinct from religious and theological endeavors of the past.[7] Despite the rupture occasioned by Kant's transformation of religion into a form compatible with reason and the critical philosophy, there remains in Kant "at least the echoes of a characteristically religious eschatology."[8] The transformation may have left Christian orthodoxy behind, but Kant retains "a pilgrim sense of life in which our present endeavours are sustained by the hope of a glorious consummation yet to come."[9]

The first section proposes that Kant felt it necessary to assert belief *over* knowledge as a consequence of his attempt to save metaphysics from the dead end of dogmatism and the scorched earth of skepticism. The making room for faith that Kant advertises as one of the primary aims of the first *Critique* allows for the restoration of a credible belief in a more than merely animal and mechanical destiny for mankind. In this light, the third *Critique*'s argument in favor of believing mankind to be the divinely ordained end of purposive nature copper-fastens a cosmology in which the relationship between God and man is asserted as an article of faith. *Toward Perpetual Peace* represents how this relationship plays out in the political sphere. The second section of the conclusion assesses the nature of Kant's reformulated metaphysical and cosmological system. Instead of revelation, Kant recasts religion in terms of a fundamental relationship between the "good principle" and mankind, a relationship that is complicated by the "evil principle" and its presence within the human species, radical evil. The final section argues that Kant's ultimate aim is soteriological, i.e., the salvation of mankind. In contrast to Schmitt's political theology of the sovereign decision, Kant's political theology is based on plotting a path to salvation on two fronts—in the postulated afterlife of the first and second *Critiques*, but also in the form of perpetual peace as an *earthly* form of salvation.

Justifying Belief: The Importance of Kant's Restoration of Metaphysics

The importance of belief throughout this book requires a thorough account of how and why it became so central to Kant's many philosophical tasks. In many respects, "What may I believe?" is the fifth great question of Kantian philosophy after "What can I know? What ought I do? What may I hope? and What is man?" Its importance is such that it relates directly to each of the preceding questions, i.e., belief is where mankind turns after knowledge has exhausted itself, belief is intrinsically tied to how we ought to act and for what we may hope, and arguably what differentiates man from other animals is his capacity to believe in both God and his own future life.

In order to get to grips with the role of belief, one must examine how it emerged as a consequence of Kant's efforts in the first *Critique* to deal with the fallout from the effect of the decline of dogmatism and the rise of skepticism in philosophy. Kant's political theology of IR is a product of his wider attempt to restore metaphysics after the crisis precipitated by Hume's skeptical revolution. Invoking the tragic fate of Hecuba, Kant claims that as a consequence of Hume's sack of metaphysics "the Queen of all the sciences" had been overthrown and that "the changed fashion of the time brings her only scorn; a matron outcast and forsaken."[10] This fall had two causes, the atrophy and degeneration of metaphysics under the administration of the dogmatists, and the final razing of the foundations of the temple of metaphysics by the skeptics, "a species of nomads, despising all settled modes of life."[11] The error of dogmatism lies in its falling victim to the transcendental illusion of mistaking "appearances, which after all are mere representations . . . for things in themselves."[12] The illegitimate extension of concepts and principles of the understanding beyond the limits of nature by the dogmatists led to a series of misleading and ultimately groundless claims about the capacity of the human mind to *know* the bases of existence in this life and the next, especially in relation to the three core themes of metaphysics, i.e., the role of God, freedom, and the afterlife. Kant's verdict on the dogmatist metaphysics of Gottfried Leibniz and Christian Wolff is damning: "there is so much deceptive in it that it is necessary to suspend this procedure."[13] Despite Kant crediting Hume with interrupting his "dogmatic slumbers," he comes to a no less negative conclusion regarding skepticism, calling it "a way of thinking in which reason moves against itself with such violence that it never could have arisen except in complete despair as regards satisfaction of reason's most important aims."[14]

The playing out of the antinomies of pure reason, in which diametrically opposed claims are made in relation to whether or not something is or is not the case, allowed the skeptics "the opportunity thereby to declare all truths of reason as uncertain, and accepted the principle that we lack certainty in all our cognitions." This situation led to the overthrow of dogmatism, but it also was one in which "skepticism affirmed no principles <*principia*> from which one could proceed," a scenario in which the "interest of human beings suffered" as a consequence of the failure of both dogmatic and skeptical metaphysics to offer a basis upon which to think about the most elemental foundations of human existence and conduct.[15] Caught between "obsolete, worm-eaten dogmatism" and the "cancer" of idealism on the one hand and the violence and rot of skepticism on the other, Kant was determined not to surrender metaphysics to these diseased, warring factions.[16] Metaphysics, according to Kant, is an "indispensable discipline," which by delineating the uses of reason "treats of the very *possibility* of some sciences, and of the *use* of all." Metaphysics also prevents errors in the use of concepts and thereby contributes to the harmony of the scientific community and points it to what Kant argues ought to be its true end, "the happiness of all mankind."[17]

Kant's restoration of metaphysics is particularly important in relation to the idea of God as the guarantor of the moral law and perpetual peace. The dogmatist makes the false claim to knowledge of God's existence, while the skeptic makes the equally unfounded claim that because God's existence cannot be known, no moral philosophy can be based on a theological foundation. In the absence of the argument for belief in God, skepticism destroys morality because the only logical outcome of the fourth antinomy would be to ignore (whatever its merits) the moral law. The skeptic comes to this conclusion because his attitude to the moral law reduces to two choices—to be a fool and obey the moral law despite knowing that no happiness will accrue to himself, or to be a knave:

> If we assume moral principles without presupposing God and another world, then we trap ourselves in a practical dilemma. Namely, if there is no God and no other world, then I must either constantly follow the rules of virtue, [and] then I am a virtuous dreamer, because I expect no consequences which are worthy of my conduct—or I will throw away and despise the law of virtue, tread over all morality because it can bring me no happiness, I will give way to my vices, enjoy these enjoyments of life while I have them, and then I form a principle through which I become a knave. We must then decide to be either fools or knaves.[18]

If the skeptic is correct then it "appears to be better that one make no effort at all to live adequately to this law, but rather attempt to promote one's happiness in the world as much as possible. In this manner the cleverest rogue is the happiest. . . . he who endeavored to live according to the moral law would be a proper fool if he set aside the advantages in the world and hankered after such things as the moral law promises him, but cannot deliver."[19] The stakes could not be higher for Kant: either he restores metaphysics or the promise offered by moral life would be fatally compromised. The primary task therefore of the first

Critique and the *Prolegomena* was to extricate metaphysics from the crisis posed by the redundancy of rationalism and the excesses of the "destructive philosophy" of Hume.

The key distinction between dogmatic and skeptical approaches and that of the critical philosophy that Kant proposes is that whereas the former both "claim to such insight into their object as is required to assert or to deny something in regard to it," the latter "confines itself to pointing out that in the making of the assertion something has been presupposed that is void and merely fictitious; and it thus overthrows the theory by removing its alleged foundation without claiming to establish anything that bears directly upon the constitution of the object."[20] The fourth antinomy of the first *Critique* is particularly important in this regard because Kant argues it is impossible to resolve whether or not there *is* a God as there are perfectly logical and rational arguments in favor of both positions. In this condition of *unknowing*, the issue devolves to perspective and belief because, as Kant claims, a "strange situation is disclosed in this antinomy," namely that the arguments both for and against God's existence are "entirely in conformity even with ordinary human reason, which frequently falls into conflict with itself through considering its object from two different points of view."[21] In such a case, according to Kant, both inferences, i.e., God's existence or nonexistence, "were correct, according to the point of view which each chose."[22] In this condition of indeterminacy, other criteria must be applied when choosing between one option and the other.

In the choice between the theses ("the *dogmatism* of pure reason") and the antitheses ("pure *empiricism*") of the antinomies, Kant argues that the *practical interest* and the *speculative interest* of reason and humanity are both best served by the theses. In the practical sphere this involves *believing* that "the world has a beginning, that my thinking self is of simple and therefore indestructible nature, that it is free in its voluntary actions and raised above the compulsion of nature, and finally that all order in the things constituting the world is due to a primordial being, from which everything derives its unity and purposive connection."[23] As if to stress the point, Kant argues that viewing appearances solely or primarily from the perspective of pure empiricism destroys the foundations of morality and religion: "[i]f there is no primordial being distinct from the world, if the world is without beginning and therefore without an Author, if our will is not free, if the soul is divisible and perishable like matter, moral ideas and principles lose all validity, and share in the fate of the transcendental ideas which served as their theoretical support."[24] In the speculative realm, reason also has an interest in choosing the thesis because "[w]hen the transcendental ideas are postulated and employed in the manner prescribed by the thesis, the entire chain of conditions and the derivation of the conditioned can be grasped completely a priori. For we then start from the unconditioned," i.e., God. The antithesis cannot perform a similar function as "it can give no answer which does not lead to the endless renewal of the same enquiry," i.e., there is an infinite regress as "every given beginning compels us to advance to one still higher; every part leads to a still smaller part; every event is preceded by another event as its cause; and the conditions of existence in general rest always again upon other conditions, without ever obtaining unconditioned footing and support in any self-subsistent thing, viewed as primordial being."[25] As a third advantage of the theses over the antitheses, they have the benefit of being comprehensible and comforting to the common understanding, whereas in "the restless ascent from the conditioned to the condition, always with one foot in the air, there can be no satisfaction."[26] Belief in God enables the vital *hope* in the human future that is necessary for the preservation of morality and at the same time political reform that in turn embodies both rational and moral principles.

Establishing the validity of belief on the grounds of practical interest allowed Kant to shift the ground of the debate with skepticism. Whereas before the skeptic was in a position to deny the possibility of knowing the existence of God and therefore the essential validity of any morality that relied on a divine foundation, Kant now argued that in the absence of definitive proof either way it was indisputably the case that it was in the practical interest of mankind to *believe* that God existed. The status of this belief gives rise to merely regulative principles of reason, but as Kant claims this is sufficient because "[i]t cannot hurt the good cause, if the dogmatic language of the overweening sophist be toned down to the more moderate and humble requirements of a belief adequate to quieten our doubts, though not to command unconditional submission."[27] Similarly, in relation to belief in the continuation of life after death, Kant recognizes that "of all this we have not the least knowledge," but that the hypothesis is useful "to meet the attack" of the skeptic who claims there is no afterlife and that there is nothing beyond what the senses reveal and the mind constructs of reality. Kant admits therefore that the claim to the possibility of an afterlife is "not even an idea of reason, but is a concept *devised* merely for the purposes of self-defence." This self-defense consists of pointing out that the skeptic "falsely represents the absence of empirical conditions as itself amounting to proof of the total impossibility of our belief, and is therefore proceeding on the assumption that he has exhausted all the possibilities," which is a mistake, according to Kant, because "[w]hat we are doing is merely to show that it is just as little possible for him to comprehend the whole field of possible things through mere laws of experience as it is for us to reach, outside experience, any conclusions justifiable for our reason."[28] Such a hypothesis may be nothing more than a "*problematic* judgment," but it cannot be refuted, even if it cannot be proven. Kant's description of the significance of these judgments is important in that it encapsulates their double-sidedness: "They are nothing but private opinions. Nevertheless, we cannot properly dispense with them as weapons against the misgivings that are apt to occur; they are necessary to secure our inner tranquillity. We must preserve to them this character, carefully guarding against the assumption of their independent authority or absolute validity, since otherwise they would drown in fictions and delusions."[29] These weapons, used properly and with due care, create the possibility of belief and thereby, at least to Kant's satisfaction, displace if not "dispose thoroughly of the Humean doubt."[30]

The other alleged fearful consequence of Humean skepticism, according to Kant, is the implication that the natural sphere is also ultimately a meaningless series of events governed by blind chance and necessity. This despairing scenario is also neutered by the shift from dogmatic knowledge of rationalism to the critical philosophy. The advantage of believing in God is that such a belief allows that "the entire chain of conditions and the derivation of the conditioned can be grasped completely *a priori*. For we then start from the unconditioned. This is not done by the antithesis [pure empiricism/skepticism], which for this reason is at a very serious disadvantage."[31] This move allows Kant to maintain that the universe is best conceived of as ordered as long as we remember that "we ought not to derive the order and systemic unity of the world from a supreme intelligence, but to obtain from the idea of a supremely wise cause the rule according to which reason in connecting empirical causes and effects in the world may be employed to best advantage, and in such a manner as to secure satisfaction of its own demands."[32] The belief is relative, not absolute; it merely allows the development of rules for comprehending an order we have the right to assume, but not to know absolutely. Kant is adamant that this "distinction has to be reckoned with in the case of a merely regulative principle. We recognise the necessity of the principle, but have no knowledge of the source of its necessity; and in assuming that it has a supreme ground, we do so solely in order to think its universality more determinately."[33] The belief in a "regulative principle and maxim" of order and systemic unity furthers and strengthens "the empirical employment of reason . . . opening out new paths which are not within the cognisance of the understanding."[34] This position has important implications for politics, which is a product of nature, and, as Kant insists in the *Idea for a Universal History*, must be understood as being determined and subject to the rules of nature in exactly the same manner as other natural processes and systems. Without a ground for belief in the purposive unity of nature, there could be no hope for the development of political systems beyond their existing forms. Natural teleology, which posits the ultimate perfection of these forms over time, depends upon the idea that there is an unconditioned origin and a systematic purpose for existence. *Toward Perpetual Peace* is notable within the corpus of Kantian texts because the belief in the convergence of moral and natural purposive unity, both of which have their foundational assumptions in the belief of a divine impetus, is a central tenet of the essay. In this sense it is the fulfillment of ideas and concepts that have their origin in the *Critique of Pure Reason*.

The final importance of belief to Kant's project lies in the extent to which it enables the critical philosophy and related political and social projects to occupy the important middle ground between rationalist dogmatism and skepticism. In the first *Critique* Kant describes belief as "the guidance which an idea gives me, and to its subjective influence in that furthering of the activities of my reason which confirms me in the idea, and which yet does so without my being in a position to give a speculative account of it."[35] The development of belief as an alternative to dogmatism and skepticism allowed Kant to present the critical philosophy as a middle way between what he saw as two extremes. A "critique of reason," wrote Kant in the *Prolegomena*, "indicates the true middle way between the dogmatism that Hume fought and the skepticism he wanted to introduce instead—a middle way that, unlike other middle ways, which we are advised to determine for ourselves as it were mechanically (something from one side, and something from the other), and by which no one is taught any better, is one, rather, that can be determined precisely, according to principles."[36] The advantage is that within the critical philosophy, the proper, limited use of skepticism allows the deflation of the puffed up claims of dogmatism without lapsing into the destructive tendency of removing all foundations of the articles of faith necessary for practical reason. The ultimate achievement of the critical philosophy is in fact *conservative*, according to Kant, because once dogmatic assertions are replaced by critical assumptions, the foundations of faith are restored on different grounds:

> The proofs which are serviceable for the world at large all preserve their entire value undiminished, and indeed, upon the surrender of these dogmatic pretensions, gain in clearness and in natural force. For reason is then located in its own peculiar sphere, namely, the order of ends, which is also at the same time an order of nature; and since it is in itself not only a theoretical but also a practical faculty, and as such is not bound down to natural conditions, it is justified in extending the order of ends, and therewith our own existence, beyond the limits of experience and of life.[37]

One of the chief achievements of the critical philosophy then for Kant is that it restored the possibility of a postskeptical belief in God, mankind and the prospect of salvation.[38] By pointing out the groundlessness of both rationalist and empiricist claims to knowledge, and by demonstrating the impossibility of ever *knowing* whether God exists or not, Kant paves the way for a legitimate reconfiguration of the idea of God as an ideal of pure reason.[39] For Donald MacKinnon the ineffability of Kant's God places his work within the tradition of negative theology, defined by "the problem of the representation of the unrepresentable."[40] Don Cupitt, building on this identification of Kant as a negative theologian, stresses that Kant's variant on this tradition is distinct from that of the Greek Fathers for whom the apophatic was the norm. The difference is instructive in that if "we who live after Kant must walk the negative way, it will certainly not be quite the same way as it was for the classical theologians," who professed faith in the existence of God, but denied knowledge of his nature. For Kant, according to Cupitt, these positions are essentially reversed, i.e., the existence of God is unknown (and unknowable) but "God's *nature* is not mysterious, for we have a clear, unproblematic and useful *idea* of God immanent within our reason"; the problematic aspect of God after Kant is that God's *existence* is unknowable.[41]

Rational Religion and the Salvation of Mankind: Perpetual Peace as Soteriological Exercise

Kant transfigures both God and mankind in the process of rescuing them from what he takes to be the worst implications of skepticism, i.e., that human beings will remain animals trapped within the confines of their passionate natures in a godless universe deprived of meaning. Kant's anthropodicy necessitates making the case for the "higher anthropological vantage point" of *Toward Perpetual Peace* or the "organized being" of the *Critique of the Power of Judgment*. Such representations are only possible, however, in the context of a rational theology predicated on an unknowable entity who nonetheless must be believed to be the omnipotent and omniscient Author of nature *and* the moral law in order to provide a ground for the *hope* that these reformed versions of mankind may be realized (or at least approximated) in phenomenal existence. Kant's God is defined not by its personality but by its power to act as a foundation for practical philosophy and rational religion. Kant strips away the dogmatic assertions and cultural accretions of the ecclesiastical religions to a set of core rational assumptions: we ought to have faith that God is the source of all things and that mankind may be believed to be the fulfillment of both purposive nature and pure practical reason. The fact that human beings as they *appear* to each other are clearly *not* the fulfillment of reason, and by their actions clearly align themselves against what can be known through reason of the will of God in creating them in the first place, brings forth an important corollary, i.e., the presence of an evil principle that opposes good within human nature and prevents mankind from moving toward the resolution Kant has identified as the consummation of its a priori history.

The Evil Principle

In contrast to the relatively clear origins of the good principle, which Kant argues we ought to believe lie in the idea of God as the author of the moral law, the origins of evil are obscure. Whereas reason leads inexorably back to belief in God as a source of rational morality, one cannot repeat the process in relation to evil. "The rational origin" of the propensity to evil, writes Kant in *Religion Within the Boundaries of Mere Reason*, "remains inexplicable . . . there is no conceivable ground . . . from which moral evil could first have come in us."[42] The scriptural account of the Fall, which attributes the introduction of evil into the human species to "a *spirit* of an originally more sublime destiny," merely demonstrates the incomprehensibility of the origin of evil, which Kant makes clear by asking if the source of evil is attributable to that spirit, from "whence the evil in that spirit?"[43] Kant further admits in his preface to the *Conflict of the Faculties* that there is a "theoretical deficiency which our pure rational belief admits" in relation to the origin of evil. Because of this deficiency, reason can turn to revelation to fill the gap left by reason, as revelation, like belief, "helps— more or less, depending on the times and the person concerned—to satisfy a rational need."[44] The biblical and other revelatory accounts of evil, therefore, have merit in that they can fill in the gaps of human knowledge of evil and allow further cognition of its role. In *Religion Within the Boundaries of Mere Reason*, Kant demonstrates the extent to which he is determined to link his project with the revelation of Christianity in that "any attempt . . . to find a meaning in scriptures in harmony with the *most holy* teachings of reason must be held not only as permissible but as duty"; although reason takes precedence, it is nonetheless a requirement to link reason to biblical themes and narratives.[45] What is certain is that Kant's "evil principle" shares with Luther's Satan the status of being "prince of this world."[46] As Karl Barth argues, it is important to recognize the ultimately Pauline nature of Kant's theorization of evil, i.e., that evil originates from a point outside nature rather than in nature itself.[47]

In what is his most revealing account of the operation of evil *within* mankind, Kant argues that

> the human being has many instincts belonging to animality, and since he has to have them if he is to continue being human, the strength of his instincts will beguile him and he will abandon himself to them, *and thus arises evil*, or rather, when the human being begins to use his reason, he falls into foolishness. *A special germ toward evil cannot be thought*, but rather *the first development of our reason toward the good is the origin of evil*. And that remainder of uncultivatedness in the progress of culture is again evil.[48]

Evil therefore emerges as a consequence of the subordination of reason to natural ends, with reason being forced to act as a handmaiden for instinct, providing answers to the question "how can I get what I consider necessary or desirable?" not "how ought I live in a manner that would be recognized as worthwhile by the deity of rational morality?" The linkage between evil and nature is established by Kant in relation to the "*natural* propensity" to radical or "genuine evil, i.e., moral evil."[49] Caught between the demands of the moral law and the natural predisposition to self-love, the human being is evil "only because he reverses the moral order of his incentives in incorporating them into his maxims."[50] The skewed priorities of the human being result in mankind being collectively unable to exercise "the moral ability to judge what to think of a human being, and renders any imputability entirely uncertain," a moral blindness that according to Kant "constitutes the foul stain of our species."[51] Within the natural world, mankind faces the ultimate problem of political life under its auspices, i.e., nature "deals despotically with man. Men destroy one another like wolves. Plants and animals overgrow and stifle one another. Nature does not observe the care and provision which they require. Wars destroy what long artifice has established and cared for."[52] If mankind is to achieve perpetual peace, it must first either declare independence from nature or accept that "the human being is a part of nature, and belongs to the sensible world, thus he is therefore also subject to the laws of appearances. All appearances are determined among themselves by certain laws, and it is just this determination of everything given in nature by universal laws that constitutes the mechanism of nature. The human being, therefore, as a part of nature is subject to this natural mechanism" and as a result mankind must submit to the ebb and flow of natural necessity, making as much sense of its existence as it can with insights derived from the senses, understanding, and technical practical reason.

Kant opens the pathway to the declaration of independence from nature by means of a quasi-Gnostic distinction between God as the *architechtus* or creator of the universe and the demiurge as "author of matter."[53] This difference between two types of godhead explains the twofold fate of mankind as being "destined for two entirely different worlds: for the realm of sense and understanding and so for this terrestrial world, but also for another world, which we do not know—a moral realm," with the demiurge predominant in the former and the genuine author of the world and God of redemption in the latter.[54] The human being "is a part of nature, and belongs to the sensible world" and as such is subject to the "mechanism of nature."[55] Salvation from the mechanism or trap of nature is however possible for humanity in that "the human race is a class of creatures which through their own nature are someday to be released and set free from their instincts . . . the whole is *some day to win through to a glorious outcome.*"[56] The path to salvation lies in the reconfiguration and redemption of nature itself by means of a dualistic perspective in which nature can be understood as both "the principle that impels us to promote our *happiness*" in the achievement of goals established by instinct or prudence, and at the same time, but from a supersensible vantage point, nature can be understood in a practical sense as "our ability to achieve certain ends by our own powers in general . . . a stimulus to good produced in us by God, the predisposition to which we did not establish in ourselves, and so, as grace."[57] By this perspectival distinction

Kant, in the manner of Origen, provides an apocatastatic redemption of nature that accords with his observation in the *Conjectural Beginning of Human History* that nature "begins from good, for that is the *work of God*."[58] Kant also shares with Origen a defining interest in the role of both providence and education (including suffering) in the eventual salvation of mankind.[59]

The Example of Jesus and the Role of Grace

Grace is defined by Kant as "the hope that good will develop in us," and he explicitly links the development of grace within mankind to the example of Jesus, to the extent that "grace can and should become more powerful than sin in us (as free beings), if only we let it act in us or let our disposition to the kind of conduct shown in that holy example become active."[60] Kant's treatment of Jesus is particularly idiosyncratic in that while he does not attribute his death with substitutionary atonement, Kant still "seeks to give to Christ's work a significance which goes far beyond that of a classic example of innocent suffering, borne with an exemplary heroism and an altogether undiminished compassion for his fellows . . . when he speaks . . . as if the coming of Christ were itself a proleptic vindication of the good man's hope," that his own efforts at moral improvement were not "doomed to frustration."[61] Stephen Palmquist also identifies a tendency in Kant's work "to affirm the traditional Christian belief that Jesus plays a unique role in the human race's ability to achieve such a moral revolution (e.g., *Religion* 80, 158–62) and that each person's salvation somehow (at least in a symbolic sense) depends on Jesus's accomplishment."[62] Yet for all that Jesus is described by Kant as opening "the portals of freedom" for mankind, his true significance lies in the fact that he represents "the archetype of the good lying in our reason," which "precedes, and is a condition of the possibility of, any judgment that a particular historical individual exemplifies this archetype."[63] The transformation of mankind in the image of God is provided with a *telos* of perfection in the person of Jesus.

If grace is to secure this transformation of the human disposition mankind must embrace faith as the means to escape nature as the operation of instinct and prudence.[64] Faith, understood as the preponderance of the moral constitution over all other aspects of mankind, is instrumental in overcoming nature because it allows confidence that "if we were or would ever become *all* that we should be and (in continued approximation) can be, nature would have to obey our wishes, which, however, would in this case never be unwise."[65] The escape from nature understood as sensibility (the domain of the demiurge) is dependent upon belief in the "three articles of moral faith, *God, freedom of the human will*, and *a moral world*," described by Kant as the means by "which it is permissible for us to transport ourselves in thought beyond all possible experience and out of the sensible world; only here may we assume and believe something from a practical point of view for which we otherwise have no adequate speculative grounds."[66] Kant's "pure religious faith" (as distinct from existing, adulterated ecclesiastical faiths) presents two prerequisites for salvation: first, that mankind believe that grace requires moral reform and a commitment to good conduct (according to Kant theoretically "we cannot make the removal of sin comprehensible in any other way"); second, that from a practical perspective the use of our free will should be determined not by physical circumstances but by reference to the moral principle that we should act in such a manner as to be worthy of God's assistance: "surely we cannot hope to partake in the appropriation of a foreign satisfying merit, and thus in salvation, except by qualifying for it through our zeal in the compliance with every human duty."[67] Gordon Michalson, however, highlights a problem with the "divine supplement" solution to the problem of radical evil and human insufficiency in that the important change in human nature that God is supposed to supplement must already have taken place, with Michalson concluding that as a result the solution "is no solution at all, but a change of subjects . . . The element of grace here is thus not only beside the point—it is, as it were, after the fact," with the effect that "Kant is slipping back and forth between human freedom and divine action."[68] One way to rescue the general concept of grace in Kant is to see it in terms of assistance rendered by God (God's *unmerited* favor) *before* the transformation of human will, "helping us to overcome the infirmity plaguing our wills."[69] It should also be remembered that Kant's God perceives human existence from a noumenal, atemporal vantage point where succession in time is not as determining of worthiness/unworthiness of the bestowal of grace as it is in our phenomenal experience.[70] Grace, like freedom, is something that transcends "the realm of possible experience to which knowledge is restricted."[71]

Salvation in *Toward Perpetual Peace*

The themes of evil and salvation that permeate Kant's work find a specifically international expression in *Toward Perpetual Peace*. In the Second Definitive Article, Kant reprises radical evil by reference to the "wickedness of human nature that shows openly in the free relationship of peoples," and employing language redolent of *Religion Within the Bounds of Mere Reason*, he further claims that man has yet to master "the evil principle in him (which he cannot disavow)."[72] The international environment is the area of political life most clearly affected by the pervasive effects of radical evil as the "wickedness that is inveterate in human nature . . . strikes the eye quite unconcealed and incontrovertible in the external relations of states to each other."[73] The very basis of the problematic relationship between moral doctrine and politics (at the subjective level of individual behavior on a universal basis, as opposed to their ultimate compatibility in objective terms) is attributable, according to Kant, to the influence of the evil principle in human beings, to the extent that virtue's courage should be expended not so much in "opposing, with firm resolve, the ills and privations that must be undergone here, as in facing and defeating the guile of the far more dangerous evil principle in ourselves, which lying and treacherous, but still rationalizing, puts up the weakness of human nature as justification of every transgression."[74]

The machinations and general influence of the evil principle within mankind complicate international politics, the operation of which Kant persistently describes as either a "status" or "mechanism" of nature. Viewing international relations as a natural mechanism allows the articulation of a certain political logic predicated on power, survival, and untrammeled ambition. The Kantian state of nature is akin to its Hobbesian equivalent in that it is "a status of war, that is, though not always an outbreak of hostilities, yet a permanent threat with them"; by contrast, the state of peace is an artificial condition that must be "instituted."[75] The state of nature is one defined by the absence of security and the injury done by the mere presence of others near one's own state. The state of nature is characterized by its lawlessness, and right is limited to those in possession of power sufficient to enforce their prerogatives. The lawlessness of the state of nature translates into a condition of fear in which states either enter into legal contracts with each other or attempt to compel each other by means of force.[76] The lawlessness of the natural condition, in which states prefer the "frenzied freedom" of individual sovereignty to the "reasonable" freedom of legal coordination, is regarded by "us," according to Kant, as "a bestial degradation of humanity . . . a depraved status," which ought to be exited as soon as possible.[77] The despotic character of nature is revealed by its use of war to drive mankind to every part of the earth. Nature is callous and does not act with care toward human beings, with war seemingly "grafted upon human nature" in order to achieve nature's presumed end of populating the earth.[78] Agreeing with the ancient Greek saying that "war is bad in that it produces more evil people than it destroys," Kant highlights that the immiseration of human beings is the consequence of following nature's imperatives, "[s]o much, then, for what nature does to further *her own end* with respect to the human race as an *animal species*" (emphasis added).[79] Insofar as it can be discerned from experience, nature has no end for humans as animals (human beings' sole identity in natural terms) other than extending their presence as far as possible over the earth by any means necessary, but most especially by the morally unacceptable practice of war.

Nature plays out its conflictual logic on many levels in global political life. The natural desire of every powerful state, according to Kant, is to become a universal monarch ("to place itself in this manner in a permanent status of peace, ruling, if possible, the whole world"), which calls forth the countervailing forces of states anxious to preserve their sovereignty.[80] Nature further "wills" division by means of segregating people according to linguistic and religious differences, "which carries with it the propensity to mutual hatred and a pretext for war."[81] The mechanism of nature, without the eventual germination of reason in the articulation of freedom and the development of morality, is a cruel despot that offers little to its subjects other than the prudential "art of using that mechanism to govern men" without reference to right, which, in this scenario, "is a thought void of anything real."[82]

The natural condition in which immoral human beings exist is that from which mankind requires salvation. Kant attributes an important role to nature itself in the process by which mankind might evolve beyond its mechanism. In what is the most crucial political-theological passage of *Toward Perpetual Peace*, Kant argues that the process of global pacification is guaranteed by "nothing less than the great artist nature . . . from the mechanical course of which purposiveness conspicuously shines forth in letting concord arise by dint of discord among men even against their will."[83] The key move that Kant makes is to introduce a perspectival distinction between the purposiveness of nature perceived as simple fate and that purposiveness regarded as a product of providence to the effect that, depending on which perspective one employs, one derives very different kinds of peace from nature's purposiveness. In simply natural terms the pacification effect that Kant identifies under the banner of "fate" (defined by Kant as "the necessitation of a cause unknown by its laws of operation") is attributable to the operation of rational self-interest as revealed by prudence/technical practical reason, i.e., the peace of fear of death or loss of earnings. In *providential* terms, however, this purposiveness may be read as the product of "the deep-seated wisdom of a higher cause directed toward the objective ultimate end of mankind."[84] In effect, Kant is replaying the fourth antinomy of the *Critique of Pure Reason* in that perpetual peace is thought simultaneously as both a purely empirical and a metaphysical (and theological) issue. Thus, although it is the great artist nature that guarantees perpetual peace, this attribution may be only at the surface level of the appearance of events and processes, and ultimately the great artist nature is revealed to be best conceived of as being preliminary to the achievement of a perpetual peace derived from God/providence: an instance of nature itself being ultimately attributed to God.[85]

At first sight it would appear that Kant is in favor of a natural as opposed to a theological understanding of perpetual peace, endorsing the use of the word nature over providence as it is "more becoming to the confines of a human reason which, in respect of effects to their causes, must keep within the bounds of possible experience, and also more modest than the expression of a providence that we can cognize, whereby one presumptuously puts on Icarian wings to get closer to the mystery of its unfathomable intention."[86] The Icarian caveat, however, comes prefaced with its own caveat, i.e., this "proper" use of nature instead of providence only applies "when as here, we have to do with theory only (not religion)."[87] Theory, for Kant, applies to the world of appearances, hence the reference to "relations of effects to their causes"—it is defined by its limits in the phenomenal realm, limits that Kant makes abundantly clear must be exceeded in the context of their ultimate incapacity to deliver true perpetual peace, which can only be delivered by the employment of pure practical reason. The criticism of providence offered by Kant is also tied to the metaphysical position staked out in the first *Critique*, as it is not providence, but the invocation of "a providence that we can cognize," that Kant rejects as Icarian. A providence in which we can believe for practical purposes is a very different matter—it is telling that it is providence, not nature, that Kant claims is vindicated by his work.[88]

The limits of nature in providing perpetual peace are linked to the shortcomings of technical practical reason and prudence as means by which to constrain or direct human inclinations and passions. Thus, although nature can come "to the aid of the revered, but practically powerless general will grounded in reason," to the extent that a nation of devils can form a republic by the combination of self-seeking inclinations allied with technical practical reason organizing the state to direct its inhabitants' forces "against each other in such a way that one curbs the others in their deleterious effect or neutralises them: so that the result turns out for reason as if both did not exist at all, and man is thus forced to be, though not a morally good man, yet a good citizen," this combination is not sufficient to resolve the problems of interstate and cosmopolitan politics on a permanent/eternal basis.

This inability of human beings as natural agents to achieve genuine peace is attributable to the fact that prudence, the technical practical reason of force and cunning, "still stands under fate, that is, reason is not elucidated enough to survey the series of predetermining causes that permit predicting the fortunate or ill result of man's commissions and omissions with certainty according to the mechanism of nature." In contrast to this contingency and uncertainty, pure practical reason offers more definite guidance, "in order to remain in the groove of duty (according to rules of wisdom), to that, and thus to the ultimate end, reason casts its light brightly enough ahead."[89] Moralizing politicians, justifying illegal but prudentially informed acts "under the pretext of a human nature not capable of the good according to the idea as prescribed by reason, *make impossible*, as much as depends on them, *a change for the better and perpetuate the violation of right*" (emphasis added).[90] Politicians such as these can only operate according to the lower anthropological level of the knowledge of men as natural entities, and not at the higher level, i.e., that of "knowing man *and what can be made of him*" (emphasis added).[91] Ultimately, the most important outcome of "all these serpentine windings of an immoral doctrine of prudence to bring about the status of peace among men out of the warlike status of nature" is the revelation of the extent to which right is the proper guide to achieve that end, to the extent that politicians "don't dare to base politics publicly on manipulations of prudence only."[92] Viewing perpetual peace as a merely technical task to be achieved instrumentally by prudence is tinged with the uncertainty that bedevils all technical practical reason in human affairs, because "much knowledge of nature is required in order to use her mechanism for the end in mind, and yet all this knowledge is uncertain in regard to its result, concerning the eternal peace, whichever of the three departments of public law [state law, the law of nations, and cosmopolitan law] one may take."[93] By way of demonstration of this unpredictability, Kant argues that "[i]t is uncertain whether in the interior, a people may be kept in obedience and at the same time in prime more successfully by severity or by baits to vanity," regardless of the *form* of state involved. The only exception is that of a true republic, which, as it "can only enter a moral politician's mind," is a product of pure practical reason and hence outside the realm of prudence.[94] An international law based solely in statutes derived from political calculation of "ministerial plans" is also unreliable in that such law "in fact is only a word without a real thing and rests on treaties that in the very act of their conclusion contain the secret reservation of their violation at the same time."[95]

Insofar as nature plays a role in furthering perpetual peace it lies in two dimensions, i.e., the breathing space for the development of legal relations offered by the equilibrium produced by states in conflict and in the commercial activities of states and their citizens at the cosmopolitan level. Kant argues that a passion for money-making is incompatible with war and instrumental in preserving peace as states will prevent war between conflicting parties because war is bad for business and therefore contrary to the interests of the whole. These two roles, however, have possible negative effects, e.g., the balance of power may not be sufficient to restrain every attempt at hegemony, with the result that a universal monarchy of "soulless despotism" could emerge, crushing right and, in its eventual demise, creating the conditions for anarchy, the worst of all social scenarios, to emerge. At another level, as the Sixth Preliminary Article makes clear, war and conflict could potentially lead to a situation in which the combatants resort to "dishonourable stratagems" to win a conflict, thereby destroying trust and the possibility of concluding peace, leading to a war of extermination and the perpetual peace of the graveyard for all mankind. In terms of commercial activity, Kant stresses that the credit system, "the ingenious invention of a trading people," is a "dangerous power of money, a treasure, namely for waging war that exceeds the treasures of all other states combined." This is a danger that is further compounded by the probable default of the debtor state, resulting in the involvement of many innocent states in the ensuing financial damage.[96] Although Kant wants both dishonorable stratagems and the use of credit outlawed under the preliminary articles, he is surely acute enough to recognize that they are products of processes inherent in the operation of nature's mechanism as outlined in the later parts of the essay. Kant was also not blind to the fact that the horrors of colonialism were the result of the inhospitable practices of "civilized, chiefly trading states."[97] Three problems then pose serious difficulties in relation to a purely natural peace that emerges organically from the operation of the politics of self-interest: unpredictability; the problem of regression, which leads at best to abderite cycles of progress and degeneration; and finally the problem of nature's means, which are cruel, callous, and reduce mankind to an animal status without any possibility of viewing itself as anything other than subject to nature and its inscrutable intentions (assuming it has any).

Providence and Perpetual Peace

The mechanical operation of nature in its morally indifferent manner and human beings in their actively immoral choices provide the valuable service of allowing the ideas that undergird true and *certain* perpetual peace—right and law—the eventual opportunity to circulate and gain traction in those communities that develop republican states and federal international societies: this is the sense in which nature can be said to *guarantee* perpetual peace, i.e., as the midwife of reason.[98] Kant, in any case, is quite clear that the guarantee is a *practical* idea, not a theoretical concept: "through the mechanism of human inclinations themselves, nature guarantees the eternal peace, with a security, it must be admitted, that is not sufficient to (theoretically) presage its future but does suffice in practical respect and makes it a duty to work toward this (not merely chimerical) end."[99]

The reform of politics according to pure practical reason begins with the idea of a republican state. In addition to the war aversion derived from technical practical reason within a representative legislature, what separates a republic from other states is "the impeccability of its origin in having sprung from the pure source of the concept of right."[100] The republican pillars of freedom, legislation, and equality within the state issue "from the idea of the original contract on which all juridical legislation of a people must be founded."[101] It is important to note that Kant argues that the "validity of these innate and inalienable rights, which necessarily belong to humanity," is put in the context of man's "legal relations even to higher beings (if he thinks such)," i.e., that man ought to conceive of himself "also as a citizen of a super-sensible world," in other words as a citizen of a transcendental order.[102] The validity of these rights, which have no necessary traction within the mechanism of nature, can only be properly secured by the embrace of the other perspective permitted to account for the purposiveness of nature, the providential analysis of the same impulse to harmonization of the international order derived from pure practical reason: a broader, deeper, and more complete idea of perpetual peace that has the further advantage of being predictable—if pursued according to its principles—even to the final, objective end of humanity.[103]

Kant refers to providence as "the deep-seated wisdom of a higher cause . . . predetermining the course of the world," before making it clear in the vein of the third *Critique* that the ideas associated with providence, i.e., "purposiveness in the course of the world," "the objective ultimate end of mankind," and the predetermination of history, are all elements that we "can and must only add in our thought to form a concept of their possibility for us as after analogy with human technical actions."[104] Thinking of providence in this manner has the advantage of recasting human destiny from being merely a part of the mechanism of nature (with an uncertain end) to participating in "the end immediately prescribed by reason," i.e., the independence of mankind from nature's imperfect organization and lack of care for the individuals and peoples that compose the species. Employing the analogy of God as an artist (a major theme of the third *Critique*), Kant admits that this idea "in theoretical respect, is transcendent indeed," but argues that the idea of a divine artist is "in practical respect however (for example, of eternal peace as a concept of duty to use the mechanism of nature to that end) dogmatic and well grounded as to its reality."[105] *Belief* in a providential arrangement of the world allows the human mind to think about how perpetual peace might be secured according to a divine will based on reason—it is therefore a vital step in the process of moving *beyond* nature.[106]

Whereas in the purely natural understanding of the processes that lead to perpetual peace the human being is essentially reduced to a passive object of nature's will, the providential perspective allows a practically necessary reorientation of both the mechanism of nature and mankind's place within it. The key move in this direction is Kant's assertion that we can only make *comprehensible* that which lies underneath the at best partial impression created by our understanding of nature "by underlaying it with the end of a world-originator who predetermines it, calling his predetermination (divine) providence."[107] Consistent with the antidogmatic position undertaken in the first *Critique*, Kant makes clear that God should not be believed to intervene directly in the course of human history, arguing that "having him who is himself the complete cause of the changes of the world complement his own predetermining providence during the course of the world (which therefore must have been deficient) . . . is firstly contradictory in itself."[108] The postula-

tion of a divine *concursus*, however, is perfectly appropriate and even necessary from a moral-practical perspective: "the belief that God will complement the lack of our own justice also by means incomprehensible to us if only
our bent of the will was genuine" is required so "that consequently we shall
not slacken in our striving for the good."[109] This striving for the good is only
achievable through the pursuit of right, which, despite his animality, is an
idea of which "man just cannot rid himself," a persistence that "sanctions the
theory of the ability to become adequate to it, everybody sees that he for his
part must act according to it, others may do as they please."[110] The linkage of
the divine *concursus* with the successful instantiation of a regime of right and
justice beyond our animal nature is a Kantian translation of what Voegelin
identifies as the "soteriological truth of Christianity" in that it "breaks with
the rhythm of existence; beyond temporal successes and reverses lies the supernatural destiny of man, the perfection through grace in the beyond. Man
and mankind now have fulfilment, but it lies beyond nature."[111]

Kant's ultimate reconciliation of the practical philosophy with itself in *Toward Perpetual Peace* revolves around this issue of *how* to achieve peace properly, which turns around this central test: "whether in tasks of practical reason
the beginning must be made from the material principle of reason, the end (as
the object of choice), or from the formal principle, that is, from that principle
(restricted to external relations) according to which it runs," which is revealed
to be a reiteration of the categorical imperative, "act that you can will your
maxim to become a universal law (whatever that end may be)."[112] Kant's answer
is unambiguous: "[w]ithout any doubt the formal principle must precede, for as
a principle of right, it has unconditional necessity," whereas any end, if is to be
properly consistent with moral right, would have to be derived from the formal
principles of external action.[113] For the moral politician, operating according to
a formal principle, the achievement of perpetual peace "is a moral task . . . a
world apart from the other [the political moralist/moralizing politician] in the
method of bringing about the eternal peace, which one now desires not merely
as a physical good but also as a status resulting from an acknowledgment of
duty."[114] Kant repeats the point more forcefully later in the essay when he states
that it is the concept of right "which alone could establish peace eternally."[115]
Prudence's role is reduced to the task of reminding the moral reformer "not to
force the end precipitately but to approach it unremittingly according to conditions of favourable circumstances."[116] In contrast to the uncertainty of the results attained by the exercise of technical practical reason and prudential judg-

ment, the means and ends of pure practical reason are clear: expose deceits and point the way to the promised land of perpetual peace. It is hardly a coincidence that Kant expresses this principle by means of a gospel paraphrase: "seek ye first the kingdom of pure practical reason and its justice, and your end (the benefit of eternal peace) will fall to you of itself."[117] In his discussion of justice Kant makes a decisive move *against* benefit and happiness by stating "political maxims must not start from a state's welfare and happiness that is to be expected from their observance, thus not from the end each of them makes its object (from volition) as the highest (yet empirical) principle of state wisdom but from pure concepts of the duty of right (from the ought, the principle of which is given a priori by pure reason), whatever the physical consequences thereof may be."[118]

In the purely rational terms of the practical philosophy "objectively (in theory) there is no conflict between moral doctrine and politics at all," although subjectively the conflict "will and may ever remain" due to the self-seeking inclinations of human beings. Belief in human moral progress enables escape from the mechanism of nature by reference to "true politics," which cannot "take a step without having already paid homage to morals, and although politics by itself is a difficult art, its union with morals is no art at all; for as soon as the two conflict with each other, morals cuts the knot that *politics cannot untie*" (emphasis added). It is only by embracing the moral and providential, according to Kant, that politics can "hope to reach, though slowly, the level where it will shine unfailingly."[119] It is for this reason that Kant advocates that providence and not nature is ultimately the foundation of perpetual peace: "for the moral principle in man is never extinguished, and reason, with pragmatic skill to execute legal ideas according to that principle, moreover grows continually through always advancing cultivation, with that, however, also the guilt of those transgressions" with the ultimate effect being the supersession of the political by the moral as a consequence of the effects of both natural and rational processes playing themselves out according to their own internal logic. In order for this culmination of nature and reason to occur, however, a leap of faith is still necessary in that the process of perpetual peace must be *believed* to be achieved. Kant provides his most eloquent expression of this requirement in *The Metaphysics of Morals*:

> The question is no longer whether perpetual peace is something real or a fiction, and whether we are not deceiving ourselves in our theoretical judgment

when we assume that it is real. Instead, we must act as if it is something real, though perhaps it is not; we must work toward establishing perpetual peace and the kind of constitution that seems to us most conducive to it (say, a republicanism of all states, together and separately) in order to bring about perpetual peace and put an end to the heinous waging of war, to which as their chief aim all states without exception have hitherto directed their internal arrangements.[120]

Once the leap of faith is made, the conclusion Kant draws is that perpetual peace, the highest political good, and in effect the final, providentially ordained kingdom of pure practical reason, "is possible only in a federative union (which union is thus given a priori according to principles of right), and all state prudence has as its legal basis the institution of this union in its greatest possible extent, without which objective all its sophistry is unwisdom and veiled injustice."[121] Kant therefore ultimately comes to his own version of the most Lutheran of conclusions: salvation—in this case true perpetual peace—is achievable by faith alone.[122] That this faith is necessary is brought home most clearly by Kant's evocation of the tragic fate suffered by righteous atheists in the *Critique of the Power of Judgment*, who although worthy of happiness would "nevertheless be subject by nature, which pays no attention to that, to all the evils of poverty, illnesses, and untimely death, just like all the other animals on earth, and will always remain thus until one wide grave engulfs them all together (whether honest or dishonest, it makes no difference here) and flings them, who *were capable of having believed themselves to be the final end of creation*, back into the abyss of the purposeless chaos of matter from which they were drawn" (emphasis added).[123]

Conclusion: "Philosophers Can Have Their Chiliasm"

Kant does not secularize theological concepts in the style of Schmitt and Löwith, nor does he seek to reoccupy intellectual positions that have been vacated in the wake of the collapse of the Middle Ages in the manner attributed to modern thinkers by Blumenberg. Kant's efforts are perhaps better understood as an attempt to *translate* previous concepts into forms compatible with his philosophy, e.g., from original sin to radical evil.[124] For Moltmann this translation is a natural consequence of Kant's socialization within the "culture-

Protestantism" of Prussia, a culture that "drew eschatology into history." Charles Taylor expands on this theme by stressing that "we cannot be surprised when we learn that Kant came from a Pietist background. His philosophy goes on breathing this sense of the stringent demands of God and the good. . . . We have a moving field of forces here, in which more than one constellation is possible, and more, in which the constellations frequently mutate."[125] Within the context of the critical philosophy, rational religion, and the political/IR theory derived from it, the key issue is whether mankind can be saved. The matter is complicated by the distance that the critical philosophy has moved rational religion from the established dogma of the "ecclesiastical" churches. There can be no real recourse in Kant's religion to the intercession of Jesus, the Virgin Mary, or the saints, and it is clear that there is little hope that human beings can escape from their depraved condition operating according to their current understandings of both themselves and others. What is needed is a reorientation of human beings, but Kant's assessment as to whether they can effect such a reorientation is pessimistic.

Two responses to this pessimistic finding emerge in Kant's work: fear of what Jacob Taubes calls "the apocalypse of man," i.e., that human beings will destroy themselves, and *hope* that this universal destruction might be averted. This hope that mankind might be saved despite its self-destructive tendencies relies on a power (a *katechon*) akin to that which restrains the "son of perdition" in St. Paul's Second Epistle to the Thessalonians, in which an interim power ("one that restraineth now") curtails the agent of destruction until such time as Jesus defeats him, whereupon the restrainer may be dispensed with ("be taken out of the way"). In Kant's philosophy, human beings in thrall to the evil principle—lying, avaricious, and motivated by the amoral pursuit of power and self-interest—play the role of the "son of perdition," threatening, by their actions, to precipitate a war of annihilation in which the entire species, and with it any hope of establishing a regime of right, is extinguished. The *katechontic* role is played by the laws of reason (primarily at first technical practical reason) restraining the destructive urges of the human being, thereby averting the apocalypse and, in time, perhaps even creating the conditions for the emergence of a Kingdom of God on earth, a salvation *without* an apocalyptic denouement.[126] Kant avoids the problem identified by Blumenberg, i.e., that God cannot be both the eschatological God of the Last Judgment and the God of the Church Fathers to whom the faithful pray to avoid that very judgment. Kant achieves this feat by removing salvation from scripture, but remaining within a theistic framework heavily influenced by Christianity.[127] By reframing religion within the boundaries of reason, Kant enabled the persistence of eschatology and soteriology as aspects of the theorization of global politics into the liberal era.[128]

The success of the translation of Christian ideals into rational-moral concepts consistent with the critical philosophy and Kant's efforts in morality provokes a final set of questions: Is this translation in itself desirable, or does it lead to a specifically Kantian form of political-theological delusion about what is possible in a political environment? Does Kant's prophetic vision, inspired in equal parts by fear and hope, agree "with a sober view of the world and of man's condition in it"?[129] In this skeptical reading of Kant the solutions he provides— the higher anthropological viewpoint, the ideal of humanity, purposeful nature, and so forth—are evasions rather than solutions, a shadow play about mankind projected on a screen at the edge of the abyss that Kant has glimpsed but refuses to confront.[130] The shadow play may have come too late, and, having seen the abyss, perhaps we recognize in it the reflection of our true selves. And in that moment of recognition we realize that, in an era when the belief prescribed by Kant is no longer persuasive, alternative answers may have to be forged to the questions: what can I know? what ought I to do? for what may I hope? Once aware of the abyss (or even its possibility), can mankind ever truly ignore or deny it again? Does the nagging doubt that, behind the image of humanity that we project onto ourselves, human beings remain "trapped" in nature ultimately scupper Kant's thought and all that follows in its wake? Becoming aware of the requirement to *believe* in Kant's God is the first step in a process that might lead the discipline of IR in Nietzschean fashion to kill this deity—but what would make us worthy of such a deed? For this task the exploration of other approaches to the relationship between politics and morality is required in order to navigate the relationship between the demands of necessity and the requirements of morality in International Relations.

Epilogue

Kant and Contemporary Cosmopolitanism

> In every system of morality . . . the author proceeds for some time in the ordinary way of reasoning, and establishes the being of a God, or makes observations concerning human affairs; when of a sudden I am surpriz'd to find, that instead of the usual copulations of propositions, *is*, and *is not*, I meet with no proposition that is not connected with an *ought*, or an *ought not*. This change is imperceptible; but is, however, of the last consequence. For as this *ought*, or *ought not*, expresses some new relation or affirmation, 'tis necessary that it shou'd be given, for what seems altogether inconceivable, how this new relation can be a deduction from others, which are currently different from it.[1]

The challenge Kant poses to contemporary cosmopolitanism lies in the completeness of his theory's integration of politics and morality. Kant's position presents an intricate response to the is/ought problem raised by Hume in the above epigraph. Kant does not deny what "is," but rather begins his account of the relationship between "is" and "ought" by placing what "is" in a new context. Kant argues that what "is" may be regarded as what *appears* to be. Political life is conducted by reference to the knowledge gained from the observation of appearances, which in turn leads technical practical reason to develop prudence as a means of dealing with the requirement for judgment in an uncertain environment. Eventually, according to Kant, a modus operandi may emerge in which prudent statesmen motivated by self-preservation and a desire to create and preserve wealth will institute a regime based on right, which they obey initially out of interest as opposed to moral conviction. Kant's hope is that over time human beings will become habituated toward moral actions as any other behavior would be imprudent as well as immoral. In this reading of the is/ought relationship, "is," for Kant, is ultimately revealed to be primarily a preliminary, preparatory phase in the realization of what "ought" to be. Kant integrates the problem into the solution by bringing technical practical reason to its logical conclusion and probing beyond its limits using pure practical reason and belief.

The coherence and completeness of Kant's political project is due to its emergence concurrently with the development of the critical philosophy. The higher and lower anthropological perspectives of *Toward Perpetual Peace* represent the viewpoints of humanity and human beings respectively. The question then becomes which should be the point of orientation in relation to the transcendental object of mankind? Kant favors the higher perspective for *practical* purposes. Kant never loses sight of the fact, however, that nature and its incentives cannot be denied and must be accommodated within any attempt to address what it means to be human. The problem with mankind's competing pictures of itself is that human beings are free to choose from incentives other than those of rational morality. That human beings consistently fail to choose rational-moral options and instead embrace political choices that are either amoral or immoral must be confronted and explained, which Kant ultimately does by reference to radical evil. It is Kant's *hope* that the species might eventually come to a point where living according to the moral law, or approximating such a condition, is a universal norm, but recognizes that such a conclusion is not tenable for human beings acting according to technical practical reason. Kant's hope in turn rests on a postulate that God has arranged matters such that salvation can be attained.

The operation of the mechanism of nature offers no hope for anything more than temporary and contingent cessations of conflict. At best, prudent human beings operating within such a structure could create a peaceful and just international society that in all likelihood would eventually decline and fall back to the standard mean of human behavior. It is necessary to step *beyond* nature in order to subject nature to rational morality, but such a step cannot be taken by human beings acting according to insights gained within nature. For Kant, the answer lies in the idea of representing nature as purposive, i.e., we must *believe* that nature has an end or purpose and that our salvation is that end. Only such a *belief* can enable us to submit nature to rational morality. Finally, for nature to be purposive belief in God is necessary as the author of nature and the moral law. In the absence of faith, life is meaningless and mankind is condemned to a

Mendelssohnian future of repeating cycles of progress and regression, with the risk of extermination rising over time.

By way of contrast, cosmopolitanism does not offer the same degree of completeness. There is a clear account of how politics "is" and how politics "ought" to be but no account of how to get from the former condition to the latter. Thomas Pogge, for example, states that "international relations have historically been brutal. The main players . . . negotiate and re-negotiate the rules of the game among themselves with each pressing vigorously for its own advantage, using war and the threat of war when this seems opportune and showing no concern for the interests or even the survival of the weakest."[2] Pogge also argues that severe global poverty persists "because we do not find its eradication morally compelling."[3] Despite acknowledging these political "realities" Pogge insists that the international political system *ought* to "be designed so that all human beings, insofar as reasonably possible, have secure access to the objects of their human rights."[4] Pogge does not, however, confront the ultimate problem facing contemporary cosmopolitanism, i.e., that the reform of the international political system would have to be carried out by the politically motivated and morally indifferent human beings who maintain and benefit from the global system of inequality that he wishes to alter. Given their established indifference toward millions of deaths in poor societies, why would they act any differently? In contrast to Kant, who attempts to bridge the gap between "is" and "ought" by integrating politics and morality, Pogge simply asserts moral duties without adequate reference to the political context.[5]

In the unlikely event of cosmopolitanism achieving its aims of establishing a new political order based on redistributive justice and the vertical dispersal of sovereignty, cosmopolitanism would still face serious difficulties. Pogge and David Held are particularly convinced that the transformation of power and sovereignty will open the gates to a more just form of society. Pogge insists that under his "institutional" cosmopolitan principles, governments and individuals would have a responsibility "to work for an institutional order and public culture that ensures that all members of society have secure access to the objects of their human rights."[6] Pogge links these duties to a revolution in the meaning of sovereignty. "Dispersing political authority over nested territorial units," Pogge affirms, "would decrease the intensity of the struggle for power and wealth within and among states, thereby reducing the incidence of war, poverty, and oppression. In such a multi-layered order, borders could be redrawn more easily to accord with the aspirations of peoples and communities."[7] The traditional arrangement in which sovereignty is concentrated at one level "is no longer defensible," according to Pogge. In place of state sovereignty, Pogge proposes "that governmental authority—or sovereignty—be widely dispersed in the vertical dimension. What we need is both centralization and decentralization."[8] Pogge's argument is that "massive violations of human rights could be reduced through a vertical dispersal of sovereignty over various layers of political units that would check and balance one another as well as publicize one another's abuses."[9] The vertical dispersal of power assures that "even when some units turn tyrannical and oppressive, there will always be other, already fully organized political units—above, below, or on the same level—which can render aid and protection to the oppressed, publicize the abuses, and if necessary, fight the oppressors," with the effect that governments would be deterred from any repression as it would result in the diminution of their power, not its increase.[10]

Held offers a similar proposal with his concept of "cosmopolitan sovereignty," a radical reinvention of sovereignty that "challenges the very idea of fixed borders and territories governed by states alone. It sees sovereignty as the networked realms of public authority shaped and delimited by an overarching cosmopolitan legal framework."[11] Held is convinced that the sovereignty revolution has already occurred in that it is "embedded in rule systems and institutions which have transformed the sovereign states system . . . States have been the initiators of, and have been pressed into, the creation of rights and duties, powers and constraints, and regimes and organizations which impinge on and react back upon them."[12] In a cosmopolitan political system, "the political authority of states is but one aspect of a complex, overlapping regime of political authority; legitimate political power in this framework embeds states in a complex network of authority relations, where networks are regularized or patterned interactions between independent but interconnected political agents, nodes of activity, or sites of political power."[13] Cosmopolitanism will produce regional and global "organizations and mechanisms which would provide a cosmopolitan framework of regulation and law-enforcement across the globe . . . a necessary supplement and complement to those of the state."[14]

The overriding assumption at play in these projections is that the cosmopolitan order, with its diffused power arrangements in which power is devolved to various sub- and supra-state entities, will somehow solve the problem of global political life being dominated by states jealously guarding or seeking to extend their national interests. This appears to be a particularly benign reading of the possibilities inherent in the diffusion of power and the proliferation of various centers of legitimate political authority. In the event of such a world order coming into being, history will be the judge of its character, effects, and ultimate outcome. The historical precedents of social systems in which sovereignty and legitimate authority were diffused in a manner akin to that suggested by cosmopolitan theorists are, however, not very encouraging. The contest between emperor and pope over the right to appoint bishops, which escalated into a series of wars regarding the exercise of legitimate authority, convulsed Europe for the best part of two centuries. Various political entities of numerous types (empire, papacy, duchies, city states, factions within cities, and finally factions within factions) fought bitterly for generations. During the Reformation, Catholic emperors and popes sought to impose their "legitimate" authority on Protestant princes and cities who rejected that authority in favor of their own faith-based claims to exercise power legitimately in their realms according to their principles. It is likewise a precedent that suggests that when authority is not clearly identified and agreed upon according to a principle like *cuius regio, eius religio*, conflicts like the Thirty Years' War are quite as likely, if not more likely, than the systems outlined by Pogge and Held. A world with a proliferation of centers of legitimate authority, all with some claim to the individual's loyalty—and the territory on which he stands—risks emulating the medieval and early modern systems' fatal flaw: In a world of diverse authorities, which one is paramount? As Hedley Bull wrote in his account of such a neomedieval arrangement, "there is no assurance that it would prove more orderly than the state system, rather than less. . . . if it were anything like the precedent of Western Christendom, it would contain more ubiquitous and continuous violence and insecurity than does the modern states system."[15] In its advocacy of the diffusion of sovereignty, therefore, cosmopolitanism seems particularly prone to what Nietzsche identifies as the hereditary defect of philosophy, i.e., a "lack of historical sense."[16] Even if Held's "layered" cosmopolitanism is treated as a political response to material interdependence and transnational phenomena within new conditions of complex interdependence, the diffusion of power will not solve what is a more fundamental political problem (i.e., conflict over competing interests) that has complex political and anthropological roots. Held mistakes symptoms (state relations) for causes—if the problems were reducible to forms of governance they would have been solved; that they have not been solved points toward deeper reasons for the failure to secure peace. Even more sophisticated attempts to develop a politically credible cosmopolitanism, e.g.,

Richard Beardsworth's *Cosmopolitanism and International Relations Theory*, fall prey to mistaking institutional innovation for genuine political transformation.[17] The impediments to cosmopolitanism are anthropological at their root and require theorists to grasp that the problems of political life are functions of mentality rather than deficient political forms.

The fundamental problem, therefore, that faces cosmopolitanism both in terms of the achievement of any future cosmopolitan order that might emerge and its maintenance is the failure or refusal of human beings to attain and then persist in practicing the moral standards such a system would require. As seen from the above account of politics, the picture that emerges of human beings in cosmopolitan theory is particularly bleak: human beings are venal, self-interested, shortsighted, morally compromised, vicious, exclusionary, particularistic, and chauvinist. According to Pogge, for example, the developing world is bedeviled by vicious tyrants who abuse the poor, who are so intellectually "stunted" they possess no mature moral or political agency. Preserving this system by means of loans to the tyrants and benefiting from the natural resources of the developing world extracted by exploited laborers, Western governments and populations are complicit in the persistence of "a world in which effective enslavement and genocides continue unabated."[18] Surveying contemporary politics, Held argues that "[t]hinking about the future of humankind on the basis of the early years of the twenty-first century does not give grounds for optimism."[19] Yet these vicious, uncaring, and exploitative creatures acting within less than propitious circumstances are somehow expected to reform a global political system of which they are the beneficiaries in order to save from poverty a section of the world's population they have hitherto been content to ignore or actively exploit. Why would they do so, when such reform would seem contrary to what Pogge and others have identified as their defining lack of moral commitment to those outside their immediate social and political environments? Even Pogge's piecemeal reforms, the global resource dividend, and his proposals regarding intellectual property rights in relation to generic medicines, are contrary to what he seems to expect of human beings in general. It would be inconsistent for hard-nosed Western negotiators, used to ruthlessly exploiting any situation in a bargaining context, to accept that they have a duty to allocate a certain percentage of their income to the welfare of the global poor. In Kant's terms, cosmopolitanism finds itself in a practical dilemma: Should political agents be fools or knaves? The practices of global politics would suggest that the vast majority of those in possession of power choose the latter rather than the former.

Cosmopolitanism then faces a quandary: according to cosmopolitan theorists human beings *are* amoral, apathetic interest seekers at best, and immoral exploiters of the less fortunate at worst. In these circumstances there seems little hope that these actors will individually or through their elected representatives strive for the cosmopolitan order proposed by Pogge, Held, Charles Beitz, and others. The efforts of those enlightened souls committed to pursuing cosmopolitanism would seem to be fated to drown in a sea of general indifference and hostile vested interests. Pogge hints that the threat of violent revolution ought to provoke our self-interested selves to accommodate the needs of the poor in the developing world, but what genuine threat can people that he asserts are "stunted" pose to those who are so utterly dominant within the existing system?[20] Given that the oppressed would have to first depose their own vicious governments, then form a global coalition of poorly armed states to oppose Western hegemony, the threat does not seem to be sufficiently compelling to provoke system-wide change or even the attainment of the piecemeal gestures Pogge proposes to alleviate suffering. In addition, Pogge rejects revolution in general as "macho" and ineffective, and Marxism in particular as "too thin a theory to explain all changes in moral norms and values, or even just the major historical shifts."[21]

One may dismiss Kant's ideas of unsocial sociability and radical evil as outmoded, but they do play an important role in that they explain *why* human beings do not conform to how they ought to act. Cosmopolitanism has to develop a theory that accounts for *why* human beings act the way they do, not simply provide accounts of how they ought to act. That cosmopolitans pin their hopes on an inexplicable moral awakening demonstrates that they are as reliant as Kant on faith—yet while his faith is the product of a coherent philosophy, theirs is a barely acknowledged, critically unexamined wish. Even in the event of a latter day miracle of moral awakening whereby a cosmopolitan order along Pogge-Beitz lines was instituted, the prospect of a Mendelssohnian regression to a state more consistent with the historical record seems an eminently likely scenario. The achievement and ongoing maintenance of cosmopolis does not seem to be consistent with the cosmopolitans' own implicit anthropology of actually existing human beings. Perhaps the most interesting attempt to confront this issue is Andrew Linklater's effort to identify a civilizing process at play in the sociology of international relations. Influenced by Norbert Elias, Linklater argues that "over recent centuries Western societies have developed constraints on aggressive or violent behaviour," more successful than previous epochs of human history, which might lead to more "cosmopolitan emotions" developing over time.[22] This scenario is, however, accompanied by one of darker hue in which globalization gives rise to a "'decivilizing counter thrust' in which groups react aggressively to alien values and to the insecurities that attend closer interdependence."[23]

The ideal theories of moral cosmopolitanism (Beitz and Pogge) may serve as the source for possible targets for reform and critical reflection, but they seem unlikely to serve as the basis for even approximation in political practice. Held's "layered" cosmopolitan governance and Linklater's "emancipatory" sociological cosmopolitanism fare little better. It might be politically advantageous on occasion for states to pay lip service and make occasional gestures toward cosmopolitan principles, but without a thorough and lasting reorientation of human beings and their society, such gestures are likely to remain within the province of public relations. The gap between how Pogge, Beitz, Held, and others present how human beings "are" and how they "ought" to be is too great to overcome, and contemporary cosmopolitan theory offers no convincing account of how that chasm might be bridged.

Accounting for *why* cosmopolitan theory fails to bridge the gap between "is" and "ought" is not simple. For Beitz and Pogge the answer may lie in the influence of Rawlsian political theory. For Sandel the central problem of Rawls's theory is that the circumstances of justice are Humean, but his deontological conception of the nature of justice is Kantian, leading Sandel to observe that "[g]iven the contrasting philosophical pedigrees of the two accounts, it is little wonder that the inconsistencies arise."[24] The significance of Sandel's identification of this tension at the heart of Rawls's project leads him to a fairly damning conclusion of Rawls's "have your cake and eat it, too" strategy in relation to Kant: "As a Kantian conception of the moral law and the kingdom of ends seems to deny justice its human situation, the Humean account of the human situation seems unable to accommodate strong claims on behalf of the primacy of justice. . . . the two aspirations of Rawls' theory, to avoid both the contingency of existing desires and the alleged arbitrariness and obscurity of the transcendent, are uncombinable after all, the Archimedean point wiped out in a litany of contradictions."[25] Onora O'Neill defends Rawls by claiming that his work "is admirable in its sustained effort not to smuggle in idealizations that establish the desired conclusions unless he can offer reasons for choosing those specific premises rather than alternatives," but argues that thinkers who follow in his wake are not so careful in their efforts to improve on Kant by eschewing "his supposedly objectionable accounts of reason, freedom and action."[26] The consequence of these attempts to "improve" on Kant is a failure to realize that at best "Kantian" theorists are "left only with the meagre starting points that they share with the Utilitarians to whose conclusions they object: an instrumental account of rationality and a preference-based conception of action which look ill chosen to develop a distinctively Kantian account of justice." In contrast to Kant and Rawls, O'Neill finds that "[m]uch recent work has indeed been predicated on unvindicated idealizations, which undermine its applicability to human life."[27] Held's layered cosmopolitanism fails as a consequence of his overreliance on the (Rawls inspired, "political not metaphysical") "metaprinciple of autonomy," an ideological construct that he substitutes for a fully worked out philosophical anthropology. Held holds that the metaprinciple of autonomy is "part of the 'deep structure' of ideas which have shaped the constitution of modern political life," when in fact all they have shaped are (influential, but not defining, and certainly not uncontested) liberal ideologies about political life—an idiom mistaken for a "reality."[28]

The contemporary distaste for metaphysics has led Kantians to neglect the most fundamental issue in Kantian philosophy, i.e., confronting the gap between "is" and "ought" and developing a theory that would narrow the distance between them. Kant's answer may be unacceptably outmoded but it nonetheless demonstrates by its completeness the shortcomings of contemporary Kantianism regarding their formulation of the problems of international politics and the gaping holes in their attempts to provide solutions to them. A critical return to Kant might assist in the recognition of the need to address these issues and to develop effective foundations upon which to build a convincing theory of international politics. One such benefit would be to demonstrate the extent to which cosmopolitanism hobbles itself when, like Beitz, it insists on purging "the traditional image of international relations as a state of nature . . . of its sceptical elements," or, in Held's formulation, "[t]he problems of democracy and social justice will only be institutionally resolved if we grasp the structural limits of the present global political arrangements, limits which can be summed up as 'realism is dead' or to put it more moderately, raison d'état must know its place."[29] Kant's method does not purge skepticism; it integrates skepticism and realism within a wider framework. Kant is concerned with understanding the political from a realist and skeptical perspective in as unflinching a manner as possible precisely because he understands that to solve the problem of political association he has to *proceed* from there—to purge skepticism or declare realism dead is to cut oneself off from the tools that are necessary to build the foundations for perpetual peace and a cosmopolitan world order.

Conclusion

Cosmopolitanism finds itself in a state of philosophical-anthropological contradiction in which its morality points in one direction while its political analysis points in another. Unlike Kant, who distinguishes between human beings and humanity as *representations* of mankind, cosmopolitanism opposes its normative theory *against* its ontology—a situation in which arguably hope can find no credible justification. Where Kant reconciles "is" and "ought" within a teleological philosophy of history, underwritten by the requirement to believe in purposive nature and acting *as if* God had ordained the salvation of mankind, cosmopolitanism offers an at times evasive ideal theory at best and self-satisfied virtue signaling at worst. Holding political reality to moral account via "ideal theory" in the manner of Beitz is doubtlessly a worthwhile intellectual and moral endeavor, but it also smacks of the impotence that Kant attributes to the good will in a natural and political context.[30]

Accounting for *why* this is the case requires a return to metaphysics and theology in Kant and their absence in contemporary cosmopolitanism. There is no recourse in cosmopolitanism to the factor of belief in purposive nature or faith in providence. That these elements are missing is *not* the problem: the fundamental flaw in cosmopolitanism is that it has not replaced these ideas with ones of comparable intellectual power, and, worse, it is seemingly blind to the requirement to do so. Cosmopolitanism has replaced critique with ideology. As a consequence, cosmopolitanism does not have a convincing answer to the is/ought problem when viewed from outside its ideological framework. Its "is" is divorced from rather than integrated with its "ought." It can offer only dogmatic assertion of its moral vision and condemnation of the existing constellation of forces arranged around the pursuit of self-interest. A contrast of Kant and contemporary cosmopolitanism reveals that contrary to their assumption of having improved on his approach they are lacking a sophisticated ontology, are epistemologically weak, and devoid of a philosophical anthropology of equivalent depth to that of Kant. Until they are aware of these shortcomings and can develop a *convincing* set of alternative positions, cosmopolitan theorists will remain in Kant's shadow, epigones of a system of thought they invoke but whose nature and legacy they fail to understand in its own terms and in relation to their projects.

Notes

Preface

1. Immanuel Kant, "Idea for a Universal History with a Cosmopolitan Aim," in *Kant's Idea for a Universal History with a Cosmopolitan Aim: A Critical Guide*, edited by Amélie Oksenberg Rorty and James Schmidt (Cambridge: Cambridge University Press, 2009), 22. Immanuel Kant, "Toward Perpetual Peace," in *Practical Philosophy*, trans. and ed. Mary Gregor (Cambridge: Cambridge University Press, 1996), 346.

2. Immanuel Kant, "On the Common Saying: That May Be Correct in Theory, but It Is of No Use in Practice," in *Practical Philosophy*, trans. and ed. Mary Gregor (Cambridge: Cambridge University Press, 1996), 308–9.

Introduction

1. The *Metaphysics of Morals* is one of the texts affected by Kant's decline. Kant biographer Manfred Kuehn describes it as "disappointing. It exhibits none of the revolutionary vigor and novelty of the two earlier works [the "Groundwork" and the "Critique of Practical Reason"]. Indeed, it reads just like the compilation of old lecture notes that it is . . . much remains cryptic and . . . some of the text is corrupt"; *Kant: A Biography* (Cambridge: Cambridge University Press, 2001), 396. Although certain passages are illuminating and useful in illustrating Kant's work in general, I am inclined to agree with Kuehn on the overall merits of this work. For Kant's struggle with his mental decline, see the last chapter of Kuehn's biography.

2. "Treaty of Peace between France and Prussia, signed at Basle, 5 April 1795," in *Parry's Consolidated Treaty Series*, vol. 52, ed. Clive Parry (Oxford: Oxford University Press, 1969), 333–39.

3. For the sake of convenience given the currency it has in the discipline, I conform to the convention of referring to this essay as *Toward Perpetual Peace*, although I take on

board the argument against the deployment of perpetual peace because it "obscures or even eliminates the semantic ambiguity inherent in the German concept '*ewig*' with its religions and metaphysical connotation"; see Andreas Behnke, "'Eternal Peace' as the Graveyard of the Political: A Critique of Kant's *Zum Ewigen Frieden*," *Millennium* 36, no. 3 (2008): 513. As the reader will discover, the theological and metaphysical aspects of *Toward Perpetual Peace* will be brought to the fore in my analysis of the text.

4. Chris Brown, *International Relations Theory: New Normative Approaches* (New York: Columbia University Press, 1993), 14.

5. Howard Williams, "Kant: the Idea of Perpetual Peace," in *International Relations in Political Theory*, ed. Howard Williams (Buckingham: Open University Press, 1991), 80.

6. Martin Wight's treatment of Kant is perhaps best developed in *Four Seminal Thinkers in International Theory: Machiavelli, Grotius, Kant and Mazzini* (Oxford: Oxford University Press, 2004). Andrew Hurrell's "Kant and the Kantian Paradigm in International Relations," *Review of International Studies* 16, no. 3 (1990), is an excellent account of both Kant's theory and its use in IR that begins from but is not restricted to the English School. Alexander Wendt identifies the Kantian as one of the three cultures of anarchy in *Social Theory of International Politics* (Cambridge: Cambridge University Press, 1999). Kant is particularly prominent as an intellectual influence on social constructivism in Nicholas Onuf's *The Republican Legacy in International Thought* (Cambridge: Cambridge University Press, 1998).

7. Andrew Linklater, *Critical Theory and World Politics: Citizenship, Sovereignty and Humanity* (Abingdon: Routledge, 2007), 4. One is wary of attaching the label of poststructuralism to their works, but insofar as it is a useful designation to mark certain traits or a shared ethos, the theorists most associated with this "movement" in IR who have addressed Kant's work in a sustained manner (albeit in very different ways) are R. B. J. Walker and Mark F. N. Franke. Walker consistently addresses the singular importance of Kant both as a theorist of global politics in his own right and his influence on the discipline of IR; to take merely one example he refers to Kant as "the key figure in any attempt to make sense of the modern international," in "Lines of Security: International, Imperial, Exceptional," *Security Dialogue* 37, no.1 (2006): 73. Franke's *Global Limits: Immanuel Kant, International Relations and Critique of World Politics* (Albany: State University Press of New York Press, 2001) is an excellent, thoughtful analysis of Kant, the effect of his texts on the development of IR theory, and the extent to which Kant's legacy is a challenge to IR as a "discipline."

8. There are of course some notable exceptions, like that of Mark Franke mentioned above, in which the relationship between Kant's wider philosophy and IR work is explored either in terms of his development or in relation to other philosophers. This is particularly the case when the ambit of IR is broadened to include (international) political theory. The doyen of such work is Howard Williams, whose work I engage with throughout this book. Other notable contributions to this area of study are Kimberly

Hutchings, *Kant, Critique and Politics* (London: Routledge, 1996); Katrin Flikschuh, *Kant and Modern Political Philosophy* (Cambridge: Cambridge University Press, 2000); Elisabeth Ellis, *Kant's Politics: Provisional Theory for an Uncertain World* (New Haven: Yale University Press, 2005); and Antonio Franceschet, *Kant and Liberal Internationalism: Sovereignty, Justice, and Global Reform* (New York: Palgrave Macmillan, 2002). I discuss Garrett Wallace Brown's *Grounding Cosmopolitanism: from Kant to the Idea of a Cosmopolitan Constitution* (Edinburgh: Edinburgh University Press, 2009) below.

9. In what is a very interesting and now sadly neglected analysis of Kant, A. C. Armstrong refers to Karl Vorländer's *Kant under der Gedanke des Völkerbundes*, which "cited passages from the posthumous papers which tend to show that Kant was thinking on the question as early as 1755–56," A. C. Armstrong, 'Kant's Philosophy of Peace and War,' *Journal of Philosophy* 28, no. 8 (1931): 197.

10. Immanuel Kant, *The Critique of Pure Reason* (Cambridge: Cambridge University Press, 1999), 643.

11. "International relations scholars have been interested in Kant for quite some time, although it has only been recently, with the promise of liberal democracy in Eastern Europe and the republics of the former Soviet Union, that references to the Kantian analysis of the conditions of international peace have proliferated." Cecelia Lynch, "Kant, the Republican Peace, and Moral Guidance in International Law," *Ethics & International Affairs* 8, no. 1 (1994): 43.

12. In *Kant, Critique and Politics* (56), Kim Hutchings makes clear "that thinkers attempting to draw on the Kantian inheritance for an account of critical social and political theory are drawing on a volatile legacy. The different aspects of Kant's political thought are not neatly separable and the logic of their relation reflects the problematic logic of critique itself."

13. Kant writes that "a long period of peace causes the spirit of mere commerce to predominate, along with base selfishness, cowardice and weakness, and usually debases the mentality of the populace," in *The Critique of the Power of Judgment*, ed. Paul Guyer, trans. Paul Guyer and Eric Matthew (Cambridge: Cambridge University Press, 2000), 146.

14. Geoffrey Waite, "Kant, Schmitt or Fues on Political Theology, Radical Evil and the Foe," *Philosophical Forum* 41, nos. 1–2 (2010): 226. Although I agree with his conclusions, I do not attribute this to the "exoteric/esoteric and therefore fearfully prudent" mode of expression that Waite attaches, in the manner of Leo Strauss, to Kant. I think this ambiguity is the product of a much more deep-rooted ambiguity and ambivalence within Kant's work.

15. Leonard Woolf, "Perpetual Peace," *New Statesman*, July 31, 1915, 398–99. For a good discussion of Woolf and interwar idealism in general, see Peter Wilson, *The International Theory of Leonard Woolf: A Study in Twentieth Century Idealism* (New York: Palgrave Macmillan, 2003).

16. Howard Williams and Ken Booth have also commented on this issue: "For decades

Kant's work was marginal and marginalised in academic international relations, though he has a justifiable claim to be the first comprehensive theorist of world politics." Howard Williams and Ken Booth, "Kant: Theorist beyond Limits," in *Classical Theories of International Relations*, ed. Ian Clark and Iver Neumann (London: Macmillan, 1996), 71.

17. Wight, *Four Seminal Thinkers in International Theory*, 72. In the contemporary English School, Andrew Hurrell and Andrew Linklater provide interesting analyses of Kant in the context of international society—often revising Wight's original position. See especially Hurrell, "Kant and the Kantian Paradigm in International Relations," and Andrew Linklater and Hidemi Suganami, *The English School: A Contemporary Reassessment* (Cambridge: Cambridge University Press, 2006).

18. The massive volume of criticism and reaction directed at *Toward Perpetual Peace* has been the subject of a large-scale sociology of knowledge and historical investigation in Eric S. Easley, *The War for Perpetual Peace: An Exploration into the History of a Foundational International Relations Text* (New York: Palgrave, 2004).

19. F. H. Hinsley, *Power and the Pursuit of Peace: Theory and Practice in the History of Relations between States* (Cambridge: Cambridge University Press, 1963), 74.

20. Ibid., 75.

21. W. B. Gallie, *Philosophers of Peace and War: Kant, Clausewitz, Marx, Engels and Tolstoy* (Cambridge: Cambridge University Press, 1978), 21.

22. Ibid., 28.

23. Michael W. Doyle, "Kant, Liberal Legacies, and Foreign Affairs," *Philosophy and Public Affairs* 12, no. 3 (1983): 227.

24. Ibid., 225.

25. Ibid., 228.

26. Ibid., 230–31.

27. Michael W. Doyle, "Kant, Liberal Legacies, and Foreign Affairs, Part Two," *Philosophy and Public Affairs* 12, no. 4 (1983): 350.

28. Bruce Russett, "The Fact of Democratic Peace," and "Why Democratic Peace?," and Christopher Layne, "Kant or Cant: The Myth of the Democratic Peace," in *Debating the Democratic Peace*, ed. Michael Edward Brown, Sean M. Lynn-Jones, and Steven E. Miller (Cambridge: MIT Press, 1996).

29. Kant evokes a form of philosophical chiliasm to serve as a spur for human progress, but not one akin to religious millenarianism: see the eighth proposition of "Idea for a Universal History with a Cosmopolitan Aim," in *Kant's Idea for a Universal History with a Cosmopolitan Aim: A Critical Guide*, edited by Amélie Oksenberg Rorty and James Schmidt (Cambridge: Cambridge University Press, 2009), 19.

30. This is particularly clear in "Michael Doyle on the Democratic Peace—Again," in *Debating the Democratic Peace* (Cambridge: MIT Press, 1996). Thomas Baum provides an important critique of Doyle's position in "A Quest for Inspiration in the Liberal Peace Paradigm: Back to Bentham," *European Journal of International Relations* 14, no. 3 (2008).

31. John Macmillan, "Immanuel Kant and the Democratic Peace," in *Classical Theory in International Relations*, ed. Beate Jahn (Cambridge: Cambridge University Press, 2006), 56.

32. Any readers curious as to the development and application of democratic peace theory should consult Piki Ish-Shalom's excellent study, *Democratic Peace: A Political Biography* (Ann Arbor: University of Michigan Press, 2013).

33. Charles Beitz identifies that "[t]rouble appears when we ask, not what moral cosmopolitanism rules out, but what it requires, for then the view seems to be far less determinate. . . . cosmopolitanism is not a complete moral conception." For Beitz, cosmopolitanism is akin to "a 'protest ideal' which operates as a basis for criticizing certain institutional arrangements rather than as a basis for choosing any particular one." Charles Beitz, "Cosmopolitanism and Global Justice," *Journal of Ethics* 9, nos. 1–2 (2005): 18.

34. Robert Fine and Robin Cohen, "Four Cosmopolitan Moments," in *Conceiving Cosmopolitanism: Theory, Context and Practice*, ed. Steven Vertovec and Robin Cohen (Oxford: Oxford University Press, 2002).

35. David Harvey, *Cosmopolitanism and the Geographies of Freedom* (New York: Columbia University Press, 2009), 17.

36. Katrin Flikschuh observes that "[m]ost Kant-inspired current cosmopolitans do not regard themselves as un-reconstituted Kantians. Most come to Kant via Rawls." Katrin Flikschuh, "Kant's Sovereignty Dilemma: A Contemporary Analysis," *Journal of Political Philosophy* 18, no. 4 (2010): 470n. There is a certain irony here in that when Rawls turned his attention to international politics in 1993's "The Law of Peoples" he explicitly rejected cosmopolitanism and denied that his principles could be effectively extended beyond their intended deployment in democratic societies. See John Rawls, "The Law of Peoples," in *Collected Papers*, ed. Samuel Freeman (Cambridge: Harvard University Press, 2001), and, for further elaboration, John Rawls, *The Law of Peoples* (Cambridge: Harvard University Press, 1999). See Thomas Pogge's response in *World Poverty and Human Rights*, 2nd ed. (Cambridge: Polity, 2008), 112ff.

37. Michael J. Sandel, *Liberalism and the Limits of Justice* (Cambridge: Cambridge University Press, 1982), 14.

38. John Rawls, "A Kantian Conception of Equality," in *Collected Papers*, ed. Samuel Freeman (Cambridge: Harvard University Press, 2001), 264.

39. John Rawls, "Kantian Constructivism in Moral Theory," in *Collected Papers*, ed. Samuel Freeman (Cambridge: Harvard University Press, 2001), 305.

40. Hutchings, *Kant, Critique and Politics*, 6.

41. Thomas W. Pogge, "Kant's Theory of Justice," *Kant Studien* 79, no. 4 (1988): 428.

42. Ibid., 433.

43. Pogge, "Is Kant's *Rechtslehre* a Comprehensive Liberalism?," in *Kant's Metaphysics of Morals: Interpretive Essays*, ed. Mark Timmons (Oxford: Oxford University Press, 2002), 150.

44. Thomas W. Pogge, "The Categorical Imperative," in *Kant's Groundwork of the Metaphysics of Morals*, ed. Paul Guyer (Totowa, NJ: Rowman and Littlefield, 1998), 198.

45. Ibid., 202–4.

46. Ibid., 206.

47. Ibid., 207.

48. Pogge, "Cosmopolitanism and Sovereignty," *Ethics* 103, no. 1 (1992): 70.

49. Charles Beitz, *Political Theory and International Relations: With a New Afterword by the Author* (Princeton: Princeton University Press, 1999), 9.

50. Ibid., 181–82.

51. Beitz's reading of Kant can be idiosyncratic; see, for example, his treatment of definitive and preliminary articles in terms of which is more basic, as opposed to which must precede the other, ibid., 82–83.

52. Sandel, *Liberalism and the Limits of Justice*, 46.

53. Hans Blumenberg, *The Legitimacy of the Modern Age*, trans. Robert M. Wallace (Cambridge: MIT Press, 1985), 69.

54. Paul Ricoeur identifies the critical power of suspicion through his engagement with Karl Marx, Friedrich Nietzsche, and especially Sigmund Freud. Ricouer finds value in suspicion as a "tearing off of masks," and as a means of demystifying illusion and fable. Paul Ricoeur, *Freud and Philosophy: An Essay on Interpretation*, trans. Denis Savage (New Haven: Yale University Press, 1970), 30, 35.

55. R. B. J. Walker, "On the Possibilities of World Order Discourse," *Alternatives* 19, no. 2 (1994): 243.

56. See, for example, Linklater's work, drawing on Norbert Elias, in Linklater, *Critical Theory and World Politics*. See also the epilogue to this volume.

57. Flikschuh, *Kant and Modern Political Philosophy*, 3.

58. Beate Jahn, "Classical Theory and International Relations in Context," in *Classical Theory in International Relations*, ed. Beate Jahn (Cambridge: Cambridge University Press, 2006).

59. Brown, *Grounding Cosmopolitanism*, 10.

60. R. B. J. Walker, *Inside/Outside: International Relations as Political Theory* (Cambridge: Cambridge University Press, 1992), 29.

61. Brown, *Grounding Cosmopolitanism*, 16.

62. Ibid., 21.

63. Ibid., 22.

64. Otfried Hoffe, *Kant's Cosmopolitan Theory of Law and Peace* (Cambridge: Cambridge University Press, 2006), 16.

65. For the use and abuse of traditions in IR in general, see Renée Jeffery, "Tradition as Invention: The 'Traditions Tradition' and the History of Ideas in International Relations," *Millennium: Journal of International Studies* 34, no. 1 (2005): 57–84.

66. Desiderius Erasmus, "On the Method of Study (*De ratione studii ac legendi inter-*

pretandique auctores)," in *Collected Works of Erasmus*, vol 24 (Toronto: University of Toronto Press, 1978), 669.

67. Michael C. Williams, "Reason and Realpolitik: Kant's 'Critique of International Politics,'" *Canadian Journal of Political Science/Revue canadienne de science politique* 25, no. 1 (1992): 100.

68. Erasmus, "On the Method of Study," 673.

69. Karl Löwith, *Meaning in History: The Theological Implications of the Philosophy of History* (Chicago: University of Chicago Press, 1949), 2.

70. Friedrich Nietzsche, *Daybreak: Thoughts on the Prejudices of Morality*, ed. Maudmarie Clark and Brian Leiter, trans. R. J. Hollingdale (Cambridge: Cambridge University Press, 1997), 205. There is an affinity here with Franke's approach, which is that Kant's "texts and ideas are emerging as a composite site in which the very stakes of international relations are being located, deliberated, and further cultivated," *Global Limits*, 18.

71. Blumenberg, *Legitimacy of the Modern Age*, 594.

72. Martin Heidegger, *Kant and the Problem of Metaphysics: Fifth Edition, Enlarged*, trans. Richard Taft (Bloomington: Indiana University Press, 1997), 140.

73. Martin Heidegger, "Appendix V: On Odebrecht's and Cassirer's Critiques of the Kant Book," in Heidegger, *Kant and the Problem of Metaphysics*, 211.

74. Kant, "Toward Perpetual Peace," in *Practical Philosophy*, 346.

75. Jean Bethke Elshtain, "Kant, Politics, and Persons: The Implications of His Moral Philosophy," *Polity* 14, no. 2 (1981): 206.

76. *Critique of the Power of Judgment*, 82.

77. Immanuel Kant, "Religion Within the Boundaries of Mere Reason," in *Religion and Rational Theology*, trans. and ed. Allen Wood and George Di Giovanni (Cambridge: Cambridge University Press, 1996), 92.

78. Kant, "Religion," 135.

79. Manfred Kuehn, *Kant: A Biography* (Cambridge: Cambridge University Press, 2001), 41.

80. Ibid., 45.

81. Ibid., 53, 138.

82. Immanuel Kant, *Correspondence*, trans. and ed. Arnulf Zweig (Cambridge: Cambridge University Press, 1999), 289–90.

83. "To divide the world into a 'real' and an apparent world, whether in the manner of Christianity or in the manner of Kant (which is, after all, that of a cunning Christian) is only a suggestion of *décadence*—a symptom of declining life," Friedrich Nietzsche, *Twilight of the Idols and The Antichrist*, trans. R. J. Hollingdale (London: Penguin, 2003), 49, 133.

84. David Boucher, *Political Theories of International Relations: From Thucydides to the Present* (Oxford: Oxford University Press, 1998), 273. For Boucher, however, "God

becomes the creature of men, created out of their need to assume him. The kingdom of ends and the idea of God are closely related. . . . The postulate of God is the ideal of perfection, with which our moral actions must strive to be in accord."

85. Howard Williams, "Kant and the Protestant Ethic," in Howard Williams, *International Relations and the Limits of Political Theory* (Houndmills: Macmillan, 2006), 14.

86. Mark Lilla, *The Stillborn God* (New York: Vintage, 2007), 3–4.

87. Mark Lilla, "Kant's Theological-Political Revolution," *Review of Metaphysics* 52 (December 1998): 397, 403.

88. Anna Schmidt argues that Schmitt developed his concept of political theology as a reaction against Mikhail Bakunin's use of the phrase as an insult; Anna Schmidt, "The Problem of Carl Schmitt's Political Theology," *Interpretations* 36, no. 3 (2009): 226. O'Donovan traces the origin of the term to Augustine's dismissal of Marcus Varro's "mendacious" *civile genus theologiae* in *The City of God*; Oliver O'Donovan, *The Desire of the Nations: Rediscovering the Roots of Political Theology* (Cambridge: Cambridge University Press, 1996), 7.

89. Carl Schmitt, *Political Theology: Four Chapters on the Concept of Sovereignty*, trans. George Schwab (Cambridge: MIT Press, 1985), 36. An interesting discussion of how this process has affected IR theory is to be found in Mika Luoma-Aho, "International Relations and the Secularisation of Theological Concepts: A Symbolic Reading," in *Perspectives* 17, no. 2 (2009).

90. Schmitt, *Political Theology*, 46.

91. Derek Simon clearly outlines the repugnant elements of Schmitt's political theology in "The *New* Political Theology of Metz: Confronting Schmitt's Decisionist Political Theology of Exclusion," *Horizons* 30, no. 2 (2003).

92. Schmitt, *Political Theology*, 52.

93. Wolfram Malte Fues addresses aspects of Kant and Schmitt's political theologies in "The Foe. The Radical Evil. Political Theology in Immanuel Kant and Carl Schmitt," *Philosophical Forum* 41, nos. 1–2 (2010). See also Geoffrey Waite's reply to Fues, "Kant, Schmitt or Fues on Political Theology, Radical Evil and the Foe," *Philosophical Forum* 41, nos. 1–2 (2010). In his postscript, "Hobbism in Kant?," Wolfgang Schwarz argues that Kant prohibits rebellion against the legislature, while allowing the possibility of rebellion against the executive in extreme circumstances. *Principles of Lawful Politics: Immanuel Kant's Philosophic Draft "Towards Eternal Peace"*, ed. Wolfgang Schwarz (Aalen: Scientia-Verlag, 1988), 137ff.

94. Schmitt, *Political Theology*, 14.

95. Ibid.

96. Jacob Taubes, *Occidental Eschatology* (Stanford: Stanford University Press, 2009), 140.

97. Jürgen Moltmann, *The Coming of God: Christian Eschatology* (London: SCM Press, 1996), 188.

98. Simon Critchley, *The Faith of the Faithless: Experiments in Political Theology* (New York: Verso, 2012), 84.

99. Lilla, *Stillborn God*, 153.

100. Carl Schmitt, *Political Theology II: The Myth of the Closure of Any Political Theology* (Cambridge: Polity, 2008), 124.

101. Ibid., 130.

102. Ibid., 128.

103. Ibid. Kantian political theorists are not alone in this; rather, it is endemic in political science, as Mika Luoma-Aho argues (with a nod toward Gilles Deleuze and Félix Guattari): "Christian theology cannot be weeded out of political science; there are too many rhizomes in the field," Mika Luoma-Aho, "Political Theology, Anthropomorphism, and Person-hood of the State: The Religion of IR," *International Political Sociology* 3, no. 3 (2009): 298.

104. Schmitt, *Political Theology II*, 57–58.

105. A good reading of the apocalyptic and *katechontic* elements of Schmitt is contained in Julia Hell, "*Katechon*: Carl Schmitt's Imperial Theology and the Ruins of the Future," *Germanic Review* 84, no. 4 (2009).

106. Clare Monagle, "A Sovereign Act of Negation: Schmitt's Political Theology and Its Ideal Medievalism," *Culture, Theory and Critique* 51, no. 2 (2010): 115 and 126. In a similar vein Phillip W. Gray also identifies the historical and political lacunae in Schmitt's understanding of the medieval and argues that the "natural" political theology of Schmitt is linked to totalitarianism in all its forms; Phillip W. Gray, "Political Theology and the Theology of Politics: Carl Schmitt and Medieval Christian Political Thought," *Humanitas* 20, nos. 1–2 (2007): 175–200.

107. Ernst Kantorowicz, *The King's Two Bodies: A Study in Mediaeval Political Theology* (Princeton: Princeton University Press, 1957), 3.

Chapter 1

1. Immanuel Kant, "Critique of Practical Reason," in *Practical Philosophy*, trans. and ed. Mary Gregor (Cambridge: Cambridge University Press, 1996), 210. Hereafter referred to as CPrR.

2. Immanuel Kant, *Critique of Pure Reason*, trans. Norman Kemp Smith, 2nd ed. (Houndmills: Palgrave Macmillan, 2007), 635. Hereafter referred to as *CPR*.

3. Kant, *Critique of Pure Reason* (*CPR*), 635–36. In a letter to Carl Friedrich Stäudlin (May 4, 1793), Kant writes, "[w]ith the enclosed work, *Religion within the Limits [of Reason Alone]*, I have tried to complete the third part of my plan. In this book I have proceeded conscientiously and with genuine respect for the Christian religion but also with a befitting candor, concealing nothing but rather presenting openly the way in which I believe that a possible union of Christianity with the purest practical reason is possible." *Correspondence*, 458.

4. Immanuel Kant, "Jasche Logic," in *Lectures on Logic*, ed. J. M. Young (Cambridge: Cambridge University Press, 1992), 538. In *Kant and the Problem of Metaphysics*, 144–52, Heidegger identifies the important connection between philosophy and anthropology (specifically a transcendental as opposed to an empirical anthropology) as essential to understanding Kant's regrounding of metaphysics. My position in this chapter inverts this relationship, arguing that the critical philosophy has anthropological (and thereby ultimately political) significance in that it offers distinct ways of understanding the possible answers to the question "what is man?"

5. This understanding of political theology is offered by Michael Jon Kessler, "Introduction: Political Theology in a Plural Context," in *Political Theology for a Plural Age*, ed. Michael Jon Kessler (Oxford: Oxford University Press, 2013), 1. Mark Lilla counts Kant's as "the third theological-political revolution in modern thought, and perhaps the most consequential," in "Kant's Theological-Political Revolution," 403.

6. Immanuel Kant, "Metaphysics of Morals," in *Practical Philosophy*, trans. and ed. Mary J. Gregor (Cambridge: Cambridge University Press, 1996).

7. Kant, *CPR*, 266. See also Kant's further treatment of the worlds of sense and understanding, 272ff. Jennifer Uleman provides a good account of phenomena and noumena in her *Introduction to Kant's Moral Philosophy* (Cambridge: Cambridge University Press, 2010), 72: "Phenomena are the basic subject matter of natural science, the data with which science works and which it explains. But noumena are not like this, and noumena do not behave according to Newtonian laws—noumena have their own laws (sometimes called, by Kant, 'the laws of freedom'). . . . the phenomenal order of appearances, governed by rigidly deterministic Newtonian law is no more or less real than the noumenal order of intelligible objects, governed by 'laws of freedom,' and accessible only to the intellect (see A537/B565). Each system has its own laws of evidence and its own set of warranted claims, and in some particularly interesting cases—the case of the will, for example—an object can belong to both systems."

8. Kant, *CPR*, 266. It should be noted here that I am not making the claim that the moral and noumenal worlds constitute "a belief in a mysterious form of supersensuous existence," Christine M. Korsgaard, *Creating the Kingdom of Ends* (Cambridge: Cambridge University Press, 1996), xi. My position is fairly close to that of Henry Allison, who argues that the "two worlds" are best understood as "two ways of considering things" and not as a contrast "between two modes of being (real and apparent)." The world of understanding, according to Kant, "is neither a transcendent metaphysical domain nor a merely heuristically adopted stance . . . it refers not to a distinct, non-natural realm of true being, but rather to a conceptual space in which reason frames a model of agency that is necessary in order to conceive itself as practical." Henry E. Allison, "We Can Act Only under the Idea of Freedom," in *Essays on Kant*, 96 and 97. See also Allison's discussion of the "epistemologically based understanding of transcendental idealism" in contrast to the "more traditional" ontological reading of the relationship between appearances and things in themselves in Henry E. Allison, *Kant's Transcendental*

Idealism: An Interpretation and a Defense, rev. ed. (New Haven: Yale University Press, 2004), 16ff. For a criticism of Allison and a defence of the alternative "two world" reading of transcendental idealism, see Paul Guyer, *Kant* (Abingdon: Routledge, 2006), 67ff.

9. Immanuel Kant. "Groundwork for the Metaphysics of Morals," in *Practical Philosophy*, trans. and ed. Mary Gregor (Cambridge: Cambridge University Press. 1996), 99.

10. Kant, *CPR*, 466.

11. Ibid.

12. Allison's treatment of freedom as an idea, i.e., "a normative principle that is a product of reason," is useful here in that freedom may be understood as a "regulative idea that governs our conception of ourselves as agents," and also allows us to understand freedom's effect on the sensible world as a product of its possessing "normative force," Henry E. Allison, "Kant's Practical Justification of Freedom," in *Essays on Kant*, 113.

13. Kant, *CPR*, 467. "Though I cannot *know*, I can yet *think* freedom, that is to say, the representation of it is at least not self-contradictory, provided due account be taken of our critical distinction between the modes of representation, the sensible and the intellectual, and of the resulting limitation of the pure concepts of understanding and of the principles which flow from them." *CPR*, 28.

14. Stephen H. Watson, "Kant on Autonomy, the Ends of Humanity, and the Possibility of Morality," *Kant Studien* 77, no. 2 (1986): 168.

15. Kant, *CPR*, 472.

16. Ibid., 473. Henry Allison expresses very well Kant's envisaged relationship between sensibility, understanding, and reason: "Just as the function of the understanding is to unify the raw material given in sensible intuition by bringing it to the objective unity of apperception, the function of reason is to unify the discrete products of the understanding (judgments) by bringing them into a coherent whole (system). The work of reason thus stands at the apex of the cognitive enterprise: if attained, the unity at which it aims would constitute the completion of knowledge," *Kant's Transcendental Idealism*, 2nd ed., 309.

17. Kant, *CPR*, 632. In the "Groundwork of the Metaphysics of Morals" (69n), Kant identifies "two senses" of prudence: "knowledge of the world" and "private prudence." Knowledge of the world "is a human being's skill in influencing others so as to use them for his own purposes," while private prudence is "insight to unite all these purposes to his own enduring advantage." The second meaning is the more important in political terms, as Kant states that "if someone is prudent in the first sense but not in the second, we might better say of him that he is clever and cunning but, on the whole, nevertheless imprudent."

18. Christine Korsgaard, "Kant's Formula of Humanity," *Kant Studien* 77, no. 2 (1986): 193.

19. Eric C. Sandberg, "Causa Noumenon and Homo Phaenomenon," *Kant Studien* 75,

no. 3 (1984): 275–76. Kant writes: "Pure practical laws, whose end is given through reason completely a priori, and which are prescribed to us not in an empirically conditioned but in an absolute manner, would be products of pure reason. Such are the moral laws; and these alone, therefore, belong to the practical employment of reason, and allow of a canon." *CPR*, 632. Sandberg (277) cautions that it must be remembered that "this intelligible world only has reality in a practical sense. The objective reality (in a practical sense) of our moral concepts allows us to think about ourselves in a different way, allows us to conceive of a world with a different order from the one which we know. To say that this world, with its different order, has practical reality is not to say that it exists independently of the empirical world but rather to say that our conception of this intelligible world influences our actions in the empirical world."

20. According to Guyer, transcendental idealism allows "for thoroughgoing determinism at the level of appearance while postulating the complete spontaneity of action at the level of reality." Guyer also describes this position as raising "one of the most vexed issues of Kant's mature philosophy—Kant himself would say that on his own theory the reality of freedom remains inexplicable or inscrutable," *Kant*, 21.

21. Kant, *CPR*, 637.

22. Ibid., 637–38. As Gilles Deleuze writes: "*There is a single dangerous misunderstanding regarding the whole of practical Reason*: believing that Kantian morality remains indifferent to its own realization. In fact the abyss between the sensible world and the suprasensible world exists only in order to be filled." Gilles Deleuze, *Kant's Critical Philosophy: The Doctrine of the Faculties*, trans. Hugh Tomlinson and Barbara Habberjam (Minneapolis: University of Minnesota Press, 2003), 39.

23. Kant, "Groundwork," 100. The seeds of this position are sown in the Transcendental Aesthetic section of the first *Critique*, in which Kant argues "that since the forms of sensory representation and any limits inherent in those forms apply only to the appearances of things, not to things as they are in themselves, we are at least free to think or conceive of things as they are in themselves independently of those forms—a possibility that Kant will require for his eventual reconstruction of metaphysics as a matter of practical rather than theoretical knowledge," Guyer, *Kant*, 53.

24. Kant, "Groundwork," 104.

25. Ibid., 108.

26. Immanuel Kant, "Critique of Practical Reason," in *Practical Philosophy*, trans. and ed. Mary Gregor (Cambridge: Cambridge University Press. 1996), 175.

27. Immanuel Kant, "An Answer to the Question: What Is Enlightenment?," in *Practical Philosophy*, trans. and ed. Mary Gregor (Cambridge: Cambridge University Press, 1996).

28. Immanuel Kant, "Critique of Practical Reason" (CPrR), 141.

29. Kant, *CPR*, 169.

30. Ibid., 136.

31. Ibid., 137. For the similarities and distinctions in Kant's use of transcendental

object, noumenon, and the thing in itself, see Henry E. Allison, "Things in Themselves, Noumena, and the Transcendental Object," *Dialectica* 32, no. 1 (1978): 41–76.

32. For an excellent account of the emergence and development of humanity as an idea and as an ideal within Kant's work, see Richard Dean, "Humanity as an Idea, as an Ideal, and as an End in Itself," *Kantian Review* 18, no. 2 (2013): 171–95. To the best of my knowledge there is no similar work dedicated to the role of human beings within the critical and practical philosophy. My intention here is simply to contrast humanity (as representative of the *homo noumenon*) against human beings (as representative of the *homo phaenomenon*) in the critical and practical philosophy and to draw out the important implications of the disparity between the thing in itself and the appearance. The human being/humanity distinction is also examined at various points throughout this book in the anthropological, teleological, and theological dimensions of Kant's work.

33. Kant, *CPR*, 486.

34. Ibid., 311.

35. Kant, "Groundwork," 54.

36. Ibid., 59–60. Kant's attitude toward happiness is ambivalent. Robert Taylor notes that in the CPrR Kant is of the opinion that "happiness achieved through the exercise of prudence is a good in itself (albeit not an unconditional one). Happiness, for example, is part of the highest good in Kant's moral theory: virtue is the *supreme* good, but the *complete* good requires happiness proportional to virtue as well, at least for sentient beings such as ourselves. Moreover, in his later writings Kant argues that our original predispositions to self-love, which have happiness as their object, are predispositions to the good, and therefore any attempt to root them out would 'not only be futile but harmful and blameworthy as well.'" Robert S. Taylor, "Kantian Personal Autonomy," *Political Theory* 33, no. 5 (2005): 608.

37. Kant, "Groundwork," 61 and 71.

38. Ibid., 77.

39. Ibid., 79.

40. The lower faculty of desire is concerned with the identification of ends, the higher faculty of desire emerges in response to what Kant conceives as the ultimate end—man's realization of his ethical self through reason in the concept of freedom. Kant, "CPrR," 155–58. In the *Critique of the Power of Judgment* Kant goes so far as to equate reason with the higher faculty of desire.

41. Kant, "CPrR," 146.

42. For an important exception to this, namely the subjectively universal pleasure derived from beauty, see chapter 2 of this volume.

43. Kant, "CPrR," 159.

44. Kant, "Metaphysics of Morals," 517.

45. Kant, "CPrR," 169.

46. Ibid.

47. Ibid., 187.

48. Ibid., 197. Despite inclinations being a "predisposition to the good, they are readily twisted into vices . . . the goodness of our original predispositions to self-love is a delicate one, a primal innocence that is easily corrupted." Taylor, "Kantian Personal Autonomy," 611.

49. Kant, "CPrR," 189.

50. Kant, "Groundwork," 98. Andreas Teuber makes the importance of this distinction very clear: "Our actual existence is not so awe-inspiring; indeed it is a source of humiliation to us. . . . What deserves respect (Kant sometimes says 'demands' respect) is 'no other than the pure moral itself.' . . . The person is an end-in-himself, but only insofar as he has within him something that is itself an end-in-itself." Andreas Teuber, "Kant's Respect for Persons," *Political Theory* 11, no. 3 (1983): 373.

51. On the importance of freedom, see Henry E. Allison, "Morality and Freedom: Kant's Reciprocity Thesis," *Philosophical Review* 95, no. 3 (1986).

52. Kant, "Groundwork," 52.

53. Ibid., 54.

54. Ibid., 55.

55. Ibid., 62.

56. Ibid., 55–56. Anne Margaret Baxley attempts to rehabilitate sympathy in Kant's moral theory in "Kantian Virtue," *Philosophy Compass* 2, no. 3 (2007): 404ff.

57. Kant, "Groundwork," 67.

58. Kant, "CPrR," 206

59. Kant, "CPrR," 238.

60. Kant, "Groundwork," 100. Kant elaborates on this theme in the "Metaphysics of Morals" (544): "The human being as a *natural being* that has reason (*homo phaenomenon*) can be determined by his reason, as a *cause*, to actions in the sensible world, and so far the concept of obligation does not come into consideration. But the same human being thought in terms of his *personality*, that is, as a being endowed with *inner freedom* (*homo noumenon*), is regarded as a being that can be put under obligation and, indeed, under obligation to himself (to the humanity in his own person). So the human being (taken in these two different senses) can acknowledge a duty to himself without falling into contradiction (because the concept of a human being is not thought in one and the same sense)."

61. Kant, "Groundwork," 102.

62. Kant, "Groundwork," 105. As Dodson writes, "The moral world, however, is not subject to the conditions of space and time, since qua moral agents we are noumena. The laws governing this world are not physical but juridical, and the body of these laws is called 'jurisprudence.'" Kevin Dodson, "Autonomy and Authority in Kant's *Rechtslehre*," *Political Theory* 25, no. 1 (1997): 98.

63. Kant, "Groundwork," 106.

64. Ibid.

65. Immanuel Kant, "Answer to the Question," 17.

66. Immanuel Kant, "Idea for a Universal History with a Cosmopolitan Intent," in *Perpetual Peace and Other Essays*, trans. Ted Humphrey (Indianapolis: Hackett, 1983), 29.

67. Kant, "Groundwork," 77.

68. Kant, "CPrR," 200. Or as Kant puts it in "The Metaphysics of Morals," "only the descent into the hell of self-cognition can pave the way to godliness," 562. Kant moderates this position by stating that "moral cognition of oneself will . . . dispel fanatical contempt for oneself as a human being. . . . it is only through the noble predisposition to the good in us, which makes the human being worthy of respect, that one can find one who acts contrary to it contemptible." "The Metaphysics of Morals," 562–63. Kant also rails against monkish "hypocritical loathing of oneself," "The Metaphysics of Morals," 597.

69. Kant, "CPrR," 206.

70. Ibid., 210.

71. Ibid. 269.

72. Ibid. For the role of the emotions, and in particular shame and humiliation, see Krista K. Thomason, "Shame and Contempt in Kant's Moral Theory," *Kantian Review* 18, no. 2 (2013): 221–40.

73. Kant, "CPrR," 269.

74. Ibid., 211.

75. Ibid., 270.

76. Kant, "On the Common Saying," 305.

77. Kant, "Toward Perpetual Peace," in *Practical Philosophy*, 346.

78. Kant, "Perpetual Peace," 339.

79. Kant, "Metaphysics of Morals," 491.

80. Kant, "Idea for a Universal History with a Cosmopolitan Intent," in *Perpetual Peace and Other Essays*, 30.

81. Kant, "Groundwork," 102. The limitations of Kant's theory of freedom are evident when placed in a political or natural-practical sense: "The problem is that freedom, in every Kantian context, is incompatible *with being an object in nature*, that is, with being a spatio-temporal object of experience." Jennifer K. Uleman, "External Freedom in Kant's Rechtslehre: Political, Metaphysical," *Philosophy and Phenomenological Research* 68, no. 3 (2004): 580. Uleman attempts to clarify Kantian freedom as the "spatio-temporal pursuit of freely-set ends free of spatio-temporal interference by others with free wills," 601. Even such a clarification, however, still leaves Kantian freedom operating in a political void.

82. Kant draws here on his resolution to the Third Antinomy in the *Critique of Pure Reason*.

83. Kant, "CPrR," 163.

84. Allison, "Kant's Practical Justification of Freedom," 123.

85. David Lindstedt, "Kant: Progress in Universal History as a Postulate of Practical Reason," *Kant Studien* 90, no. 2 (1999): 138.

86. Autonomy has two components, "that no authority external to ourselves is needed to constitute or inform us of the demands of morality" and "that in self-government we can effectively control ourselves." J. B. Schneewind, "Autonomy, Obligation, and Virtue: An Overview of Kant's Moral Philosophy," in *The Cambridge Companion to Kant*, ed. Paul Guyer (Cambridge: Cambridge University Press, 1992), 309.

87. Kant, "CPrR," 217.

88. Ibid., 217.

89. Ibid., 218.

90. Ibid., 231. In the essay "Kant on Freedom of the Will," Henry Allison notes that "unlike most present-day conceptions of autonomy, Kant's is an all or nothing affair: either the will has it or it does not. Moreover, if it does not, morality must be rejected as a phantom of the brain," *Essays on Kant*, 146.

91. Kant, "Groundwork," 107.

92. Kant, "CPrR," 163.

93. Ibid., 166.

94. Kant, "CPrR," 153. Kant sees mankind cosmologically as in effect a member of the community of rational beings, from mankind (after exiting self-incurred minority through the redemption of reason) through angels and on to God. Ian Hunter has termed this Kant's "metaphysical anthropology," "The Morals of Metaphysics: Kant's 'Groundwork' as Intellectual '*Paideia*,'" *Critical Inquiry* 28, no. 4 (2002): 911ff.

95. Kant, "CPrR," 153.

96. Ibid., 154, 162.

97. Uleman, *Introduction*, 11.

98. Kant, "CPrR," 175.

99. Ibid., 207.

100. Allison, "Kant on the Freedom of the Will," 393.

101. Schneewind, "Autonomy, Obligation, and Virtue," 330.

102. Kant, *CPR*, 46.

103. Ibid., 323–25.

104. "It is rational to pursue a goal only if we have good reason to believe that this goal can be realized; that the goal imposed by morality obviously is not always realizable *in the natural world*, which has no place for God or immortality, because of the wayward inclinations of others or even ourselves; so we must therefore postulate an as it were unnatural world, beyond the temporal frame of ordinary existence and ruled by a wise, benevolent, and powerful God, in which the ideal result of morality will become actual." Guyer, *Kant*, 232.

105. Kant, *CPR*, 354.

106. Ibid., 377.

107. Ibid., 619.

108. Ibid. Again, it must be stressed that Kant is not making the case that we have knowledge of this condition; it is a position he stresses that the practical theorist can

adopt in self-defense against the attacks of skeptical atheism. This position may be developed in self-defence, yet Kant stresses that "[n]one the less we are here proceeding in entire conformity with reason."

109. Kant, CPrR, 246.

110. Kant, *CPR*, 415.

111. Ibid., 419. "Reason proceeds by one path in its empirical use, and by yet another path in its transcendental use," *CPR*, 482.

112. Ibid., 425.

113. Ibid., 430.

114. Ibid., 505.

115. Ibid., 517.

116. "The law of reason which requires us to seek for this unity, is a necessary law, since without it we should have no reason at all, and without reason, no coherent employment of the understanding, and in the absence of this no sufficient criterion of empirical truth. In order, therefore, to secure an empirical criterion, we have no option save to presuppose the systematic unity of nature as objectively valid and necessary." Kant, *CPR*, 538.

117. Kant, *CPR*, 556. "The idea is posited only as being the point of view from which alone that unity, which is so essential to reason and so beneficial to the understanding, can be further extended. In short, this transcendental thing is only the schema of the regulative principle by which reason, so far as lies in its power, extends systematic unity over the whole field of experience." 557.

118. Ibid., 566.

119. Ibid., 567.

120. Ibid., 639.

121. Ibid., 597.

122. Ibid., 635.

Chapter 2

1. On the importance of hope, and specifically religious hope, see Christopher Insole, "The Irreducible Importance of Religious Hope in Kant's Conception of the Highest Good," *Philosophy* 83, no. 3 (2008). Insole makes the important observation that "[w]e might not like it, but religious hope seems to play an independently important role in Kant's moral thought. Where we excise this from Kant's thought, we should be clear that we are engaged in reconstruction, not interpretation," 337.

2. Henry E. Allison also draws a closer connection between the third *Critique* and *Perpetual Peace* than is usual in the literature in "The Gulf between Nature and Freedom and Nature's Guarantee of Perpetual Peace," in Allison, *Essays on Kant*, 224–26.

3. Kant, *Critique of the Power of Judgment*, 3–4.

4. Ibid., 6.

5. On the development of the faculty of the power of judgment from its limited use in the *Critique of Pure Reason* to the expanded capabilities of the *Critique of the Power of Judgment*, see Thomas Teufel, "What Does Kant Mean by 'Power of Judgment' in His *Critique of the Power of Judgment*," in *Kantian Review* 17, no. 2 (2012): 301ff.

6. Kant, *Critique of the Power of Judgment*, 8.

7. Ibid., 82.

8. Henry E. Allison, *Kant's Theory of Taste: A Reading of the Critique of Aesthetic Judgement* (Cambridge: Cambridge University Press, 2001), 203–4.

9. For Allison the purposiveness of nature represents the a priori principle of the reflective power of judgment, *Kant's Theory of Taste*, 5, 14.

10. Kant, *Critique of the Power of Judgment*, 7.

11. Ibid., 8–9.

12. Avner Baz, "Kant's Principle of Purposiveness and the Missing Point of (Aesthetic) Judgements," *Kantian Review* 10, no. 1 (2005): 9.

13. "We need to presuppose nature's systematicity, if our reflection on it is to be systematic. . . . Unless the questions we pose to nature are posed systematically, we have no hope of discovering a system in nature; and we cannot make our questioning of nature systematic, without, in effect, assuming *nature* to *be* systematic." Baz, "Kant's Principle of Purposiveness," 10.

14. As Pheng Cheah writes: "Chance is inimical to freedom because it is also blind. To ground freedom's realization on chance is to abolish freedom. It deprives the final end of rational lawfulness, making it the outcome of a fortunate accident. . . . Likewise, Kant repeatedly stresses that organisms cannot be explained by chance. As an objective end, the organism is the natural exorcism of chance as a governing principle in nature." Pheng Cheah, "Human Freedom and the Technic of Nature: Culture and Organic Life in Kant's Third Critique," *differences: a Journal of Feminist Cultural Studies* 14, no. 2 (2003): 8.

15. Kant, *Critique of the Power of Judgment*, 15.

16. Kristi Sweet, "Reflection: Its Structure and Meaning in Kant's Judgments of Taste," *Kantian Review* 14, no. 1 (2009): 55.

17. Allison, *Kant's Theory of Taste*, 41.

18. Kant, *Critique of the Power of Judgment*, 17.

19. Ibid., 19.

20. Ibid., 15–16.

21. That the power of judgment legislates for itself and not for nature is an important point, because "the possibility still remains open that the order of nature is such that it is not cognizable by the human mind. . . . to exorcize this second spectre . . . we are constrained to approach [the empirical world] as if it were purposive. Thus, judgment, unlike understanding, legislates not to nature but to itself. What it governs is our 'way of thinking' about nature, insofar as we are engaged in the project of empirical enquiry." Allison, *Kant's Theory of Taste*, 205.

22. Sweet, "Reflection," 76–77.

23. Kant, *Lectures on Logic* (LD-W 24:710:447), quoted in Allison, *Kant's Theory of Taste*, 48. In the *Critique of Pure Reason*, Kant identifies the imagination as the "blind though indispensable function of the soul, without which we would have no cognition at all, but of which we are seldom even conscious" (CPR A78/B104), quoted in Allison, *Kant's Theory of Taste*, 281.

24. Rachel Zuckert, "Kant's Rationalist Aesthetics," *Kant Studien* 98, no. 4 (2007): 461–62.

25. Kristin Gjesdal, "Reading Kant Hermeneutically: Gadamer and the *Critique of Judgement*," *Kant Studien* 98, no. 3 (2007): 355.

26. Baz, "Kant's Principle of Purposiveness," 4–5, 10.

27. Kant, "Metaphysics of Morals," 487.

28. Ryan Johnson, "An Accord in/on Kantian Aesthetics," *Kritike: An Online Journal of Philosophy* 5, no. 1 (2011).

29. Kyriaki Goudeli, "Kant's Reflective Judgement: The Normalization of Political Judgement," *Kant Studien* 94, no. 1 (2003): 67.

30. Willi Goetschel, "Kant and the Christo Effect: Grounding Aesthetics," *New German Critique* 79 (2000): 144.

31. Although Kant's work is revolutionary in terms of method and epistemology it is nonetheless quite conservative in intent and there is a great deal of continuity with rationalist philosophy; see Zuckert, "Kant's Rationalist Aesthetics," 444.

32. Gjesdal, "Reading Kant Hermeneutically," 354.

33. "[W]e must assume that cognitive abilities are universal among mankind. Further we must appreciate that cognition, on Kant's account, is a matter of organizing manifolds of the imagination by the understanding. Thus so the argument goes, since recognizing free harmony (by the feeling of pleasure) is also recognizing a relation between understanding and imagination, we have good reason to suppose that this recognition will work out in the same way for all persons. Thus, we have good reason to suppose that all persons will recognize free harmony by the same feeling of pleasure. As such, we have shown that free harmony is universally pleasing." Kenneth Rogerson, "Pleasure and Fit in Kant's Aesthetics," *Kantian Review* 2, no. 1 (1998): 120.

34. Zuckert, "Kant's Rationalist Aesthetics," 454. Baz expresses the requirement succinctly: "In calling something beautiful, we express a liking for what we see, Kant says. But this is not all: we also 'demand' or 'require' that others like it as well. This inter-subjective appeal is essential to what we say when we call something 'beautiful,' and so essential to what beauty is. It would not occur to anyone to use the term 'beautiful,' Kant argues, 'without thinking of a universal validity.'" Baz, "Kant's Principle of Purposiveness," 8. See also Paul Guyer's discussion of the universality of taste in *Kant and the Claims of Taste*, 2nd ed. (Cambridge: Cambridge University Press, 1997), 134ff.

35. Joseph Cannon, "Nature as the School of the Moral World: Kant on Taking an Interest in Natural Beauty," in *The Environment: Philosophy, Science, and Ethics*, ed. Wil-

liam P. Kabasenche, Michael O'Rourke, and Matthew H. Slater (Cambridge: MIT Press, 2012), 121.

36. Henry E. Allison, "Beauty and Duty in Kant's Critique of Judgement," *Kantian Review* 1, no. 1 (1997): 67–68.

37. Michael Rohlf, "The Transition from Nature to Freedom in Kant's Third Critique," *Kant Studien* 99, no. 3 (2008): 357; Allison, "Beauty and Duty in Kant's Critique of Judgement," 67.

38. Allison, *Kant's Theory of Taste*, 264.

39. Nature is, according to Kant, "not a thing in itself but is merely an aggregate of appearances, so many representations of the mind," *CPR*, 140, and as such it may be transformed as a consequence of a shift in perspective. Currently, the understanding dictates what appears to be, "the source of the laws of nature, and so of its formal unity . . . in keeping with the object to which it refers, namely, experience," *CPR*, 148, but this does not necessarily have to remain the case; reason and the reflective power of judgment may enable a fundamental redefinition of nature in addition to the definition provided by the understanding.

40. Kant, *Critique of the Power of Judgment*, 130.

41. Ibid., 134. Allison makes the important observation that "since what is properly termed sublime cannot be contained in any sensible form but concerns ideas of reason, Kant insists that true sublimity is to be found only in the mind, and all that may be said about an object is that it is suitable for exhibiting or evoking such sublimity," *Kant's Theory of Taste*, 310.

42. "Sublimity can play a moral role by accustoming us to how the moral agent's response to the moral law feels, by giving us a palpable awareness of our transcendental and practical freedom," Robert R. Clewis, *The Kantian Sublime and the Revelation of Freedom* (Cambridge: Cambridge University Press, 2009), 226. This preparatory aspect is particularly the case when viewed in the context of Kant's linkage of the moral law and the starry heavens—an example of the sublime in nature that occasions awe and respect.

43. Kant, *Critique of the Power of Judgment*, 145.

44. Ibid. For Allison, "The basic idea is that in the experience of the sublime, the self is aware of its independence of nature and of all its limitations and vulnerability as a merely natural being because it also becomes conscious of a capacity and a vocation that transcends nature. . . . in the face of the raw power of external nature, we become directly aware of our independence, as persons, from our entire nature as sensuous beings, and therefore, of our superiority to any power that threatens merely the latter." *Kant's Theory of Taste*, 329.

45. In Allison's formulation, "the sublime puts us in touch (albeit merely aesthetically) with our 'higher self'; and, as such, it may help clear the ground, as it were, for genuine moral feeling and, therefore, like the sensitivity to natural beauty, though in a very different way, function as a moral facilitator." *Kant's Theory of Taste*, 343.

46. Kant, *Critique of the Power of Judgment*, 148.

47. Ibid., 176–77.

48. Ibid., 192.

49. Ibid., 230.

50. Ibid., 233.

51. As Jeffrey Wattles writes, "[a]ccording to Kant, although a mechanist cannot ask what things are for, if we think teleologically it is impossible to stop short of the question of an ultimate purpose." "Teleology Past and Present," *Zygon* 41, no. 2 (2006): 453.

52. Kant, *Critique of the Power of Judgment*, 234.

53. Marie Zermatt Scutt draws the connection between pure reason and teleology: "For Kant, the only way to preclude the indifference of nature to the inferred necessary connection between adherence to the law of pure reason and the realization of the highest good is to conceive of the world in a teleological manner that is commensurate with the moral teleology that arises from the analysis of pure reason as a practical faculty." "Kant's Moral Theology," *British Journal for the History of Philosophy* 18, no. 4 (2010): 624.

54. Kant, *Critique of the Power of Judgment*, 243.

55. Ibid., 246–47.

56. Guyer writes (with a hint of disapproval) that "[t]he belief that intelligible form or proportion requires the action of an intelligent creator goes back to the roots of Western philosophy, and Kant may well have been in its grasp when he supposed that regular forms were obviously appearances of design." *Kant and the Claims of Taste*, 233. For an argument in favor of Kant's commitment to a form of theism, and opposition to atheism, see Lara Dennis, "Kant's Criticism of Atheism," *Kant Studien* 94, no. 2 (2003).

57. Kant, *Critique of the Power of Judgment*, 259. On the antinomy, see Henry E. Allison, "Kant's Antinomy of Teleological Judgment," in *Essays on Kant*, ed. Henry E. Allison (Cambridge: Cambridge University Press, 2006).

58. Kant, *Critique of the Power of Judgment*, 260. For Guyer, "from a theoretical point of view the assumption of the existence of God would be, as a ground of explanation, a mere 'hypothesis,' although with regard to 'an object set for us by the moral law' it can be a 'belief and even a pure belief of reason.'" Paul Guyer, "Unity of Nature and Freedom: Kant's Conception of the System of Philosophy," in *Kant's System of Nature and Freedom: Selected Essays* (Cambridge: Cambridge University Press, 2005), 291.

59. Kant, *Critique of the Power of Judgment*, 269.

60. "If we think the world as the creation of a great artist, as experience obliges us to do, we can develop and expand our cognitive powers. If we deny the argument from design, we cannot comprehend our experience, nor can we grasp our roles as cognitive agents in the world. The consequence would be frustration of our desires and abilities, not their further development. Thus, if the argument from design is to be looked at as a fiction, it must be seen as a necessary fiction. It is a necessary condition for the satisfaction of basic human interests." Michael Kraft, "Thinking the Physico-Teleological Proof," *International Journal for Philosophy of Religion* 12, no. 2 (1981): 74.

61. Wattles expresses this issue well: "There are rational motives to posit Ideas that cannot be proven but that can nevertheless guide the progress of a discipline. We can work with an Idea of God as an unconditioned Cause of nature, for example, even though science and philosophy do not let us know God," "Teleology Past and Present," 451–52.

62. Kant, *Critique of the Power of Judgment*, 303.

63. For an argument stressing the continuity, but also the changes, within Kant's approach to the role of God as "the Wise Author of Nature" from the *Critique of Pure Reason* to the *Critique of the Power of Judgment*, see Lawrence Pasternack, "Regulative Principles and the 'Wise Author of Nature,'" *Religious Studies* 47, no. 4 (2011).

64. Kant, *Critique of the Power of Judgment*, 282–83.

65. Ibid., 287.

66. Ibid., 298.

67. On the importance of culture within Kant's teleology and philosophy, and the distinction between the culture of skill and the culture of discipline, see Henry E. Allison, "Teleology and History in Kant: The Critical Foundations of Kant's Philosophy of History," in *Kant's Idea for a Universal History with a Cosmopolitan Aim: A Critical Guide*, ed. Amélie Oksenberg Rorty and James Schmidt, 24–45 (Cambridge: Cambridge University Press, 2009).

68. Kant, *Critique of the Power of Judgment*, 299–300.

69. Kant had already written on politics by this stage, and even touched on many themes that would feature in his later works, but the works after the third *Critique* have been indelibly marked by its concerns and display a greater thematic unity.

70. Kant, *Critique of the Power of Judgment*, 192.

71. Ibid., 303.

72. Guyer expresses this in terms of a difference between ultimate and final ends of mankind in nature: "there must be an *ultimate* end *within* nature that is connected with but not identical to human freedom as the *final* end of nature, and which we can conceive of as being brought about by natural processes but also as providing the point of connection between nature and the unconditional value of freedom." Paul Guyer, "Purpose in Nature: What Is Living and Dead in Kant's Teleology?," in *Kant's System of Nature and Freedom* (Oxford: Oxford University Press, 2005), 366. I will argue in chapter 3 that *Perpetual Peace* is an attempt to develop an ultimate end within nature that in turn provides the opportunity for mankind to achieve its apotheosis.

Chapter 3

1. Immanuel Kant, "Idea for a Universal History with a Cosmopolitan Aim," in *Kant's Idea for a Universal History with a Cosmopolitan Aim: A Critical Guide*, ed. Amélie Oksenberg Rorty and James Schmidt (Cambridge: Cambridge University Press, 2009), 11.

2. Ibid., 10. R. B. J. Walker stresses that "despite the rather fragmentary nature of his explicitly political writings on war and peace, there is a close connection between his general philosophical position and his observations on international relations. His analysis of the movement from war to peace parallels his more general philosophical discussion of the movement from diversity and conflict to unity," Walker, *Inside/Outside*, 137. Kimberly Hutchings argues that Kant's wider political thought is an "extension of his critical philosophy, combining both the critical task of establishing the ground and limits of political right and the metaphysical task of spelling out the implications for the nature of a legitimate state and government." *Kant, Critique and Politics*, 29.

3. The Copernican revolution to which Kant refers in the first *Critique* compares the effect of his proposal that objects must conform to our knowledge, as opposed to our knowledge must conform to objects, to the innovations in astrophysics relating to heliocentricity and the rotation of the Earth on its axis by Nicholas Copernicus. In "Idea for a Universal History with a Cosmopolitan Aim" he is obviously trying to draw a parallel between his work on politics and history and that of Tycho Brahe and Isaac Newton in physics.

4. Kant, "Idea for a Universal History with a Cosmopolitan Aim," in *Kant's Idea for a Universal History with a Cosmopolitan Aim: A Critical Guide*, ed. Rorty and Schmidt, 10.

5. Howard Williams, *Kant's Political Philosophy* (Oxford: Blackwell, 1983), 20. In Mark Franke's formulation, for Kant "[t]he past in itself is not available as an object. He suggests, rather, that any history offered as such can provide only a systemic report of events where no system as such prevails," Franke, *Global Limits*, 84.

6. Jens Bartelson, "The Trial of Judgment: A Note on Kant and the Paradoxes of Internationalism," *International Studies Quarterly* 39, no. 2 (1995): 273.

7. Steven M. Delue, "Kant's Politics as an Expression of the Need for His Aesthetics," *Political Theory* 13, no. 3 (1985): 425.

8. Kant, "Idea for a Universal History with a Cosmopolitan Aim," in *Kant's Idea for a Universal History with a Cosmopolitan Aim: A Critical Guide*, ed. Rorty and Schmidt, 10–11.

9. Franke makes the important observation that "the central debate over whether nature serves humanity or whether nature has its own mechanical dynamics which have only incidentally served humans in certain ways cannot be concluded decisively and, thereby, really only goes to show that human beings cannot conceive the movement of nature without view to final causes. And this substrate to nature, since it cannot be found within nature but only underlying it, must itself be supersensible. Hence, reason needs to create for itself an idea of such a principle of purposiveness." Franke, *Global Limits*, 121.

10. Howard Williams, "Back from the USSR: Kant, Kaliningrad and World Peace," *International Relations* 20, no. 1 (2006): 28.

11. Howard Williams notices the importance of the higher anthropological standpoint or perspective, but he does not oppose it to a lower anthropological perspective or

put them in tension as a means to explore the anthropological dimensions of the problem of politics. See Howard Williams, "The Torture Convention, Rendition and Kant's Critique of 'Pseudo-Politics,'" *Review of International Studies* 36, no. 1 (2010): 210.

12. Kant, *Critique of the Power of Judgment*, 298.

13. Kant, "Religion Within the Boundaries of Mere Reason," 129. See Allen Wood, "Kant's Fourth Proposition: The Unsociable Sociability of Human Nature," in *Kant's Idea for a Universal History with a Cosmopolitan Aim: A Critical Guide*, ed. Amélie Oksenberg Rorty and James Schmidt (Cambridge: Cambridge University Press, 2009), 126–27.

14. Kant, "Metaphysics of Morals," 452.

15. Ibid. See also Pauline Kleingeld, "Kant's Theory of Peace," in *The Cambridge Companion to Kant and Modern Philosophy*, ed. Paul Guyer (Cambridge: Cambridge University Press, 2006), 488.

16. Immanuel Kant, *Lectures on Ethics*, ed. Peter Heath and J. B. Schneewind, trans. Peter Heath (Cambridge: Cambridge University Press, 1997), 340.

17. Kant, "Metaphysics of Morals," 484, compare with "Toward Perpetual Peace," 349, see Georg Cavallar, *Kant and the Theory and Practice of International Right* (Cardiff: University of Wales Press, 1999), 95.

18. Kant, "Metaphysics of Morals," 484.

19. Kant, *Lectures on Ethics*, 340.

20. Hurrell, "Kant and the Kantian Paradigm in International Relations," 186.

21. See Susan Meld Shell, "Kant on Just War and 'Unjust Enemies': Reflections on a 'Pleonasm,'" *Kantian Review* 10 (2005), and the response by Georg Cavallar, "Commentary on Susan Meld Shell, 'Kant on Just War and Unjust Enemies': Reflections on a 'Pleonasm,'" *Kantian Review* 11 (2006).

22. See Williams, "Back from the USSR," 35.

23. Kant, "On the Common Saying," 309.

24. Ibid., 307. Kant, "Metaphysics of Morals," 455–56.

25. Kant, "On the Common Saying," 308. See Gunnar Beck, "Kant's Theory of Rights," *Ratio Juris* 19, no. 4 (2006): 397.

26. Kant, "On the Common Saying," 308. Elsewhere, the role of education is afforded more importance, cf. Immanuel Kant, "Lectures on Pedagogy," in *Anthropology, History and Education*, ed. Robert B. Louden and Günter Zöller, trans. Mary Gregor, Paul Gregor, Robert B. Louden, and others (Cambridge: Cambridge University Press, 2007).

27. Kant, "On the Common Saying," 307.

28. Kant, "Idea for a Universal History with a Cosmopolitan Intent," 32. In "The End of all Things," in Kant, *Perpetual Peace and Other Essays*, Kant elaborates on this point: "In the natural progress of the human race, talents, skills, and tastes (along with its result, voluptuousness) become cultured before morality develops. . . . However, humanity's moral capacity . . . will someday overtake them," 96.

29. Immanuel Kant, "Idea for a Universal History with a Cosmopolitan Aim," in Im-

manuel Kant, *Anthropology, History and Education*, ed. Robert B. Louden and Günter Zöller (Cambridge: Cambridge University Press, 2007), 108. This point is also noted by Lea Ypi, "*Natura Daedela Rerum?* On the Justification of Historical Progress in Kant's Guarantee of Perpetual Peace," *Kantian Review* 14, no. 2 (2010): 129. Garrett Wallace Brown is particularly worried by what he sees as the deterministic elements of Kant's philosophy of history, concluding that "a tenable conception of Kantian cosmopolitanism must reject the inherent complications involved in understanding Kant's theory of history as promoting a determined natural teleology. . . . any practical construction of Kantian cosmopolitanism must distance itself from the possible teleological ramifications of 'guaranteed' human progression." *Grounding Cosmopolitanism*, 41

30. As Larry Krasnoff writes, "Kant himself insists that teleology is not something that can be inferred from natural or historical experience by a kind of empirical or inductive analysis; there is simply no theoretical justification for an appeal to historical progress. . . . teleology is nothing more than an assumption imposed on empirical history to suit our own ends . . . ends we have as moral and political agents." "The Fact of Politics: History and Teleology in Kant," *European Journal of Philosophy* 2, no. 1 (1994): 22.

31. Kant, "Idea for a Universal History with a Cosmopolitan Aim," in *Anthropology, History and Education*, ed. Louden and Zöller, 111.

32. Ibid., 116.

33. Ibid., 112. See Krasnoff, "Fact of Politics," 27.

34. See Bruce Buchan, "Explaining War and Peace: Kant and Liberal IR Theory," *Alternatives* 27 (2002): 419–22.

35. Kant, "Idea for a Universal History with a Cosmopolitan Aim," in *Anthropology, History and Education*, ed. Louden and Zöller, 113.

36. Brad Evans, *Liberal Terror* (Cambridge: Polity, 2013), 199.

37. See Georg Cavallar, "Kantian Perspectives on Democratic Peace," *Review of International Studies* 27, no. 2 (2001): 247.

38. Kant, "Idea for a Universal History with a Cosmopolitan Aim," in *Anthropology, History and Education*, ed. Louden and Zöller, 114.

39. Ibid., 114–15.

40. Ibid., 116. Kant changes his mind regarding the balance of power in *Toward Perpetual Peace*; see Doyle, "Kant, Liberal Legacies, and Foreign Affairs, Part 2," 345. See also Hans Saner, *Kant's Political Thought: Its Origins and Development* (Chicago: University of Chicago Press, 1973), 246.

41. See Allison, "Teleology and History in Kant," 30.

42. Kant, "Idea for a Universal History with a Cosmopolitan Aim," in *Anthropology, History and Education*, ed. Louden and Zöller, 119. In the essay "On the Use of Teleological Principles in Philosophy," *Anthropology, History and Education*, trans. and ed. R. Louden and G. Zöller (Cambridge: Cambridge University Press, 2007), Kant links "pure practical teleology" to a "*doctrine of pure ends* (which can be no other doctrine than that

of *freedom*) . . . since a pure practical teleology, i.e., a morals, is destined to realize its ends in the world, it may not neglect their *possibility* in the world, both as regards the *final* causes given in it and the suitability of the *supreme cause of the world* to a whole of all ends as effect—hence natural *teleology* as well as the possibility of a nature in general, i.e., transcendental philosophy. This serves to secure objective reality to the doctrine of practically pure ends with respect to the possibility of the object in exercise, namely the objective reality of the end that this doctrine prescribes as to be effectuated in the world," 217.

43. Kant, "Idea for a Universal History with a Cosmopolitan Aim," in *Anthropology, History and Education*, ed. Louden and Zöller, 119.

44. Kant, "Idea for a Universal History with a Cosmopolitan Aim," in *Kant's Idea for a Universal History with a Cosmopolitan Aim: A Critical Guide*, ed. Rorty and Schmidt, 11.

45. Ibid., 12.

46. Ibid., 17.

47. Moses Mendelssohn, *Jerusalem: Or on the Religious Power and Judaism*, trans. Allan Arkush, introduction and commentary Alexander Altmann (Hanover, NH: University Press of New England, 1983), 42.

48. Ibid., 95.

49. As Mendelssohn writes, "In reality, the human race is—if the metaphor is appropriate—in almost every century, child, adult, and old man at the same time, though in different places and regions of the world," *Jerusalem*, 96.

50. Kant, "Idea for a Universal History with a Cosmopolitan Aim," in *Kant's Idea for a Universal History with a Cosmopolitan Aim: A Critical Guide*, ed. Rorty and Schmidt, 17–18.

51. Moses Mendelssohn, *Jerusalem*, section II, 44–47, quoted in Immanuel Kant, "On the Common Saying: That May Be Correct in Theory, But It Is of No Use in Practice," in *Practical Philosophy*, 305.

52. Kant, "On the Common Saying," 305–6.

53. Mendelssohn, *Jerusalem*, 96.

54. Kant's interpretation of Mendelssohn is problematic. In his introduction to Mendelssohn's *Jerusalem*, Alexander Altmann (26) refers to Kant's tendency to project "his own ideas upon Mendelssohn," in relation to religion. In my reading, Kant also seems to have projected his own fears about the purposelessness of nature onto Mendelssohn.

55. Kant, "On the Common Saying," 305.

56. Ibid., 306–7.

57. Ibid., 308–9.

58. Mendelssohn, *Jerusalem*, 97, 120.

59. Williams, *Kant's Political Philosophy*, 5.

60. Kant, "Toward Perpetual Peace," in *Practical Philosophy*, 340.

61. Ibid., 341.

62. Ibid., 342.

63. Ibid., 340.

64. Ibid., 341.

65. Kant, "On the Common Saying," 306.

66. Ibid., 307.

67. Howard Williams correctly identifies the significance of *Toward Perpetual Peace* as being "not simply a book commenting from a philosophical perspective on what can be done about politics. It represents a point of culmination of Kant's critical enterprise, at least in so far as its practical aspect is concerned," "Back from the USSR," 28.

68. Kant, "Toward Perpetual Peace," in *Practical Philosophy*, 326.

69. Ibid.

70. Ibid.

71. Williams, *Kant's Political Philosophy*, 59–60.

72. Ibid., 60.

73. Pierre Laberge, "Kant on Justice and the Law of Nations," in *International Society: Diverse Ethical Perspectives*, ed. David R. Mapel and Terry Nardin (Princeton: Princeton University Press, 1999), 84.

74. Kant, "Metaphysics of Morals," 387.

75. Flikschuh, *Kant and Modern Political Philosophy*, 11.

76. Ibid., 89, 90–91.

77. Ibid., 101. To those who might object that such a finding contradicts Kant's strict criteria regarding morally worthy action, Elisabeth Ellis counters that "respect of the moral law in general provides sufficient incentive for human beings to follow it. . . . Regarding legal, as opposed to moral, action, however, Kant argues that material incentives, such as threat of punishment, are the appropriate motivation for human actions." Elisabeth Ellis, *Kant's Politics: Provisional Theory for an Uncertain World* (New Haven: Yale University Press, 2005), 117.

78. Ellis, *Kant's Politics*, 112.

79. Ibid., 114.

80. Ibid., 80.

81. Flikschuh, *Kant and Modern Political Philosophy*, 176.

82. Ellis, *Kant's Politics*, 135.

83. Mark N. Franke, *Global Limits*, 108.

84. Pierre Laberge, "Kant on Justice and the Law of Nations," 85.

85. Kant, "Toward Perpetual Peace," in *Practical Philosophy*, 321.

86. Ibid., 321n.

87. Ibid., 323.

88. Ibid., 322n.

89. Ibid., 325.

90. Ibid., 326.

91. Ibid., 336.

92. Ibid., 328.

93. Ibid., 327.

94. Ibid.

95. Ibid., 326–27.

96. Ibid.

97. Ibid., 329.

98. Ibid., 329–30.

99. Ibid., 327. See Sharon Anderson Gold, *Unnecessary Evil: History and Moral Progress in the Philosophy of Immanuel Kant* (Albany: State University of New York Press, 2001).

100. Kant, "Toward Perpetual Peace," in *Practical Philosophy*, trans. and ed. Gregor, 320.

101. Ibid., 335.

102. Ibid.

103. Ibid.

104. Kant, "Idea for a Universal History with a Cosmopolitan Aim," in *Anthropology, History and Education*, ed. Zöller and Louden, 113.

105. Kant, "Toward Perpetual Peace," in *Practical Philosophy*, 320, 336.

106. Ibid., 328.

107. Ibid.

108. Williams and Booth, "Kant: Theorist beyond Limits."

109. Kant, "Toward Perpetual Peace," in *Practical Philosophy*, trans. and ed. Gregor, 328. The substitution is controversial among Kantians. Howard Williams, for example, regards Kant's position as "paradoxical and almost contradictory . . . He is both advocating an international state as the ultimate goal, but not advocating it as something to be realized in the immediate or near future. It is an objective to be put to the back of our minds, but it is an objective we always must have *in mind*. This seeming paradox is unavoidable, he thinks, if we are to adhere to a political course of action that will succeed," *Kant's Political Philosophy*, 256.

110. Kant, "Toward Perpetual Peace," in *Practical Philosophy*, 328. Kant "becomes less optimistic regarding the possibility of the complete realization of peace," Pauline Kleingeld, "Six Varieties of Cosmopolitanism in Late Eighteenth-Century Germany," *Journal of the History of Ideas* 60, no. 3 (1999): 510. For a good treatment of Kant's decision to frame his international project in terms of a federation, see Kjartan Koch Mikalsen, "In Defense of Kant's League of States," *Law and Philosophy* 30, no. 3 (2011).

111. Kant, "Toward Perpetual Peace," in *Practical Philosophy*, 331.

112. Ibid., 335.

113. Ibid., 336.

114. Williams, *Kant's Political Philosophy*, 261.

115. See Pauline Kleingeld, "Kant's Changing Cosmopolitanism," in *Kant's Idea for a Universal History with a Cosmopolitan Aim: A Critical Guide*, ed. Amélie Oksenberg Rorty and James Schmidt (Cambridge: Cambridge University Press, 2009), 172.

116. In "Proclamation of the Imminent Conclusion of a Treaty of Perpetual Peace in Philosophy," Kant writes that "nature is presented in man even prior to his humanity, and thus in its generality, just as it acts in the beast, merely in order to evolve forces which can subsequently turn man to laws of freedom; though this activity, and its arousal are not practical, but still merely mechanical." In Immanuel Kant, *Theoretical Philosophy after 1781*, ed. Henry Allison and Peter Heath, trans. Gary Hatfield and Michael Friedman (Cambridge: Cambridge University Press, 2002), 453. See J. B. Schneewind, "Good out of Evil: Kant and the Idea of Unsocial Sociability," in *Kant's Idea for a Universal History with a Cosmopolitan Aim: A Critical Guide*, ed. Amélie Oksenberg Rorty and James Schmidt (Cambridge: Cambridge University Press, 2009), 95.

117. Immanuel Kant, *Observations on the Feeling of the Beautiful and Sublime*, trans. John T. Goldthwait (Berkeley: University of California Press, 1960), 62–63.

118. Kant, *Anthropology from a Pragmatic Point of View*, ed. R. B. Louden (Cambridge: Cambridge University Press, 2006), 43.

119. Kant, "Toward Perpetual Peace," in *Practical Philosophy*, 337.

120. On this point, see Katrin Flikschuh, "Reason and Nature: Kant's Teleological Argument in *Perpetual Peace*," in *A Companion to Kant*, ed. Graham Bird (Oxford: Blackwell, 2010), 390.

121. Kant, *Critique of the Power of Judgment*, 146

122. Kant, "Toward Perpetual Peace," in *Practical Philosophy*, 330.

123. For Kant's troubling equation of the happy but "undeveloped" Tahitians with mere animals, see Behnke, "'Eternal Peace' as the Graveyard of the Political."

124. Kant, "Toward Perpetual Peace," in *Practical Philosophy*, trans. and ed. Gregor, 339.

125. Ibid., 339–40.

126. Ibid., 340.

127. Ibid., 345.

128. Kant, *Critique of the Power of Judgment*, 300.

129. Paul Guyer, "The Crooked Timber of Mankind," in *Kant's Idea for a Universal History with a Cosmopolitan Aim: A Critical Guide*, ed. Amélie Oksenberg Rorty and James Schmidt (Cambridge: Cambridge University Press, 2009), 131ff.

130. Howard Williams, *Kant's Political Philosophy*, 22.

131. Ibid., 135.

132. Stanley Hoffmann, *Duties beyond Borders: On the Limits and Possibilities of Ethical International Politics* (Syracuse: Syracuse University Press, 1981), 140.

133. Williams, "Kant: The Idea of Perpetual Peace."

134. Niccolò Machiavelli, "The Prince," in *Machiavelli: The Chief Works and Others*, vol. 1, trans. Allan Gilbert (Durham: Duke University Press, 1957), 26.

135. Kant, *Anthropology from a Pragmatic Point of View*, 103.

136. See Joseph M. Knippenberg, "The Politics of Kant's Philosophy," in *Kant and Po-*

206 NOTES TO PAGES 98–104

litical Philosophy: The Contemporary Legacy, ed. Ronald Beiner and William James Booth (New Haven: Yale University Press, 1993), 167.

137. Kant's most developed treatment of the transformative effect of the Enlightenment on political life is "An Answer to the Question: What Is Enlightenment?," in Practical Philosophy. See Yirimahu Yovel, Kant and the Philosophy of History (Princeton: Princeton University Press, 1980), 153. See also Ciaran Cronin, "Kant's Politics of Enlightenment," Journal of the Philosophy of History 41, no. 1 (2003): 51–80.

138. Kant, "Toward Perpetual Peace," in Practical Philosophy, trans. and ed. Gregor, 340.

139. Ibid. See also Kant, "On a Supposed Right to Lie From Philanthropy," in Practical Philosophy, trans. and ed. Mary Gregor (Cambridge: Cambridge University Press, 1996): "Right must never be accommodated to politics, but politics must always be accommodated to right," 614. See Williams, Kant's Political Philosophy, 41–49.

140. See Rohlf, "Transition from Nature to Freedom," 357.

141. David Hume, A Treatise of Human Nature, ed. David Fate Norton and Mary J. Norton (Oxford: Oxford University Press, 2000), 302.

142. Kant, "Metaphysics of Morals," 482.

143. Kimberly Hutchings, "The Possibility of Judgement: Moralizing and Theorizing in International Relations," Review of International Studies 18, no. 1 (1992): 53.

144. Kant, Critique of Pure Reason, xxx.

145. Kant, "Critique of Practical Reason," in Practical Philosophy, 209.

146. Flikschuh, Kant's Political Philosophy, 81.

147. As William Rasch has argued, "Even when law structures and limits violence, peace is not the fullness, the absence of which would be war. Rather, peace as public security is a continuous war against war, a pacification of war, not peace in the emphatic sense that Kant has in mind." William Rasch, "Kant's Project of Perpetual Pacification," Law & Critique 19, no. 1 (2008), 29.

148. Kant, "Toward Perpetual Peace," in Practical Philosophy, 331.

149. Ibid., 341.

Chapter 4

1. Immanuel Kant, "Conjectural Beginning of Human History," in Anthropology, History and Education, ed. R. Louden and G. Zöller (Cambridge: Cambridge University Press, 2007), 169.

2. Immanuel Kant, "Review of Moscati's work Of the Corporeal Essential Differences Between the Structure of Animals and Humans," in Anthropology, History and Education, ed. R. Louden and G. Zöller (Cambridge: Cambridge University Press, 2007), 79.

3. The human body's unnaturalness does not prevent Kant from elsewhere making the argument that the human being is at the same time "the most noble of animals. He is built in such a way that his posture and limbs show that he is laid out for more actions

than any other animal," Immanuel Kant, *Physische Geographie Hesse*, quoted in Robert Louden, "The Second Part of Morals," in *Essays on Kant's Anthropology*, ed. B. Jacobs and P. Kain (Cambridge: Cambridge University Press, 2003), 96.

4. Immanuel Kant, *Universal Natural History and Theory of the Heavens*, trans. S. L. Jaki (Edinburgh: Scottish Academic Press, 1981), 187.

5. Ibid., 188.

6. Ibid., 196.

7. Kant, *Anthropology from a Pragmatic Point of View*, 30.

8. Immanuel Kant, "Metaphysik Mrongovius," in *Lectures on Metaphysics*, trans. and ed. K. Ameriks and S. Nargon (Cambridge: Cambridge University Press, 1997).

9. See Rudolf Makkreel, "Kant on the Scientific Status of Psychology, Anthropology, and History," in *Kant and the Sciences*, ed. Eric Watson (Oxford: Oxford University Press, 2001).

10. Kant, *Observations on the Feeling of the Beautiful and the Sublime*, 60.

11. Ibid., 61.

12. Ibid., 74.

13. Kant, *Anthropology*, 177mn. Explanatory note: mn refers to Kant's handwritten manuscript notes. For the interrelationship of aesthetics and morality in a teleological context, see Paul Guyer, "Beauty, Freedom, and Morality: Kant's Lectures on Anthropology and the Development of His Aesthetic Theory," in *Essays on Kant's Anthropology*, ed. B. Jacobs and P. Kain (Cambridge: Cambridge University Press, 2003).

14. Immanuel Kant, "Essay on the Maladies of the Head," in *Anthropology, History and Education*, ed. R. Louden and G. Zöller (Cambridge: Cambridge University Press), 65.

15. Ibid. Reflecting on Arsenij Goulyga's biography of Kant, Monique David-Menard and Alison Ross describe this rarely discussed essay as a "reflection on the interconnected development of the state of society and the troubles of the mind," in "Kant's 'An Essay on the Maladies of the Mind' and *Observations on the Feeling of the Beautiful and the Sublime*," *Hypatia* 15, no. 4 (2000): 83.

16. Kant, "Essay on the Maladies of the Head," 67.

17. Ibid., 68.

18. Roger J. Sullivan draws the obvious parallel with original sin: "[t]he historical record confirmed in Kant's mind the fundamental rightness of the Christian doctrine of Original Sin in which he had been reared." Sullivan goes on to locate Kant within "the Augustinian tradition in Christianity, with its deep belief in the pervasive reality of human concupiscence." "The Influence of Kant's Anthropology on His Moral Theory," *Review of Metaphysics* 49, no. 1 (1995): 86 and 92.

19. Kant's treatment of "I" is complex. In the *Anthropology*, Kant outlines the differences between the various aspects of "I": "The I in every judgment is neither an intuition nor a concept, and not at all a determination of an object, but an act of understanding by the determining subject as such, and the consciousness of oneself; pure apperception

itself therefore belongs merely to logic (without any matter and content). On the other hand, the I of inner sense, that is, of the perception and observation of oneself is not the subject of judgment, but an object," 31n.

20. Thomas Sturm, "Freedom and the Human Sciences: Hume's Science of Man versus Kant's Pragmatic Anthropology," *Kant Yearbook* 3 (2011): 37.

21. Kant, *Anthropology*, 16.

22. Ibid., 18.

23. Ibid.

24. Ibid., 20.

25. Ibid., 28–29.

26. Gary Hatfield, "Kant and Empirical Psychology in the 18th Century," *Psychological Science* 9, no. 6 (1998): 426.

27. Kant, *Anthropology*, 29.

28. Ibid., 32.

29. Ibid., 33.

30. Job Zinkstok, "Anthropology, Empirical Psychology, and Applied Logic," *Kant Yearbook* 3 (2011): 126.

31. Zöller, "Kant's Political Anthropology," *Kant Yearbook* 3, no. 1 (2011): 147.

32. Kant, *Anthropology*, 42.

33. Ibid., 44.

34. Alix Cohen, "Kant's Concept of Freedom and the Human Sciences," *Canadian Journal of Philosophy* 39, no. 1 (2009): 132.

35. Patrick Frierson, "The Moral Importance of Politeness in Kant's Anthropology," *Kantian Review* 9 (2005): 116.

36. Kant, *Anthropology*, 75.

37. Ibid., 103.

38. Emil Fackenheim, "Kant's Concept of History," *Kant Studien* 48, nos. 1–4 (1957): 397.

39. Immanuel Kant, "Conflict of the Faculties," in *Religion and Rational Theology*, trans. and ed. Allen Wood and George Di Giovanni (Cambridge: Cambridge University Press, 1996), 298.

40. Kant, *Anthropology*, 126.

41. Susan Meld Shell identifies the writings of Count Verri as the source of Kant's embrace of pain as the primary motivator of human action. "Kant's 'True Economy of Human Nature': Rousseau, Count Verri, and the Problem of Happiness," in *Essays on Kant's Anthropology*, ed. B. Jacobs and P. Cain (Cambridge: Cambridge University Press, 2003), 195.

42. Kant, *Anthropology*, 130–31.

43. On this issue, see Sidney Axinn, "Ambivalence: Kant's View of Human Nature," *Kant Studien* 72, no. 2 (1981): 169, and Sullivan, "Influence of Kant's Anthropology on His Moral Theory," 81.

44. Kant, *Anthropology*, 134.

45. Ibid., 137.

46. Ibid., 140–41.

47. Ibid., 149.

48. Ibid.

49. Ibid., 151. Passions are uniquely human qualities and presented as insurmountable problems: "The manias for honor, revenge, and so forth, just because they are never completely satisfied, are therefore counted among the passions as illnesses for which there is only a palliative remedy," 166.

50. Ibid., 166.

51. Ibid.

52. Ibid., 170.

53. Ibid.

54. Kant maintains that "the passions in general, as violent as they may be as sensible incentives, are still sheer weaknesses in view of what reason prescribes to the human being," ibid., 172. This may be the case in relation to reason, but the political is not always a rational aspect of human life, at least not in the case of human beings.

55. Ibid., 173.

56. Ibid., 174.

57. Ibid., 175.

58. Ibid., 177 (square brackets and parentheses in original).

59. In an important marginal note, Kant claims that the "highest level of culture is when the state of war between peoples is in equilibrium, and the means to this is the question of who among them shall inquire whether war shall be or not." Ibid.

60. Ibid.

61. See Louden's account of the role that character plays in Kant's anthropology in *Kant's Impure Ethics*, 74ff.

62. Kant, *Anthropology*, 226.

63. Ibid.

64. Ibid., 228.

65. Ibid., 229.

66. Ibid., 231.

67. Ibid., 232.

68. Ibid.

69. Immanuel Kant, "Idea for a Universal History," in *Anthropology, History and Education*, ed. R. Louden and G. Zöller, 117.

70. G. Felicitas Munzel, "Kant on Moral Education, or 'Enlightenment' and the Liberal Arts," *Review of Metaphysics* 57, no. 1 (2003): 54.

71. Immanuel Kant, "Essays regarding the Philanthropinum," in *Anthropology, History and Education*, trans. R. Louden and G. Zöller (Cambridge: Cambridge University Press, 2007), 103; see also Georg Cavallar's excellent paper, "Cosmopolitan Education in the 1770s: Basedow and Kant," delivered at the Annual Conference of the Philosophy of

Education Society of Great Britain, New College, Oxford, March 30, 2012. http://www.philosophy-of-education.org/uploads/papers2012/Cavallar.pdf

72. Immanuel Kant, "Lectures on Pedagogy," in *Anthropology, History and Education*, ed. R. Louden and G. Zöller (Cambridge: Cambridge University Press, 2007), 439.

73. Ibid., 442.

74. Ibid., 443. This is true of human beings before the propensity to evil takes effect.

75. On the difference between predisposition and propensity, and the precedence of the latter over the former, see Kant, "Religion Within the Boundaries of Mere Reason," 121.

76. Ibid., 95.

77. Kant, "Lectures on Pedagogy," 459–60.

78. Ibid., 473.

79. Ibid., 474–76. See also Kate A. Moran, "Can Kant Have an Account of Moral Education?," *Journal of Philosophy of Education* 43, no. 4 (2009): 471–84.

80. Kant, "Lectures on Pedagogy," 476.

81. Kant, *Anthropology*, 230.

82. Ibid., 233.

83. Ibid., 235.

84. Ibid., 236 (square brackets in original).

85. Ibid., 236–37.

86. Ibid., 238.

87. Ibid., 233.

88. Kant, "On the Common Saying," *Practical Philosophy*, 308–9. See also Martin A. Bertman, "Kant's Orientation," *History of European Ideas* 28, no. 4 (2002): 263–80.

89. See Sharon Anderson-Gold, "Kant's Ethical Anthropology and the Critical Foundations of the Philosophy of History," *History of Philosophy Quarterly* 11, no. 4 (1994): 405–19.

90. Kant, *Anthropology*, 233.

91. Immanuel Kant, "Toward Perpetual Peace," *Practical Philosophy*, 332.

Chapter 5

1. Kant, *Critique of Pure Reason*, trans. and ed. Guyer and Wood, 117.

2. Immanuel Kant, "On the Miscarriage of all Philosophical Trials in Theodicy," in *Religion and Rational Theology*, trans. and ed. Allen Wood and George Di Giovanni (Cambridge: Cambridge University Press, 1996), 36–37.

3. On this point, see Matthew Caswell, "The Value of Humanity and Kant's Conception of Evil," *Journal of the History of Philosophy* 44, no. 4 (2006): 645.

4. Paul Formosa, "Kant on the Radical Evil of Human Nature," *Philosophical Forum* 38, no. 3 (2007): 235.

5. Immanuel Kant, "Religion Within the Boundaries of Mere Reason," in *Religion*

and Rational Theology, trans. and ed. Allen Wood and George Di Giovanni (Cambridge: Cambridge University Press, 1996), 77.

6. Ibid., 78.

7. Ibid, 83–84.

8. Ibid., 85.

9. Ibid., 89ff. Stephen R. Grimm, "Kant's Argument for Radical Evil," *European Journal of Philosophy* 10, no. 2 (2002).

10. Kant, *Religion and Rational Theology*, 92.

11. Henry E. Allison, "On the Very Idea of a Propensity to Evil," *Journal of Value Inquiry* 36 (2002): 347. In his excellent account of the continued influence of original sin in international political theory, Vassilios Paipais identifies a key issue: "Kant here proposes a mystery as solution to a puzzle. It appears that the only possible way to reconcile the fact of sin with the rational conditions of moral accountability is to posit a profound disjunction at the core of human identity." "First Image Revisited: Human Nature, Original Sin and International Relations," *Journal of International Relations and Development* (2016).

12. Kant, "Religion Within the Boundaries of Mere Reason," 95.

13. Ibid., 93. Kant presents the original disposition as being prior to the evil propensity and thus as having "precedence of domicile in humankind," 121.

14. Kant, "Religion Within the Boundaries of Mere Reason," 103.

15. Ibid., 107. Kant makes the case that the best mankind can hope to achieve is the *approximation* of Christ's standards of behavior. For a good discussion of Kant's use of Christ as moral exemplar, see Daniel Whistler, "Kant's *Imitatio Christi*," *International Journal of the Philosophy of Religion* 67 (2010).

16. Kant, "Religion Within the Boundaries of Mere Reason," 105.

17. Ibid., 108.

18. Ibid., 113. On Kant's use of Christian phraseology, see Gordon E. Michalson, "The Inscrutability of Moral Evil in Kant," *Thomist: A Speculative Quarterly Review* 51, no. 2 (1987): 267–68.

19. Kant, "Religion Within the Boundaries of Mere Reason," 109.

20. Ibid., 121.

21. Ibid., 129.

22. Ibid. Allison, "On the Very Idea of a Propensity to Evil," 344–45.

23. Kant, "Religion Within the Boundaries of Mere Reason," 81.

24. Ibid., 153.

25. Ibid., 130.

26. Ibid., 131.

27. Ibid., 130.

28. Ibid., 133.

29. Ibid., 135.

30. Ibid. See Robert S. Taylor, "Kant's Political Religion: The Transparency of Perpetual Peace and the Highest Good," *Review of Politics* 72, no. 1 (2010): 6.

31. Kant, "Religion Within the Boundaries of Mere Reason," 135.

32. Ibid., 139.

33. Ibid., 140.

34. Ibid., 146.

35. Ibid., 152.

36. Ibid., 153.

37. Kant, "Conflict of the Faculties," 297.

38. Ferenc Fehér, "Practical Reason in the Revolution: Kant's Dialogue with the French Revolution," *Social Research* 56, no. 1 (1989): 168.

39. Kant, "Conflict of the Faculties," 300.

40. Ibid., 301.

41. Ibid., 302.

42. Ibid.

43. Ibid., 304.

44. Ibid., 304–5.

45. Lewis White Beck, "Kant and the Right of Revolution," *Journal of the History of Ideas* 32, no. 3 (1971): 422.

46. Kant, "Conflict of the Faculties," 300.

47. Ibid., 307.

48. Ibid.

49. Ibid.

50. Louis Dupré recognizes abderitism is "logically irrefutable," but Kant rejects it on moral grounds because abderite pessimism "rules out what the moral imperative requires, namely, that moral life follow an ascending line in the human community as well as in the individual." Louis Dupré, "Kant's Theory of History and Progress," *Review of Metaphysics* 51, no. 4 (1998): 821.

51. Immanuel Kant, "The Only Possible Argument in Support of a Demonstration of the Existence of God," in *Theoretical Philosophy: 1755–1770*, trans. and ed. David Walford in collaboration with Ralf Meerbote (Cambridge: Cambridge University Press, 1992), 201.

52. Kant, *CPR*, 493.

53. Ibid., 585.

54. Ibid., 611.

55. Kant, *Critique of Pure Reason*, trans. Werner S. Pluhar (Indianapolis: Hackett, 1996), 616. Immanuel Kant, *Opus Postumum*, ed. Eckart Förster, trans. Eckart Förster and Michael Rosen (Cambridge: Cambridge University Press, 1993). "It is an ideal: There is not and cannot be a question as to whether such an object exists, since the concept is transcendent," 231.

56. Kant, "Religion Within the Boundaries of Mere Reason," 165: "Since by himself the human being cannot realize the idea of the supreme good inseparably bound up with the pure moral disposition, either with respect to the happiness which is part of that good or with respect to the union of the human beings necessary to the fulfilment

of the end, and yet there is also in him the duty to promote the idea, he finds himself driven to believe in the cooperation of the management of a moral ruler of the world, through which alone this end is possible." Notice the phrase "driven to believe"—driven to believe to plug the gaps in the rest of the Kantian project.

57. Kant, "Religion Within the Boundaries of Mere Reason," 135.

58. Ibid., 133.

59. Ibid., 60n.

60. Ibid., 133–34.

61. Ibid., 165–66.

62. Kant, *Critique of Pure Reason*, trans. Werner S. Pluhar, 753: "And I am sure that nothing can shake this faith; for that would overturn my moral principles themselves, which I cannot renounce without being detestable in my own eyes."

63. Kant, "Religion Within the Boundaries of Mere Reason," 207.

64. On the (occasionally problematic) consistency of Kant's theological concepts, see Ian Logan, "Whatever Happened to Kant's Ontological Argument?," *Philosophy and Phenomenological Research* 74, no. 2 (March 2007).

65. See the discussion of God in chapter 3 of Pamela Sue Anderson and Jordan Bell, *Kant and Theology* (London: Continuum, 2010).

66. Peter Byrne, *Kant on God* (Farnham: Ashgate, 2007), 89.

67. Kant, "Lectures on the Philosophical Doctrine of Religion," in *Religion and Rational Theology*, trans. and ed. Allen Wood and George Di Giovanni (Cambridge: Cambridge University Press, 1996), 356.

68. Kant, "Lectures on the Philosophical Doctrine of Religion," 356.

69. Ibid., 357. On God as a postulate of practical reason, see Wood, *Kant's Moral Religion*. See also Dennis Vanden Auweele, "Atheism, Radical Evil, and Kant," *Philosophy & Theology* 22, nos. 1–2 (2010): 168.

70. Kant, "Lectures on the Philosophical Doctrine of Religion," 407.

71. Ibid.

72. Ibid.

73. Allen Wood, "Rational Theology, Moral Faith, and Religion," in *The Cambridge Companion to Kant*, edited by Paul Guyer (Cambridge: Cambridge University Press, 1992), 403–4.

74. Kant, "Lectures on the Philosophical Doctrine of Religion," 409.

75. Ibid., 421.

76. Ibid., 427.

77. Ibid., 428.

78. Ibid., 430.

79. Kant, *Opus Postumum*, 200.

80. Kant, "Lectures on the Philosophical Doctrine of Religion," 442.

81. Kant, *Opus Postumum*, 223.

82. Allen Wood, *Kant's Moral Religion* (Ithaca: Cornell University Press, 1970), 166.

83. Anderson and Bell, *Kant and Theology*, 53.

84. Wood, *Kant's Moral Religion*, 178.

85. Ibid., 236.

Conclusion

1. Kant, "Lectures on Pedagogy," 480.

2. Kant, "Conflict of the Faculties," 288.

3. On the distinction between secular *Weltgeschichte* and soteriological *Heilsgeschichte*, see Löwith, *Meaning in History*, v.

4. Jacob Taubes, *Occidental Eschatology*, trans. David Ratmoko (Stanford: Stanford University Press, 2009), 13.

5. Jürgen Moltmann, *Theology of Hope: On the Ground and the Implications of a Christian Eschatology* (Minneapolis: Fortress Press, 1993), 46. Moltmann identifies the key role of the ideas contained within the "almost forgotten treatise on *Das Ende Aller Dinge*" in the development of post-Kantian German theology, most especially in the works of Karl Barth and Rudolf Bultmann.

6. Taubes, *Occidental Eschatology*, 132.

7. Although distinct in nature from his eschatological predecessors, as a philosopher "concerned with a unity of universal history and with its progress toward an ultimate goal or at least toward a 'better world,'" Kant is "still in the line of prophetic and messianic monotheism," Löwith, *Meaning in History*, 19.

8. Donald MacKinnon, *A Study in Ethical Theory* (London: Black, 1957), 103.

9. Don Cupitt, "Kant and the Negative Theology," in *The Philosophical Frontiers of Christian Theology: Essays Presented to D.M. MacKinnon*, ed. Brian Hebblethwaite and Stewart Sutherland (Cambridge: Cambridge University Press, 1982), 65.

10. *CPR*, 7–8.

11. Ibid., 8.

12. Kant, *Prolegomena to Any Future Metaphysics That Will Be Able to Come Forward as Science with Selections from the Critique of Pure Reason*, trans. and ed. Gary Hatfield, rev. ed. (Cambridge: Cambridge University Press, 2004), 51.

13. Kant, "Lectures on Metaphysik L2," in *Lectures on Metaphysics*, trans. and ed. K. Ameriks and S. Nargon (Cambridge: Cambridge University Press, 1997), 306.

14. Kant, *Prolegomena*, 25.

15. Kant, "Metaphysik Vigilantius," in *Lectures on Metaphysics*, trans. and ed. K. Ameriks and S. Nargon (Cambridge: Cambridge University Press, 1997), 429.

16. Kant, *Critique of Pure Reason*, trans. Werner S. Pluhar (Indianapolis: Hackett, 1996), 7; "Metaphysik Dohna," in *Lectures on Metaphysics*, trans. and ed. K. Ameriks and S. Nargon (Cambridge: Cambridge University Press, 1997), 362. In a nautical metaphor Kant writes that Hume "deposited his ship on the beach of scepticism for safekeeping, where it could then lie and rot," *Prolegomena*, 12.

17. *CPR*, 665. In contrast to Mendelssohn, who viewed Kant as the destroyer of metaphysics, Barth argues that "Kant does not think that in clarifying the relationship of knowledge by pure reason to empirical perception he has destroyed metaphysics, but rather that he has first and foremost made it possible as a science: metaphysics as knowledge by means of practical reason—That then is the true use of pure reason as it at last and finally emerged from the fire of Kant's critique of reason," Karl Barth, *Protestant Theology in the Nineteenth Century: Its Background and History* (London: SCM Press, [1959] 1972), 278.

18. Kant, "Metaphysik Mrongovius," 133.

19. Kant, "Lectures on Metaphysik L1," in *Lectures on Metaphysics*, trans. and ed. K. Ameriks and S. Nargon (Cambridge: Cambridge University Press, 1997), 97.

20. *CPR*, 357.

21. Ibid., 419.

22. Ibid., 420.

23. Ibid., 424.

24. Ibid., 425.

25. Ibid., 424–25.

26. Ibid., 425.

27. Ibid., 521.

28. Ibid., 620.

29. Ibid.

30. Kant, *Prolegomena*, 62.

31. *CPR*, 425.

32. Ibid., 551.

33. Ibid., 553–54.

34. Ibid., 556.

35. Kant's definition of belief can be found in *CPR*, 650.

36. Kant, *Prolegomena*, 111.

37. *CPR*, 379.

38. Kant's traditionalism or conservatism is also noted by Löwith in relation to his understanding of history, *Meaning in History*, 62, 231n. Kant is possibly even more conservative in this regard than Löwith realizes as Kant's "theology of history" does not ultimately relate to "a hidden design of nature," but nature itself is in the final analysis attributable to God, particularly from the viewpoint of practical philosophy and the culmination of history associated with it. Milbank stresses the extent to which Kant's "practical reason" remains Leibnizian in that although Kant denies "a rationalist, 'univocal' grasp of finite and infinite in the sphere of understanding," nonetheless he puts forward that mankind is able "in the sphere of reason, to 'determine' the supersensible in our practical willing . . . Only on this basis are we then permitted to posit the ultimate 'transcendental object' (God) as analogically the 'cause' of phenomenal nature," John Milbank, *Theology and Social Theory*, 2nd ed. (Oxford: Blackwell, 2006), 152–53.

39. Philip Clayton argues that the later Kant goes further in works such as *The Critique of Practical Reason*, which he states "makes a plea for the 'objective reality' of God (e.g., V, 135), at least in the context of practical reason, and perhaps beyond it as well." The most important instance of the erosion of the distinction between regulative and constitutive principles is that of the final purpose of creation explored in *The Critique of the Power of Judgment*, in which Kant, according to Clayton, "is clearly casting into question the very boundary between regulative and constitutive . . . his treatment of teleology has introduced a new perspective over against the earlier Critiques, significantly altering the status and function of the concept of God. . . . Second, Kant himself now acknowledges the haziness of the boundary between regulative and constitutive. These two developments . . . point in the direction of a new scope and stronger status for the notion of God," *The Problem of God in Modern Thought* (Grand Rapids: Eerdmans, 2000), 291. Clayton comes to the conclusion that "[f]or Kant, there will always be severe limitations on the knowability of this being. But if Kant is indeed able to speak of God's (transsubjective) existence, then it cannot be that, in the strictest sense, no knowledge of God is possible. . . . Kantians are compelled to treat the concept of God as more than a mere idea of reason," 300–301. One does not have to agree with Clayton's conclusions, but the argument he makes certainly demonstrates the importance of God's role within Kant's philosophy, a role that cannot be easily dismissed without serious ramifications for both Kant's work and even more so for those who disregard the theological and metaphysical elements that underpin its architectonic unity.

40. Donald MacKinnon, *The Problem of Metaphysics* (Cambridge: Cambridge University Press, 1974), 57.

41. Cupitt, "Kant and the Negative Theology," 58.

42. Kant, "Religion within the Boundaries of Mere Reason," in *Religion and Rational Theology*, trans. and ed. A. Wood and G. Di Giovanni (Cambridge: Cambridge University Press, 1996), 88.

43. Ibid., 89.

44. Kant, "Conflict of the Faculties," 242.

45. Kant, "Religion Within the Boundaries of Mere Reason," 122. For Kant's appreciation of the Bible and its "sublime teachings," see Blumenberg, *Legitimacy of the Modern Age*, 114.

46. Kant refers to the evil principle as "the prince of this world" in "Religion Within the Boundaries of Mere Reason," 121. Taubes describes how in both "Gnostic literature and in Paul's writings, the demonic powers are 'the rulers of this world,' and Satan is the 'Prince of this World,'" *Occidental Eschatology*, 28–29. Michael Gillespie points out the importance of Satan's governance of the world for Luther, probably Kant's most pervasive cultural influence from a young age, *The Theological Origins of Modernity* (Chicago: University of Chicago Press), 106.

47. "In opposition to the Stoics Kant declares himself in due form for the words of St Paul in Ephesians 6.12: 'For we wrestle not against flesh and blood (the natural inclina-

tion), but against principalities and powers—against spiritual wickedness,'" Karl Barth, *Protestant Theology*, 295.

48. Kant, "Lectures on the Philosophical Doctrine of Religion," in *Religion and Rational Theology*, ed. Wood and Di Giovanni, 411. Despite what Philip Quinn identifies as Kant's opposition to the "inept" model of inherited evil associated with Augustine, "Original Sin, Radical Evil and Moral Identity," *Faith and Philosophy* 1, no. 2 (1984): 189, Kant translates the Bishop of Hippo's concept of original sin into a form compatible with his philosophy. Original sin, according to Blumenberg, "took for man and upon man the responsibility for the burden oppressing the world," *Legitimacy of the Modern Age*, 133. This burden is actually magnified by the move to radical evil, which "intensified guilt that is both innate in all humans, as far as we know, and inextirpable by human power," Philip L. Quinn, "Saving Faith from Kant's Remarkable Antinomy," *Faith and Philosophy* 7, no. 4 (1990): 421. See also Gillespie, *Theological Origins of Modernity*, 142.

49. Kant, "Religion within the Boundaries of Mere Reason," 77, 79–80. Although it must also be remembered that "[c]onsidered in themselves natural inclinations are good, i.e., not reprehensible, and to want to extirpate them would not only be futile but harmful and blameworthy as well; we must rather only curb them, so that they will not wear each other out but will instead be harmonized into a whole called happiness. Now the reason that accomplishes this is called prudence," 102.

50. Ibid., 83.

51. Ibid., 85.

52. Kant, *Opus Postumum*, 221.

53. On the demiurge: "If one goes by experience, and wishes to judge from it the character of the author, it appears that he has taken no account of happiness, but acts as a despot." Kant, *Opus Postumum*, 175. The Gnostic account of the relationship between the demiurge and the God of redemption revolves around a cosmic confrontation between the two. One could certainly draw an analogy between what Blumenberg refers to as the Gnostic reading of the cosmos as an "order opposed to salvation, the system of a fall" and Kant's systematic mistrust of appearances, *Legitimacy of the Modern Age*, 128. Although Kant's diagnosis of "reality" shares much with Gnosticism's belief in the deceptiveness of the cosmos, his position regarding the ultimate goodness and salvation of nature as a part of divine creation (albeit in need of redemption and harmonization with the will of God) is ultimately closer to that of the post-Gnostic apocatastatic Christianity of Origen.

54. Kant, "Religion within the Boundaries of Mere Reason," 289. "In Marcion's writings the God of creation is indivisible from existence in this world. Apparently Marcion makes no further mention of the creator God preexisting the world. . . . The creator God, who really is the spirit of this world, stands over against the God of that world, who is the God of redemption," Taubes, *Occidental Eschatology*, 29.

55. Kant, "Lectures on the Philosophical Doctrine of Religion," 401–2.

56. Ibid., 412.

57. Kant, "Conflict of the Faculties," 268.

58. "Conjectural Beginning of Human History," in *Anthropology, History and Education*, 169. For Origen, "[c]orporeal matter comes into being as a consequence of the Fall. Although the body becomes the prison of the soul, it is not the case that spirit and matter embody the antithetical principle of good and evil. Matter is also God's creation. The world as place of punishment and a consequence of sin, and the world as God's creation, destined for God, are connected by Origen's idea of punishment as paideusis," Taubes, *Occidental Eschatology*, 74. The similarity between Origen's and Kant's ideas may not be accidental: apocatastasis, according to Taubes, "reemerges" in Pietism (the faith in which Kant was raised, but ultimately rejected), so the idea of an ultimate redemption of nature itself would have been familiar to him. The apocatastatic "doctrine of the 'restoration of all things' inspires not only the mystical elements within Pietism but the Pietistic Enlightenment too. Pietism and the Enlightenment both put their faith in the final abolition of evil," Taubes, *Occidental Eschatology*, 73, 128.

59. "The cornerstones of Origen's theodicy of history are *pronoia* and *paideusis*: providence and education. When providence is understood as an educative process, God's purpose can be fulfilled without hurting [kränken] man's sense of freedom. Punishment means cleansing and is therefore only an episode within the economy of salvation, whose purpose is to disclose the logos," Taubes, *Occidental Eschatology*, 74.

60. Kant, "Conflict of the Faculties," 268. Kant expands on the proper form of the *imitatio Christi* in "Religion Within the Boundaries of Mere Reason," 149.

61. Donald MacKinnon, "Kant's Philosophy of Religion," *Philosophy* 50, no. 192 (1975): 140. Barth makes the interesting observation that "the name of Jesus or Christ never, so far as I can see, flowed from his pen in any of his writings, and that he even found a way of avoiding it in the numerous quotations from the bible which he used in 'Religion'," *Protestant Theology*, 287.

62. Stephen Palmquist, "Kant's Ethics of Grace: Perspectival Solutions to the Moral Difficulties with Divine Assistance," *Journal of Religion* 90, no. 4 (2010): 551.

63. Jacqueline Mariña, "Kant on Grace: A Reply to His Critics," *Religious Studies* 33, no. 4 (1997): 393.

64. In "Religion Within the Boundaries of Mere Reason," Kant advises that the concept of grace must be used sparingly and cautiously, 207. Taubes makes the important point that following the Copernican revolution, "under an empty heaven man's efforts are totally insignificant as far as salvation is concerned. In the Copernican world salvation can only be the work of grace, to which man cannot contribute anything." Taubes also makes clear the links between Kant and Luther in terms of grace: "Kantian philosophy, like Luther's theology, is predicated on the aporia of grace, which alone 'makes possible the victory of good over evil and establishes the Kingdom of God on Earth'," *Occidental Eschatology*, 108, 146.

65. Kant, "Religion within the Boundaries of Mere Reason," 211n.

66. Kant, "Lectures on the Philosophical Doctrine of Religion," 421.

67. Kant, "Religion within the Boundaries of Mere Reason," 148. "Thus, there is a place in Kant's theology for what has traditionally been referred to as prevenient and peculiar grace: we must do as much as lies within our power to become better people. It is only when we have done this that we can hope that God will provide that which is lacking in us," E. C. Galbraith, "Kant and Erasmus," *Scottish Journal of Theology* 46, no. 2 (1993): 196.

68. G. E. Michalson, "Moral Regeneration and Divine Aid in Kant," *Religious Studies* 25, no. 3 (1989): 269–70.

69. Jacqueline Mariña, "Kant on Grace: A Reply to His Critics," *Religious Studies* 33: 385. Radical evil for Mariña "can be defined in terms of a decision not to be receptive of God's grace," 385.

70. According to Philip Quinn, "we must postulate an atemporal source for human freedom if it is to be rendered compatible with the complete determinism of the temporal realm of phenomena." Quinn, "Saving Faith from Kant's Remarkable Antinomy," 419.

71. Ibid., 421.

72. Immanuel Kant, "Toward Eternal Peace," in *Principles of Lawful Politics: Immanuel Kant's Philosophic Draft "Towards Eternal Peace"*, ed. Wolfgang Schwarz (Aalen: Scientia-Verlag, 1988), 76.

73. Kant, "Toward Eternal Peace," 115.

74. Ibid., 123.

75. Ibid., 59.

76. Ibid.

77. Ibid., 75.

78. Ibid., 96–97.

79. Kant, "Toward Perpetual Peace," in *Political Writings*, 2nd ed., ed. Hans Reiss, trans. H. B. Nisbet (Cambridge: Cambridge University Press, 1991), 112.

80. Kant, "Toward Eternal Peace," 101.

81. Ibid., 101–2.

82. Ibid., 110.

83. Ibid., 88.

84. Ibid. Kant's distinction—and the significance of the distinction in terms of what it means for human existence—is almost identical to that of Giambattista Vico: "What distinguishes the belief in providence from that in fate or chance is that divine providence uses for the attainment of its universal ends the free, though corrupted, will of man. The doctrine of fate ignores the dialectic between providential necessity and the freedom of the will, while the Epicurean doctrine of chance reduces freedom to mere capriciousness. The principles of providence and freedom are, however, equally true and important," Löwith, *Meaning in History*, 124.

85. Kant, "Lectures on Pedagogy," in *Immanuel Kant, Anthropology, History and Education*, 480. Here Kant reveals an affinity with Augustine, in whose work "[t]he historical process as such, the *saeculum*, shows only the hopeless succession and cessation of gen-

erations. If seen with the eyes of faith, however, the whole historical process of sacred and secular history appears as a preordained *ordinatio Dei*," Löwith, *Meaning in History*, 170.

86. Kant, "Toward Eternal Peace," 88.

87. Ibid.

88. This providential reading of the future avoids the problem Taubes identifies in relation to the "passive style of apocalypticism . . . motivated by a lack of faith in mankind. The long period of suffering, the repeated disappointments, the crushing power of evil, the enormous colossus of the demonic kingdom of this world would all contribute to the despair apocalypticism felt about redemption, if redemption were at the mercy of mankind," *Occidental Eschatology*, 34. Kant avoids despair by investing faith *ultimately* in providence and God rather than human beings.

89. Kant, "Toward Eternal Peace," 107.

90. Ibid., 112.

91. Ibid., 112–13. "The history of human evolution itself warrants only cultural progress. . . . But does not warrant moral improvement, which is founded upon the principle of holiness. . . . Moral progress is not founded upon the improvement of mores but on the transformation of the mind. . . . The divine spark in the depths of the soul, which radical evil is unable to destroy, enables the revolution to come about," Taubes, *Occidental Eschatology*, 145.

92. Kant, "Toward Eternal Peace," 116.

93. Ibid., 119.

94. Ibid. The republic of devils is not a "true" republic as it is not the product of good will and rational morality.

95. Ibid., 119.

96. Ibid., 49–50.

97. Ibid., 84.

98. Ibid., 100: "nature irresistibly wills that right finally gain the upper hand. What one here neglects to do will at last generate itself, though with much discomfort."

99. Ibid., 103.

100. Ibid., 67.

101. Ibid., 62.

102. Ibid., 64.

103. Objective end of humanity: "This ultimate purpose of pure practical reason is the highest good, so far as it is possible in the world, though it is to be sought not merely in what Nature can furnish, namely happiness (the greatest amount of pleasure); it lies, rather, in what is also the supreme requirement, or condition, under which alone reason can accord happiness to the rational world-being, namely that the latter's behavior should simultaneously conform to the utmost with the moral law." Immanuel Kant, "What Real Progress has Metaphysics Made in Germany Since the Time of Leibniz and Wolff?," in *Theoretical Philosophy After 1781*, ed. and trans. Henry E. Allison and Peter

Heath, and trans. Gary Hatfield and Michael Friedman (Cambridge: Cambridge University Press, 2002), 383.

104. A good analysis of *Toward Perpetual Peace* in the light of the third *Critique* is to be found in Irmgard Scherer, "Kant's Eschatology in *Zum Ewigen Frieden*: The Concept of Purposiveness to Guarantee Perpetual Peace," in *Proceedings of the Eighth Annual Kant Conference*, vol. 2, part 1, ed. Hoke Robinson (Milwaukee: Marquette University Press, 1995), 437–44. In this short piece, Scherer correctly identifies the importance of purposiveness but conflates or is unaware of the difference between the purposiveness of nature and that of providence.

105. Kant, "Toward Eternal Peace," 88.

106. In this sense Kant's distinction between theory/nature and faith/providence is analogous to the distinction between *theoria* and *pistis*, in which "*theoria* is literally a vision or contemplation of what is visible and thereby demonstrable or capable of being shown, while Christian faith or *pistis* is a firm trust in what is invisible and thereby undemonstrable, though capable of being professed by a commitment," Löwith, *Meaning in History*, 161. The primary difference between Christian and Kantian faith is that the former is based on trust and the latter in fear.

107. Kant, "Toward Eternal Peace," 90n.

108. Ibid., 91–92n.

109. Ibid., 92n.

110. Ibid., 116.

111. Eric Voegelin, *The New Science of Politics*, 2nd ed. (Chicago: University of Chicago Press, 1987), 119–20.

112. Kant, "Toward Eternal Peace," 117.

113. Ibid., 118.

114. Ibid., 118–19.

115. Ibid., 123.

116. Ibid., 119.

117. Ibid.

118. Ibid., 122.

119. Kant, "Toward Perpetual Peace," in *Practical Philosophy*, 347.

120. Kant, "Metaphysics of Morals," in *Practical Philosophy*, 491.

121. Kant, "Toward Eternal Peace," 131. Kant's position is an instance of what Taubes identifies as the eschatological perspective common to both "theistic-transcendental" and "atheistic, materialist" viewpoints, i.e., "Both perspectives require a leap: from above into the absurdity below; from below, the realm of necessity, up into the realm of freedom," *Occidental Eschatology*, 7.

122. This is Kant's answer to the questions of both the meaning of human existence and the ultimate conclusion of the process of history as a purposeful progression toward moral-rational order, an answer that recognizes what Löwith identifies as the "problem of history as a whole," i.e., "Historical processes as such do not bear the least evidence of

a comprehensive and ultimate meaning. History as such has no outcome. There never has been and never will be an immanent solution of the problem of history, for man's historical experience is one of steady failure. Christianity, too, as a historical world religion, is a complete failure," *Meaning in History*, 191. Only from an eschatological vantage point can reason find a meaning for history that can then be retrospectively read back into the past or into the future.

123. Kant, *Critique of the Power of Judgment*, 317–18.

124. Jürgen Moltmann also identifies this process as one of translation: "Kant was aware that the fundamental ideas of the teleological philosophy of history—development, progress, goal—were derived from the salvation-history theology of chiliasm, and are translations of salvific plan, economy of salvation, world aeon, and the reign of Christ as the completion of history," *Coming of God*, 188. On the transition from Original Sin to radical evil, see Rudolf Bultmann, *History and Eschatology* (Edinburgh: University of Edinburgh Press, 1957), 67.

125. Charles Taylor, *A Secular Age* (Cambridge: Harvard University Press, 2007), 312.

126. The contrast between Schmitt and Kant in their deployment of *katechontic* roles is interesting in this regard. Schmitt identifies the Roman Empire and its successors as the *katechontic* restraining force against "the overwhelming power of evil," and bemoans the disappearance of a "tremendous historical monolith like that of the Christian empire of the German kings" in a modernity that is characterized by a lack of *katechontic* responsibility. Carl Schmitt, *The Nomos of the Earth in the International Law of the* Jus Publicum Europaeum, trans. G. L. Ulmen (New York: Telos, 2006), 60–61, 65. By contrast, Kant displaces his resolution of the tensions between the destructive and preservative aspects of mankind to a point in the distant future, effectively beyond history, in order to posit a possible solution based in reason rather than sovereign power.

127. This would put Kant beyond the pale of legitimate political theology in the strictly scriptural understanding professed by Oliver O'Donovan in *Desire of the Nations*, 15. O'Donovan describes Kant's moral theory as being "modelled on the thought of conscience as a form of divine revelation," which "makes it a surrogate for theology," 7. For Iris Murdoch, however, "Kant is still so close to Christianity that theistic terminology is a natural, perhaps the only clear, mode of explanation. . . . His puritanical Protestantism favours simplicity and clarity," *Metaphysics as a Guide to Morals* (London: Chatto and Windus, 1992).

128. In his assessment of Kant, Jürgen Moltmann observes that "[t]he kingdom of God is coming, but it will not be the result of an apocalyptic revolution brought about by God; it will come through the growth of reason and morality among human beings. . . . These postulates distinguish 'philosophical chiliasm' from theological chiliasm, but the underlying assumptions about the unified and planned course of history, its progress and its ultimate goal of completion, are the same," *Coming of God*, 189.

129. Löwith, *Meaning in History*, 204.

130. Heidegger expresses the issue well in relation to Kant's ultimate refusal of his own

insights into metaphysics: "Kant brought the 'possibility' of metaphysics to this abyss. He saw the unknown. He had to shrink back," *Kant and the Problem of Metaphysics*, 118.

Epilogue

1. Hume, *A Treatise of Human Nature*, 302.

2. Thomas Pogge, *World Poverty and Human Rights: Cosmopolitan Responsibilities and Reform*, 2nd ed. (Cambridge: Polity, 2008), 134.

3. Ibid., 3.

4. Ibid., 56.

5. Pogge's efforts to accommodate the interests of multinational pharmaceutical corporations represent at least some awareness of the requirement to acknowledge vested interests, but he is overoptimistic regarding the willingness of these multinationals to sacrifice their positions of dominance for the sake of the populations of the developing world.

6. Ibid., 71.

7. Ibid., 174–75.

8. Ibid., 184.

9. Ibid., 188.

10. Ibid., 189.

11. David Held, *Cosmopolitanism: Ideals and Realities* (Cambridge: Polity, 2010), 19.

12. Ibid., 50.

13. Ibid., 100.

14. Ibid., 105.

15. Hedley Bull, *The Anarchical Society: A Study of Order in World Politics*, 4th ed. (Basingstoke: Palgrave, 2012), 246.

16. Friedrich Nietzsche, *Human, All Too Human: A Book for Free Spirits*, ed. R. J. Hollingdale (Cambridge: Cambridge University Press, 1996), 13.

17. Richard Beardsworth, *Cosmopolitanism and International Relations Theory* (Cambridge: Polity, 2011). Despite his considerable efforts to acknowledge and incorporate realism into a cosmopolitan framework, Beardsworth ultimately ends up expressing how actors "should" and "ought" to act without fully addressing the gap between these desired standards of behavior and the practices of existing global politics.

18. Pogge, *World Poverty and Human Rights*, 6.

19. Held, *Cosmopolitanism*, 93.

20. On the issue of why the developing world should take the lead in reforming the existing world order, Pogge states that "[t]he landholders of feudal France or Russia could have asked likewise," *World Poverty and Human Rights*, 264. This facile historical comparison neglects the very real differences between the capacities of an already economically dominant bourgeois class to challenge a bankrupt regime, and the alliance of interests and forces that allowed the Bolsheviks to capitalize on the February Revolu-

tion. The Bolshevik Revolution itself failed in its global task, despite advantages that seem unlikely to be at the disposal of Pogge's future potential revolutionaries.

21. Pogge's attitude to revolution as being macho and unproductive is outlined in Gwilym David Blunt, "Is Global Poverty a Crime against Humanity?," *International Theory* 7, no. 3 (2015). Blunt finds Pogge's theory of gradual reform using moral persuasion to be unfit for purpose given Pogge's successful identification of global poverty as a crime against humanity, which due to its especial odiousness requires extraordinary measures on an emergency basis. For Pogge's dismissal of Marxism, see *Human Rights and World Poverty*, 4.

22. Linklater, *Critical Theory and World Politics*, 164.

23. Ibid., 176.

24. Sandel, *Liberalism and the Limits of Justice*, 35. As Sandel correctly argues, "For Kant, the deontologically given notion of right which Rawls seeks to recapture derives its force from a moral metaphysics that rules out precisely the appeal to contingent human circumstances on which Hume's account of the virtue of justice is based," 35–36.

25. Ibid., 40.

26. Onora O'Neill, *Bounds of Justice* (Cambridge: Cambridge University Press, 2000), 73.

27. Ibid., 73, 80.

28. Held, *Cosmopolitanism*, 82.

29. Beitz, *Political Theory and International Relations*, vii; Held, *Cosmopolitanism*, 172.

30. Kant addresses the impotence of good will in "Toward Perpetual Peace," *Practical Philosophy*, 335. Beitz argues that ideal theory "supplies a set of criteria for the formulation and criticism of strategies of political action in the nonideal world," but also recognizes that it "may be that the solution to problems of political change in radically unjust situations must rely on a consequentialist calculation of costs and benefits. If this is true, then political change in conditions of great injustice marks one kind of limit of the contract doctrine, for in these cases the principles of justice collapse into consequentialism," *Political Theory and International Relations*, 170 and 171.

Bibliography

Works by Immanuel Kant

"An Answer to the Question: What Is Enlightenment?" In *Practical Philosophy*, translated and edited by Mary Gregor. Cambridge: Cambridge University Press, 1996.

Anthropology from a Pragmatic Point of View. Edited by Robert B. Louden. Cambridge: Cambridge University Press, 2006.

"Conflict of the Faculties." In *Religion and Rational Theology*, translated and edited by Allen W. Wood and George Di Giovanni. Cambridge: Cambridge University Press, 1996.

"Conjectural Beginning of Human History." In *Anthropology, History and Education*, translated and edited by Robert B. Louden and Günter Zöller. Cambridge: Cambridge University Press, 2007.

Correspondence. Translated and edited by Arnulf Zweig. Cambridge: Cambridge University Press, 1999.

"Critique of Practical Reason." In *Practical Philosophy*, translated and edited by Mary Gregor. Cambridge: Cambridge University Press, 1996.

Critique of Pure Reason. Translated by Werner S. Pluhar. Indianapolis: Hackett, 1996.

Critique of Pure Reason. Translated by Norman Kemp Smith. 2nd ed. Houndmills: Palgrave Macmillan, 2007.

The Critique of Pure Reason. Translated and edited by Allen W. Wood and Paul Guyer. Cambridge: Cambridge University Press, 1999.

Critique of the Power of Judgment. Edited by Paul Guyer, translated by Paul Guyer and Eric Matthew. Cambridge: Cambridge University Press, 2000.

"The End of All Things." In *Perpetual Peace and Other Essays on Politics, History and Morals*, translated by Ted Humphrey. Indianapolis: Hackett, 1983.

"Essay on the Maladies of the Head." In *Anthropology, History and Education*, translated and edited by Robert B. Louden and Günter Zöller. Cambridge: Cambridge University Press, 2007.

"Essays regarding the Philanthropinum." In *Anthropology, History and Education*, translated and edited by Robert B. Louden and Günter Zöller. Cambridge: Cambridge University Press, 2007.

"Groundwork for the Metaphysics of Morals." In *Practical Philosophy*, translated and edited by Mary Gregor. Cambridge: Cambridge University Press, 1996.

"Idea for a Universal History with a Cosmopolitan Aim." In *Anthropology, History and Education*, edited by Robert B. Louden and Günter Zöller. Cambridge: Cambridge University Press, 2007.

"Idea for a Universal History with a Cosmopolitan Aim." In *Kant's Idea for a Universal History with a Cosmopolitan Aim: A Critical Guide*, edited by Amélie Oksenberg Rorty and James Schmidt. Cambridge: Cambridge University Press, 2009.

"Idea for a Universal History with a Cosmopolitan Intent." In *Perpetual Peace and Other Essays on Politics, History and Morals*, translated by Ted Humphrey. Indianapolis: Hackett, 1983.

"Jasche Logic." In *Lectures on Logic*, edited by J. M. Young. Cambridge: Cambridge University Press, 1992.

Lectures on Ethics. Translated by Peter Heath, edited by Peter Heath and J. B. Schneewind. Cambridge: Cambridge University Press, 1997.

"Lectures on Metaphysik L1." In *Lectures on Metaphysics*, translated and edited by K. Ameriks and S. Nargon. Cambridge: Cambridge University Press, 1997.

"Lectures on Pedagogy." In *Immanuel Kant: Anthropology, History and Education*, edited by Robert B. Louden and Günter Zöller. Cambridge: Cambridge University Press, 2007.

"Lectures on the Philosophical Doctrine of Religion." *Religion and Rational Theology*, edited by Allan W. Wood and George Di Giovanni. Cambridge: Cambridge University Press, 1996.

"Metaphysics of Morals." In *Practical Philosophy*, translated and edited by Mary Gregor. Cambridge: Cambridge University Press, 1996.

"Metaphysik Dohna." In *Lectures on Metaphysics*, translated and edited by K. Ameriks and S. Nargon. Cambridge: Cambridge University Press, 1997.

"Metaphysik Mrongovius." In *Lectures on Metaphysics*, translated and edited by K. Ameriks and S. Nargon. Cambridge: Cambridge University Press, 1997.

"Metaphysik Vigilantius." In *Lectures on Metaphysics*, translated and edited by K. Ameriks and S. Nargon. Cambridge: Cambridge University Press, 1997.

Observations on the Feeling of the Beautiful and Sublime. Translated by John T. Goldthwait. Berkeley: University of California Press, 1960.

"On a Supposed Right to Lie From Philanthropy." In *Practical Philosophy*, translated and edited by Mary Gregor. Cambridge: Cambridge University Press, 1996.

"The Only Possible Argument in Support of a Demonstration of the Existence of God." In *Theoretical Philosophy: 1755–1770*, translated and edited by David Walford in collaboration with Ralf Meerbote. Cambridge: Cambridge University Press, 1992.

"On the Common Saying: That May Be Correct in Theory, but It Is of No Use in Practice." In *Practical Philosophy*, translated and edited by Mary Gregor. Cambridge: Cambridge University Press, 1996.

"On the Miscarriage of all Philosophical Trials in Theodicy." In *Religion and Rational Theology*, translated and edited by Allen W. Wood and George Di Giovanni. Cambridge: Cambridge University Press, 1996.

"On the Use of Teleological Principles in Philosophy." In *Anthropology, History and Education*, translated and edited by Robert B. Louden and Günter Zöller. Cambridge: Cambridge University Press, 2007.

Opus Postumum. Edited by Eckart Förster, translated by Eckart Förster and Michael Rosen. Cambridge: Cambridge University Press, 1993.

"Proclamation of the Imminent Conclusion of a Treaty of Perpetual Peace in Philosophy." In *Theoretical Philosophy after 1781*, edited and translated by Henry E. Allison and Peter Heath, and translated by Gary Hatfield and Michael Friedman, 451–60. Cambridge: Cambridge University Press, 2002.

Prolegomena to Any Future Metaphysics That Will Be Able to Come Forward as Science with Selections from the Critique of Pure Reason. Translated and edited by Gary Hatfield, rev. ed. Cambridge: Cambridge University Press, 2004.

"Religion Within the Boundaries of Mere Reason." In *Religion and Rational Theology*, translated and edited by Allen W. Wood and George Di Giovanni. Cambridge: Cambridge University Press, 1996.

"Review of Moscati's work *Of the Corporeal Essential Differences Between the Structure of Animals and Humans*." In *Anthropology, History and Education*, translated and edited by Robert B. Louden and Günter Zöller. Cambridge: Cambridge University Press, 2007.

"Toward Perpetual Peace." In *Political Writings*, 2nd ed., edited by Hans Reiss, translated by H. B. Nisbet, 112. Cambridge: Cambridge University Press, 1991.

"Toward Perpetual Peace." In *Practical Philosophy*, translated and edited by Mary Gregor. Cambridge: Cambridge University Press, 1996.

"Towards Eternal Peace." In *Principles of Lawful Politics: Immanuel Kant's Philosophic Draft "Towards Eternal Peace"*, edited by Wolfgang Schwarz. Aalen: Scientia-Verlag, 1988.

Universal Natural History and Theory of the Heavens. Translated by S. L. Jaki. Edinburgh: Scottish Academic Press, 1981.

"What Real Progress has Metaphysics Made in Germany Since the Time of Leibniz and Wolff?" In *Theoretical Philosophy after 1781*, edited and translated by Henry E. Allison and Peter Heath, and translated by Gary Hatfield and Michael Friedman, 337–424. Cambridge: Cambridge University Press, 2002.

Secondary Sources

Allison, Henry E. 1978. "Things in Themselves, Noumena, and the Transcendental Object." *Dialectica* 32 (1): 41–76.

Allison, Henry E. 1986. "Morality and Freedom: Kant's Reciprocity Thesis." *Philosophical Review* 95 (3): 393–425.

Allison, Henry E. 1997. "Beauty and Duty in Kant's Critique of Judgement." *Kantian Review* 1 (1): 53–81.

Allison, Henry E. 2001. *Kant's Theory of Taste: A Reading of the Critique of Aesthetic Judgement.* Cambridge: Cambridge University Press.

Allison, Henry E. 2002. "On the Very Idea of a Propensity to Evil." *Journal of Value Inquiry* 36:337–48.

Allison, Henry E. 2004. *Kant's Transcendental Idealism: An Interpretation and a Defense.* Rev. ed. New Haven: Yale University Press.

Allison, Henry E. 2005. "Kant on the Freedom of the Will." In *The Cambridge Companion to Kant and Modern Philosophy*, edited by Paul Guyer, 381–415. Cambridge: Cambridge University Press.

Allison, Henry E. 2009. "Teleology and History in Kant: The Critical Foundations of Kant's Philosophy of History." In *Kant's Idea for a Universal History with a Cosmopolitan Aim: A Critical Guide*, edited by Amélie Oksenberg Rorty and James Schmidt, 24–45. Cambridge: Cambridge University Press.

Allison, Henry E. 2012. "We Can Act Only under the Idea of Freedom." In *Essays on Kant*, edited by Henry E. Allison, 87–98. Oxford: Oxford University Press.

Allison, Henry E. 2012. "Kant's Practical Justification of Freedom." In *Essays on Kant*, edited by Henry E. Allison, 110–23. Oxford: Oxford University Press.

Allison, Henry E. 2012. "Kant on Freedom of the Will." In *Essays on Kant*, edited by Henry E. Allison, 137–61. Oxford: Oxford University Press.

Anderson, Pamela Sue, and Jordan Bell. 2010. *Kant and Theology.* London: Continuum.

Armstrong, A. C. 1931. "Kant's Philosophy of Peace and War." *Journal of Philosophy* 28 (8): 197–204.

Auweele, Dennis Vanden. 2010. "Atheism, Radical Evil, and Kant." *Philosophy & Theology* 22 (1–2): 155–76.

Axinn, Sidney. 1981. "Ambivalence: Kant's View of Human Nature." *Kant Studien* 72 (2): 169–74.

Bartelson, Jens. 1995. "The Trial of Judgment: A Note on Kant and the Paradoxes of Internationalism." *International Studies Quarterly* 39 (2): 255–79.

Barth, Karl. 1959–72. *Protestant Theology in the Nineteenth Century: Its Background and History.* London: SCM Press.

Baum, Thomas. 2008. "A Quest for Inspiration in the Liberal Peace Paradigm: Back to Bentham." *European Journal of International Relations* 14 (3): 431–53.

Baxley, Anne Margaret. 2007. "Kantian Virtue." *Philosophy Compass* 2 (3): 396–410.

Baz, Avner. 2005. "Kant's Principle of Purposiveness and the Missing Point of (Aesthetic) Judgements." *Kantian Review* 10 (1): 1–32.

Beardsworth, Richard. 2011. *Cosmopolitanism and International Relations Theory.* Cambridge: Polity.

Beck, Gunnar. 2006. "Kant's Theory of Rights." *Ratio Juris* 19 (4): 371–401.

Beck, Lewis White. 1971. "Kant and the Right of Revolution." *Journal of the History of Ideas* 32 (3): 411–22.

Behnke, Andreas. 2008. "'Eternal Peace' as the Graveyard of the Political: A Critique of Kant's *Zum Ewigen Frieden*." *Millennium: Journal of International Studies* 36 (3): 513–31.

Beitz, Charles. 1999. *Political Theory and International Relations: With a New Afterword by the Author*. Princeton: Princeton University Press.

Beitz, Charles. 2005. "Cosmopolitanism and Global Justice." *Journal of Ethics* 9, nos. 1–2: 11–27.

Bertman, Martin A. 2002. "Kant's Orientation." *History of Ideas* 28 (4): 263–80.

Blumenberg, Hans. 1985. *The Legitimacy of the Modern Age*. Translated by Robert M. Wallace. Cambridge: MIT Press.

Blunt, Gwilym David. 2015. "Is Global Poverty a Crime against Humanity?" *International Theory* 7 (3): 539–71.

Boucher, David. 1998. *Political Theories of International Relations: From Thucydides to the Present*. Oxford: Oxford University Press.

Brown, Chris. 1993. *International Relations Theory: New Normative Approaches*. New York: Columbia University Press.

Brown, Garrett Wallace. 2009. *Grounding Cosmopolitanism: From Kant to the Idea of a Cosmopolitan Constitution*. Edinburgh: Edinburgh University Press.

Buchan, Bruce. 2002. "Explaining War and Peace: Kant and Liberal IR Theory." *Alternatives* 27: 419–22.

Bull, Hedley. 2012. *The Anarchical Society: A Study of Order in World Politics*. 4th ed. Basingstoke: Palgrave.

Bultmann, Rudolf. 1957. *History and Eschatology*. Edinburgh: University of Edinburgh Press.

Byrne, Peter. 2007. *Kant on God*. Farnham: Ashgate.

Cannon, Joseph. 2012. "Nature as the School of the Moral World: Kant on Taking an Interest in Natural Beauty." In *The Environment: Philosophy, Science, and Ethics*, edited by William P. Kabasenche, Michael O'Rourke, and Matthew H. Slater, 151–70. Cambridge: MIT Press.

Caswell, Matthew. 2006. "The Value of Humanity and Kant's Conception of Evil." *Journal of the History of Philosophy* 44 (4): 635–63.

Cavallar, Georg. 1999. *Kant and the Theory and Practice of International Right*. Cardiff: University of Wales Press.

Cavallar, Georg. 2001. "Kantian Perspectives on Democratic Peace: Alternatives to Doyle." *Review of International Studies* 27 (2): 229–48.

Cavallar, Georg. 2006. "Commentary on Susan Meld Shell, 'Kant on Just War and 'Unjust Enemies': Reflections on a 'Pleonasm.'" *Kantian Review* 11:117–24.

Cavallar, Georg. 2012. "Cosmopolitan Education in the 1770s: Basedow and Kant." Delivered at the Annual Conference of the Philosophy of Education Society of Great Britain, New College, Oxford, March 30. http://www.philosophy-of-education.org/uploads/papers2012/Cavallar.pdf

Cheah, Pheng. 2003. "Human Freedom and the Technic of Nature: Culture and Organic Life in Kant's Third Critique." *differences: A Journal of Feminist Cultural Studies* 14 (2): 1–26.

Clayton, Philip. 2000. *The Problem of God in Modern Thought.* Grand Rapids, MI: Eerdmans.

Clewis, Robert R. 2009. *The Kantian Sublime and the Revelation of Freedom.* Cambridge: Cambridge University Press.

Cohen, Alix. 2009. "Kant's Concept of Freedom and the Human Sciences." *Canadian Journal of Philosophy* 39 (1): 113–35.

Critchley, Simon. 2012. *The Faith of the Faithless: Experiments in Political Theology.* New York: Verso.

Cronin, Ciaran. 2003. "Kant's Politics of Enlightenment." *Journal of the Philosophy of History* 41 (1): 51–80.

Cupitt, Don. 1982. "Kant and the Negative Theology." In *The Philosophical Frontiers of Christian Theology: Essays Presented to D. M. MacKinnon,* edited by Brian Hebblethwaite and Stewart Sutherland, 55–67. Cambridge: Cambridge University Press.

David-Menard, Monique, and Alison Ross. 2000. "Kant's 'An Essay on the Maladies of the Mind' and *Observations on the Feeling of the Beautiful and the Sublime.*" *Hypatia* 15 (4): 82–98.

Dean, Richard. 2013. "Humanity as an Idea, as an Ideal, and as an End in Itself." *Kantian Review* 18 (2): 171–95.

Deleuze, Gilles. 2003. *Kant's Critical Philosophy: The Doctrine of the Faculties.* Translated by Hugh Tomlinson and Barbara Habberjam. Minneapolis: University of Minnesota Press.

Delue, Steven M. 1985. "Kant's Politics and an Expression of the Need for His Aesthetics." *Political Theory* 13 (3): 425.

Dennis, Lara. 2003. "Kant's Criticism of Atheism." *Kant Studien* 94 (2): 198–219.

Dodson, Kevin. 1997. "Autonomy and Authority in Kant's *Rechtslehre.*" *Political Theory* 25 (1): 93–111.

Doyle, Michael W. 1983. "Kant, Liberal Legacies and Foreign Affairs." *Philosophy and Public Affairs* 12 (3): 205–35.

Doyle, Michael W. 1983. "Kant, Liberal Legacies, and Foreign Affairs, Part 2." *Philosophy and Public Affairs* 12 (4): 323–53.

Doyle, Michael W. 1996. "Michael Doyle on the Democratic Peace—Again." In *Debating the Democratic Peace,* edited by Michael E. Brown, Sean M. Lynn-Jones, and Steven E. Miller, 364–73. Cambridge: MIT Press.

Dupré, Louis. 1998. "Kant's Theory of History and Progress." *Review of Metaphysics* 51 (4): 813–28.

Easley, Eric S. 2004. *The War for Perpetual Peace: An Exploration into the History of a Foundational International Relations Text*. New York: Palgrave.

Ellis, Elisabeth. 2005. *Kant's Politics: Provisional Theory for an Uncertain World*. New Haven: Yale University Press.

Elshtain, Jean Bethke. 1981. "Kant, Politics, and Persons: The Implications of His Moral Philosophy." *Polity* 14 (2): 205–21.

Erasmus, Desiderius. 1978. "On the Method of Study (*De ratione studii ac legend interpretandique auctores*)." In *Collected Works of Erasmus, Vol. 24*. Toronto: University of Toronto Press.

Fackenheim, Emil. 1956–57. "Kant's Concept of History." *Kant Studien* 48 (1–4): 381–98.

Fehér, Ferenc. 1989. "Practical Reason in the Revolution: Kant's Dialogue with the French Revolution." *Social Research* 56 (1): 161–85.

Fine, Robert, and Robin Cohen. 2002. "Four Cosmopolitan Moments." In *Conceiving Cosmopolitanism: Theory, Context and Practice*, edited by Steven Vertovec and Robin Cohen, 137–62. Oxford: Oxford University Press.

Flikschuh, Katrin. 2000. *Kant and Modern Political Philosophy*. Cambridge: Cambridge University Press.

Flikschuh, Katrin. 2010. "Kant's Sovereignty Dilemma: A Contemporary Analysis." *Journal of Political Philosophy* 18 (4): 469–93.

Flikschuh, Katrin. 2010. "Reason and Nature: Kant's Teleological Argument in Perpetual Peace." In *A Companion to Kant*, edited by Graham Bird, 383–96. Oxford: Blackwell.

Formosa, Paul. 2007. "Kant on the Radical Evil of Human Nature." *Philosophical Forum* 38, no. 3: 221–45.

Franceschet, Antonio. 2002. *Kant and Liberal Internationalism: Sovereignty, Justice, and Global Reform*. New York: Palgrave Macmillan.

Franke, Mark F. N. 2001. *Global Limits: Immanuel Kant, International Relations and Critique of World Politics*. Albany: State University Press of New York.

Frierson, Patrick. 2005. "The Moral Importance of Politeness in Kant's Anthropology." *Kantian Review* 9:105–27.

Fues, Wolfram Malte. 2010. "The Foe. The Radical Evil. Political Theology in Immanuel Kant and Carl Schmitt." *Philosophical Forum* 41, nos. 1–2: 181–204.

Galbraith, E. C. 1993. "Kant and Erasmus." *Scottish Journal of Theology* 46 (2): 191–212.

Gallie, W. B. 1978. *Philosophers of Peace and War: Kant, Clausewitz, Marx, Engels and Tolstoy*. Cambridge: Cambridge University Press.

Gillespie, Michael. 2008. *The Theological Origins of Modernity*. Chicago: University of Chicago Press.

Gjesdal, Kristin. 2007. "Reading Kant Hermeneutically: Gadamer and the *Critique of Judgement*." *Kant Studien* 98: 351–74.

Goetschel, Willi. 2000. "Kant and the Christo Effect: Grounding Aesthetics." *New German Critique* 79:137–56.

Gold, Sharon Anderson. 1994. "Kant's Ethical Anthropology and the Critical Foundations of the Philosophy of History." *History of Philosophy Quarterly* 11 (4): 405–19.

Gold, Sharon Anderson. 2001. *Unnecessary Evil: History and Moral Progress in the Philosophy of Immanuel Kant*. Albany: State University of New York Press.

Goudeli, Kyriaki. 2003. "Kant's Reflective Judgement: The Normalization of Political
Judgement." *Kant Studien* 94:51–68.

Gray, Philip W. 2007. "Political Theology and the Theology of Politics: Carl Schmitt and
Medieval Christian Political Thought." *Humanitas* 20, nos. 1–2: 175–200.

Grimm, Stephen R. 2002. "Kant's Argument for Radical Evil." *European Journal of Philosophy* 10 (2): 160–77.

Guyer, Paul. 1997. *Kant and the Claims of Taste*. 2nd ed. Cambridge: Cambridge University Press.

Guyer, Paul. 2000. "Unity of Nature and Freedom: Kant's Conception of the System of
Philosophy." In *The Reception of Kant's Critical Philosophy*, edited by Sally Sedge-
wick, 19–53. Cambridge: Cambridge University Press.

Guyer, Paul. 2003. "Beauty, Freedom, and Morality: Kant's Lectures on Anthropology
and the Development of His Aesthetic Theory." In *Essays on Kant's Anthropology*,
edited by B. Jacobs and P. Kain, 135–63. Cambridge: Cambridge University Press.

Guyer, Paul. 2005. *Kant's System of Nature and Freedom*. Oxford: Oxford University
Press.

Guyer, Paul. 2006. *Kant*. Abingdon: Routledge.

Guyer, Paul. 2009. "The Crooked Timber of Mankind." In *Kant's Idea for a Universal
History with a Cosmopolitan Aim: A Critical Guide*, edited by Amélie Oksenberg
Rorty and James Schmidt, 129–49. Cambridge: Cambridge University Press.

Harvey, David. 2009. *Cosmopolitanism and the Geographies of Freedom*. New York: Columbia University Press.

Hatfield, Gary. 1998. "Kant and Empirical Psychology in the 18th Century." *Psychological
Science* 9 (6): 423–28.

Heidegger, Martin. 1997. *Kant and the Problem of Metaphysics. Fifth Edition, Enlarged.*
Translated by Richard Taft. Bloomington: Indiana University Press.

Held, David. 2010. *Cosmopolitanism: Ideals and Realities*. Cambridge: Polity.

Hell, Julia. 2009. "*Katechon*: Carl Schmitt's Imperial Theology and the Ruins of the Future." *Germanic Review* 84 (4): 283–327.

Hinsley, F. H. 1963. *Power and the Pursuit of Peace: Theory and Practice in the History of
Relations between States*. Cambridge: Cambridge University Press.

Hoffe, Otfried. 2006. *Kant's Cosmopolitan Theory of Law and Peace*. Cambridge: Cambridge University Press.

Hume, David. 2007. *A Treatise of Human Nature: Being an Attempt to Introduce the Ex-
perimental Method of Reasoning Into Moral Subjects*. Edited by David Fate Norton
and Mary J. Norton. Oxford: Oxford University Press.

Hunter, Ian. 2002. "The Morals of Metaphysics: Kant's 'Groundwork' as Intellectual '*Paideia*.'" *Critical Inquiry* 28 (4): 908–29.

Hurrell, Andrew. 1990. "Kant and the Kantian Paradigm in International Relations." *Review of International Studies* 16 (3): 183–205.

Hutchings, Kimberly. 1992. 'The Possibility of Judgement: Moralizing and Theorizing in International Relations.' *Review of International Studies* 18 (1): 51–62.

Hutchings, Kimberly. 1996. *Kant, Critique and Politics*. London: Routledge.

Insole, Christopher. 2008. "The Irreducible Importance of Religious Hope in Kant's Conception of the Highest Good." *Philosophy* 83 (3): 333–51.

Jahn, Beate. 2006. "Classical Theory and International Relations in Context." In *Classical Theory in International Relations*, edited by Beate Jahn, 1–24. Cambridge: Cambridge University Press.

Jeffrey, Renée. 2005. "Tradition as Invention: The 'Traditions Tradition' and the History of Ideas in International Relations." *Millennium: Journal of International Studies* 34 (1): 57–84.

Johnson, Ryan. 2011. "An Accord in/on Kantian Aesthetics." *Kritike: An Online Journal of Philosophy* 5 (1): 117–35.

Kantorowicz, Ernst H. 1957. *The King's Two Bodies: A Study in Mediaeval Political Theology*. Princeton: Princeton University Press.

Kessler, Michael Jon. 2013. "Introduction: Political Theology in a Plural Context." In *Political Theology for a Plural Age*, edited by Michael Jon Kessler, 1–10. Oxford: Oxford University Press.

Kleingeld, Pauline. 1999. "Six Varieties of Cosmopolitanism in Late Eighteenth-Century Germany." *Journal of the History of Ideas* 60 (3): 505–24.

Kleingeld, Pauline. 2006. "Kant's Theory of Peace." In *The Cambridge Companion to Kant and Modern Philosophy*, edited by Paul Guyer, 477–504. Cambridge: Cambridge University Press.

Kleingeld, Pauline. 2009. "Kant's Changing Cosmopolitanism." In *Kant's Idea for a Universal History with a Cosmopolitan Aim: A Critical Guide*, edited by Amélie Oksenberg Rorty and James Schmidt, 171–86. Cambridge: Cambridge University Press.

Knippenberg, Joseph M. 1993. "The Politics of Kant's Philosophy." In *Kant and Political Philosophy: The Contemporary Legacy*, edited by Ronald Beiner and William James Booth, 155–72. New Haven: Yale University Press.

Korsgaard, Christine. 1986. "Kant's Formula of Humanity." *Kant Studien* 77 (2): 183–202.

Korsgaard, Christine M. 1996. *Creating the Kingdom of Ends*. Cambridge: Cambridge University Press.

Kraft, Michael. 1981. "Thinking the Physico-Teleological Proof." *International Journal for Philosophy of Religion* 12 (2): 65–74.

Krasnoff, Larry. 1994. "The Fact of Politics: History and Teleology in Kant." *European Journal of Philosophy* 2 (1): 22–40.

Kuehn, Manfred. 2001. *Kant: A Biography*. Cambridge: Cambridge University Press.

Laberge, Pierre. 1999. "Kant on Justice and the Law of Nations." In *International Society: Diverse Ethical Perspectives*, edited by David R. Mapel and Terry Nardin, 82–102. Princeton: Princeton University Press.

Layne, Christopher. 1996. "Kant or Cant: The Myth of the Democratic Peace." In *Debating the Democratic Peace*, edited by Michael E. Brown, Sean M. Lynn-Jones, and Steven E. Miller, 157–201. Cambridge: MIT Press.

Lilla, Mark. 1998. "Kant's Theological-Political Revolution." *Review of Metaphysics* 52: 397–403.

Lilla, Mark. 2007. *The Stillborn God*. New York: Vintage.

Lindstedt, David. 1999. "Kant: Progress in Universal History as a Postulate of Practical Reason." *Kant Studien* 90 (2): 129–147.

Linklater, Andrew. 2007. *Critical Theory and World Politics: Citizenship, Sovereignty and Humanity*. Abingdon: Routledge.

Linklater, Andrew, and Hidemi Suganami. 2006. *The English School: A Contemporary Reassessment*. Cambridge: Cambridge University Press.

Logan, Ian. 2007. "Whatever Happened to Kant's Ontological Argument?" *Philosophy and Phenomenological Research* 74 (2): 346–63.

Louden, Robert. 2000. *Kant's Impure Ethics: From Rational Beings to Human Beings*. Oxford: Oxford University Press.

Löwith, Karl. 1949. *Meaning in History*. Chicago: University of Chicago Press.

Luoma-Aho, Mika. 2009. "International Relations and the Secularisation of Theological Concepts: A Symbolic Reading." *Perspectives* 17 (2): 71–92.

Luoma-Aho, Mika. 2009. "Political Theology, Anthropomorphism, and Person-hood of the State: The Religion of IR." *International Political Sociology* 3 (3): 293–309.

Lynch, Cecelia. 1994. "Kant, the Republican Peace, and Moral Guidance in International Law." *Ethics & International Affairs* 8 (1): 39–58.

Machiavelli, Niccolò. 1957. "The Prince." In *Machiavelli: The Chief Works and Others*, vol. 1, translated by Allan Gilbert. Durham: Duke University Press.

MacKinnon, Donald. 1957. *A Study in Ethical Theory*. London: Black.

MacKinnon, Donald. 1974. *The Problem of Metaphysics*. Cambridge: Cambridge University Press.

MacKinnon, Donald. 1975. "Kant's Philosophy of Religion." *Philosophy* 50:131–44.

Macmillan, John. 2006. "Immanuel Kant and the Democratic Peace." In *Classical Theory in International Relations*, edited by Beate Jahn, 52–73. Cambridge: Cambridge University Press.

Makkreel, Rudolf. 2001. "Kant on the Scientific Status of Psychology, Anthropology, and History." In *Kant and the Sciences*, edited by Eric Watson, 185–201. Oxford: Oxford University Press.

Mariña, Jacqueline. 1997. "Kant on Grace: A Reply to His Critics." *Religious Studies* 33:379–400.

Mendelssohn, Moses. 1983. *Jerusalem: Or on the Religious Power and Judaism*. Translated by Allan Arkush, introduction and commentary by Alexander Altmann. Hanover, NH: University Press of New England, for Brandeis University.

Michalson, Gordon E. 1987. "The Inscrutability of Moral Evil in Kant." *Thomist: A Speculative Quarterly Review* 51 (2): 246–69.

Michalson, Gordon E. 1989. "Moral Regeneration and Divine Aid in Kant." *Religious Studies* 25 (3): 259–70.

Mikalsen, Kjartan Koch. 2011. "In Defense of Kant's League of States." *Law and Philosophy* 30 (3): 291–317.

Millbank, John. 2006. *Theology and Social Theory*. 2nd ed. Oxford: Blackwell.

Moltmann, Jürgen. 1993. *Theology of Hope: On the Ground and the Implications of a Christian Eschatology*. Minneapolis: Fortress Press.

Moltmann, Jürgen. 1996. *The Coming of God: Christian Eschatology*. London: SCM Press.

Monagle, Clare. 2010. "A Sovereign Act of Negation: Schmitt's Political Theology and Its Ideal Medievalism." *Culture, Theory and Critique* 51 (2): 115–27.

Moran, Kate A. 2009. "Can Kant Have an Account of Moral Education?" *Journal of Philosophy of Education* 43 (4): 471–84.

Munzel, G. Felicitas. 2003. "Kant on Moral Education, or 'Enlightenment' and the Liberal Arts." *Review of Metaphysics* 57 (1): 43–73.

Murdoch, Iris. 1992. *Metaphysics as a Guide to Morals*. London: Chatto and Windus.

Nietzsche, Friedrich. 1996. *Human, All Too Human: A Book for Free Spirits*. Translated by R. J. Hollingdale. Cambridge: Cambridge University Press.

Nietzsche, Friedrich. 1997. *Daybreak: Thoughts on the Prejudices of Morality*. Edited by Maudmarie Clark and Brian Lester, translated by R. J. Hollingdale. Cambridge: Cambridge University Press.

Nietzsche, Friedrich. 2003. *Twilight of the Idols and The Anti-Christ*. Translated by R. J. Hollingdale. London: Penguin.

O'Donovan, Oliver. 1996. *The Desire of the Nations: Rediscovering the Roots of Political Theology*. Cambridge: Cambridge University Press.

O'Neill, Onora. 2000. *Bounds of Justice*. Cambridge: Cambridge University Press.

Onuf, Nicholas. 1998. *The Republican Legacy in International Thought*. Cambridge: Cambridge University Press.

Paipais, Vassilios. 2016. "First Image Revisited: Human Nature, Original Sin and International Relations." *Journal of International Relations and Development*. http://dx.doi.org/10.1057/s41268-016-0072-y

Palmquist, Stephen. 2010. "Kant's Ethics of Grace: Perspectival Solutions to the Moral Difficulties with Divine Assistance." *Journal of Religion* 90 (4): 530–53.

Parry, Clive, ed. 1969. *Parry's Consolidated Treaty Series*. Vol. 52. Oxford: Oxford University Press.

Pasternack, Lawrence. 2011. "Regulative Principles and the 'Wise Author of Nature.'" *Religious Studies* 47 (4): 411–29.

Pogge, Thomas W. 1988. "Kant's Theory of Justice." *Kant Studien* 79 (4): 407–33.

Pogge, Thomas W. 1992. "Cosmopolitanism and Sovereignty." *Ethics* 103 (1): 48–75.

Pogge, Thomas W. 1998. "The Categorical Imperative." In *Kant's Groundwork of the Metaphysics of Morals: Critical Essays*, edited by Paul Guyer, 189–213. Totowa, NJ: Rowman and Littlefield.

Pogge, Thomas W. 2002. "Is Kant's *Rechtslehre* a Comprehensive Liberalism?" In *Kant's Metaphysics of Morals: Interpretive Essays*, edited by Mark Timmons, 133–58. Oxford: Oxford University Press.

Pogge, Thomas W. 2008. *World Poverty and Human Rights: Cosmopolitan Responsibilities and Reform*. Cambridge: Polity.

Quinn, Philip L. 1984. "Original Sin, Radical Evil and Moral Identity." *Faith and Philosophy* 1 (2): 188–202.

Quinn, Philip L. 1990. "Saving Faith from Kant's Remarkable Antinomy." *Faith and Philosophy* 7 (4): 418–33.

Rasch, William. 2008. "Kant's Project of Perpetual Pacification." *Law & Critique* 19 (1): 19–34.

Rawls, John. 1999. *The Law of Peoples*. Cambridge: Harvard University Press.

Rawls, John. 2001. "A Kantian Conception of Equality." In *Collected Papers*, edited by Samuel Freeman, 254–66. Cambridge: Harvard University Press.

Rawls, John. 2001. "The Law of Peoples." In *Collected Papers*, edited by Samuel Freeman, 529–64. Cambridge: Harvard University Press.

Ricoeur, Paul. 1970. *Freud and Philosophy: An Essay on Interpretation*. Translated by Denis Savage. New Haven: Yale University Press.

Rogerson, Kenneth F. 1998. "Pleasure and Fit in Kant's Aesthetics." *Kantian Review* 2:117–33.

Rohlf, Michael. 2008. "The Transition from Nature to Freedom in Kant's Third Critique." *Kant Studien* 99 (3): 339–60.

Russett, Bruce. 1996. "The Fact of Democratic Peace." In *Debating the Democratic Peace*, edited by Michael Edward Brown, Sean M. Lynn-Jones, and Steven E. Miller, 58–81. Cambridge: MIT Press.

Sandberg, Eric C. 1984. "Causa Noumenon and Homo Phaenomenon." *Kant Studien* 75 (3): 267–27.

Sandel, Michael J. 1982. *Liberalism and the Limits of Justice*. Cambridge: Cambridge University Press.

Saner, Hans. 1973. *Kant's Political Thought: Its Origins and Development*. Chicago: University of Chicago Press.

Scherer, Irmgard. 1995. "Kant's Eschatology in *Zum Ewigen Frieden*: The Concept of Purposiveness to Guarantee Perpetual Peace." In *Proceedings of the Eighth Annual Kant Conference, Vol II, Part 1*, edited by Hoke Robinson, 437–44. Milwaukee: Marquette University Press.

Schmidt, Anna. 2009. "The Problem of Carl Schmitt's Political Theology." *Interpretations* 36 (3): 219–52.

Schmitt, Carl. 1985. *Political Theology: Four Chapters on the Concept of Sovereignty.* Translated by George Schwab. Cambridge: MIT Press.

Schmitt, Carl. 2006. *The* Nomos *of the Earth in the International Law of the* Jus Publicum Europaeum. Translated by G. L. Ulmen. New York: Telos.

Schmitt, Carl. 2008. *Political Theology II: The Myth of the Closure of Any Political Theology.* Cambridge: Polity.

Schneewind, J. B. 1992. "Autonomy, Obligation, and Virtue: An Overview of Kant's Moral Philosophy." In *The Cambridge Companion to Kant*, edited by Paul Guyer, 309–41. Cambridge: Cambridge University Press.

Schneewind, J. B. 2009. "Good out of Evil: Kant and the Idea of Unsocial Sociability." In *Kant's Idea for a Universal History with a Cosmopolitan Aim: A Critical Guide*, edited by Amélie Oksenberg Rorty and James Schmidt, 94–111. Cambridge: Cambridge University Press.

Schwarz, Wolfgang. 1988. "Translator's Postscript—Hobbism in Kant?" In *Principles of Lawful Politics: Immanuel Kant's Philosophic Draft "Towards Eternal Peace"*, edited by Wolfgang Schwarz, 137–51. Aalen: Scientia-Verlag.

Scutt, Marie Zermatt. 2010. "Kant's Moral Theology." *British Journal for the History of Philosophy* 18 (4): 611–33.

Shell, Susan Meld. 2003. "Kant's 'True Economy of Human Nature': Rousseau, Count Verri, and the Problem of Happiness." In *Essays on Kant's Anthropology*, edited by B. Jacobs and P. Kain, 194–229. Cambridge: Cambridge University Press.

Shell, Susan Meld. 2005. "Kant on Just War and 'Unjust Enemies': Reflections on a 'Pleonasm.'" *Kantian Review* 10 (1): 82–111.

Simon, Derek. 2003. "The *New* Political Theology of Metz: Confronting Schmitt's Decisionist Political Theology of Exclusion." *Horizons* 30 (2): 227–54.

Sturm, Thomas. 2011. "Freedom and the Human Sciences: Humes's Science of Man versus Kant's Pragmatic Anthropology." *Kant Year Book* 3:23–42.

Sullivan, Roger J. 1995. "The Influence of Kant's Anthropology on His Moral Theory." *Review of Metaphysics* 49 (1): 77–94.

Sweet, Kristi. 2009. "Reflection: Its Structure and Meaning in Kant's Judgements of Taste." *Kantian Review* 14 (1): 53–80.

Taubes, Jacob. 2009. *Occidental Eschatology.* Translated by David Ratmoko. Stanford: Stanford University Press.

Taylor, Charles. 2007. *A Secular Age.* Cambridge: Harvard University Press

Taylor, Robert S. 2005. "Kantian Personal Autonomy." *Political Theory* 33 (5): 602–28.

Taylor, Robert S. 2010. "Kant's Political Religion: The Transparency of Perpetual Peace and the Highest Good." *Review of Politics* 72 (1): 1–24.

Teuber, Andreas. 1983. "Kant's Respect for Persons." *Political Theory* 11 (3): 369–92.

Teufel, Thomas. 2012. "What Does Kant Mean by 'Power of Judgement' in His Critique of the Power of Judgement." *Kantian Review* 17 (2): 297–326.

Thomason, Krista K. 2013. "Shame and Contempt in Kant's Moral Theory." *Kantian Review* 18 (2): 221–40.

Uleman, Jennifer K. 2004. "External Freedom in Kant's Rechtslehre: Political, Metaphysical." *Philosophy and Phenomenological Research* 68 (3): 578–601.

Uleman, Jennifer. 2010. *Introduction to Kant's Moral Philosophy*. Cambridge: Cambridge University Press.

Voegelin, Eric. 1987. *The New Science of Politics*. 2nd ed. Chicago: University of Chicago Press

Waite, Geoffrey. 2010. "Kant, Schmitt or Fues on Political Theology, Radical Evil and the Foe." *Philosophical Forum* 41 (1–2): 205–27.

Walker, R. B. J. 1992. *Inside/Outside: International Relations as Political Theory*. Cambridge: Cambridge University Press.

Walker, R. B. J. 1994. "On the Possibilities of World Order Discourse." *Alternatives* 19 (2): 237–45.

Walker, R. B. J. 2006. "Lines of Security: International, Imperial, Exceptional." *Security Dialogue* 37 (1): 65–82.

Watson, Stephen H. 1986. "Kant on Autonomy, the Ends of Humanity, and the Possibility of Morality." *Kant Studien* 77 (2): 165–82.

Wattles, Jeffrey. 2006. "Teleology Past and Present." *Zygon* 41 (2): 445–64.

Wendt, Alexander. 1999. *Social Theory of International Politics*. Cambridge: Cambridge University Press.

Whistler, Daniel. 2010. "Kant's *imitatio Christi*." *International Journal for Philosophy of Religion* 67 (1): 17–36.

Wight, Martin. 2004. *Four Seminal Thinkers in International Theory: Machiavelli, Grotius, Kant, and Mazzini*. Oxford: Oxford University Press.

Williams, Howard. 1983. *Kant's Political Philosophy*. Oxford: Blackwell.

Williams, Howard. 1991. "Kant: The Idea of Perpetual Peace." In *International Relations in Political Theory*, edited by Howard Williams, 80–91. Buckingham: Open University Press.

Williams, Howard. 2006. "Back from the USSR: Kant, Kaliningrad and World Peace." *International Relations* 20 (1): 27–48.

Williams, Howard. 2006. "Kant and the Protestant Ethic." In *International Relations and the Limits of Political Theory*, edited by Howard Williams, 3–18. Houndmills: Macmillan.

Williams, Howard. 2010. "The Torture Convention, Rendition and Kant's Critique of 'Pseudo-Politics.'" *Review of International Studies* 36 (1): 195–214.

Williams, Howard, and Ken Booth. 1996. "Kant: Theorist beyond Limits." In *Classical Theories of International Relations*, edited by Ian Clark and Iver Neumann, 71–98. Houndmills: Macmillan.

Williams, Michael C. 1992. "Reason and Realpolitik: Kant's 'Critique of International Politics.'" *Canadian Journal of Political Science/Revue canadienne de science politique* 25 (1): 99–119.

Wilson, Peter. 2003. *The International Theory of Leonard Woolf: A Study in Twentieth Century Idealism*. New York: Palgrave Macmillan.

Wood, Allen. 1970. *Kant's Moral Religion*. Ithaca: Cornell University Press.

Wood, Allen. 1992. "Rational Theology, Moral Faith, and Religion." In *The Cambridge Companion to Kant*, edited by Paul Guyer, 394–416. Cambridge: Cambridge University Press.

Wood, Allen. 2009. "Kant's Fourth Proposition: The Unsociable Sociability of Human Nature." In *Kant's Idea for a Universal History with a Cosmopolitan Aim: A Critical Guide*, edited by Amélie Oksenberg Rorty and James Schmidt, 112–28. Cambridge: Cambridge University Press.

Woolf, Leonard. 1915. "Perpetual Peace." *New Statesman*, July 31, 398–99.

Yovel, Yirimahu. 1980. *Kant and the Philosophy of History*. Princeton: Princeton University Press.

Ypi, Lea. 2010. "Natura Deadela Rerum? On the Justification of Historical Progress in Kant's Guarantee of Perpetual Peace." *Kantian Review* 2:118–48.

Zinkstok, Job. 2011. "Anthropology, Empirical Psychology, and Applied Logic." *Kant Yearbook* 3:107–30.

Zöller, Günter. 2011. "Kant's Political Anthropology." *Kant Yearbook* 3:131–62.

Zuckert, Rachel. 2007. "Kant's Rationalist Aesthetics." *Kant Studien* 98 (4): 443–63.

Index

belief, 14, 19, 20, 22, 26, 28, 31, 46, 67, 75, 78,
    82, 99, 101, 133, 136–37, 140–41, 143, 145–
    46, 149, 152, 159, 164, 166
  in God, 48–49, 64, 77, 132–34, 136, 144–45,
    147–48
  in purposeful nature, 81
  rational, 31, 34
Blumenberg, Hans, 13, 17, 162–63, 217n48
Blunt, Gwilym David, 224n21
body politic, 104, 129
Booth, Ken, 92, 179n16, 180n16
Boucher, David, 23, 183n84
Brennus, 73
Brown, Chris, 3
Brown, Garrett Wallace, 14, 201n29
Bull, Hedley, 169
Bultmann, Rudolf, 214n5

Carr, E. H., 6
categorical imperative, 11, 84, 136
causality, 32–33, 38, 62–63
chance, 26, 42, 75, 78–79, 80, 82, 145, 219n84
chaos, 54, 75
character, 36, 117
Cheah, Pheng, 194n14
chiliasm, 25, 77, 162, 222n124, 222n128
choice, 46, 85, 123, 160
Christ, 25, 97, 124, 211n15. *See also* Jesus
Christian, 25–26, 140, 151, 164, 207n18,
    221n106
church, 121, 126–27
civic society, 7, 21, 66
civil
  constitution, 74, 77, 84, 87, 115, 119, 128
  order, 25, 86
  society, 74, 76, 107, 110, 118
civilizations, 21, 76, 78, 114
Clayton, Philip, 216n39
cognition, 37, 108–9, 131
  faculty of, 19, 52, 55, 109
  reflective, 21
Cohen, Alix, 110
Cohen, Robert, 10
Cold War, 4, 6
colonialism, 157
commerce, 8, 90, 95
commercial
  activities, 157

earnings, 3, 20
common sense, 59
compassion, 151
competition, 76, 107
comprehension, 21
concept
  of freedom, 19, 52
  of nature, 19, 52
  of right, 82, 87–88
  of understanding, 109
conflict, 8, 91–92, 100, 157, 166
  of interest, 70
Conflict of the Faculties, 21, 127, 148
confrontation, 28, 94
Conjectural Beginning of Human History, 103,
    151
consciousness, 45–46, 50, 60
consequences, 83
constitution, 84, 87, 125, 127, 162
  writer, 24
constructivists, 3
contemptibility, 42
contract theory, 84
cooperation, 88
corruption, 126
Cortés, Juan Donoso, 24
Cosmopolitan, 16, 66, 74, 77, 79, 82, 89, 119,
    125, 127, 129, 131, 156, 157, 170
  emotions, 172
  governance, 172
  international society, 96
  law, 2, 8, 156
  literature, ix
  order, 20, 119, 174
  right, 90
  sovereignty, 168
  theorist, x, 169, 175
cosmopolitanism, xi, 3–4, 6, 9–10, 12–16, 26–
    27, 114, 116, 121, 136, 165, 167–69, 170–71,
    174, 201n29
  layered, 173
  Kantian, 10
  sociological, 172
creation, 42, 62, 65, 118, 124, 162, 216n39
creator, 53, 64, 76, 217n54
Critchley, Simon, 25
critical
  -historical, 17

theory (*continued*)
  of human nature, 19
  international political, 3, 4, 11–12, 16, 19, 22,
    57, 120, 139, 173
  IR, 13, 16, 78, 103, 136, 163
  liberal, 7, 9
  of the mind, 109
  moral, 12, 18, 136
  normative, 9, 174
  political, x, 9, 19, 22, 58, 77, 103, 163
  of progress, 70
  social, 22
  soteriological, 120
thesis, 47, 92
Third *Critique*, 51, 55, 57, 68, 84, 140, 159,
  193n2, 198n69, 221n104
Third Reich, 24
thought, 131
time, 32, 43, 45, 47, 80
Toward Perpetual Peace, ix–x, xii, 1–3, 5, 9, 17,
  20, 25, 29, 35, 44, 49, 51, 53, 56–58, 60, 66,
  70–71, 82, 84–87, 90–91, 96, 101–2, 103,
  117, 129, 139, 140, 146, 148, 152, 154, 160,
  166, 177n3, 180n18, 193n2, 221n104
totalitarian, 8
trade, 95
tradition, 13, 15
transcendental, 36, 45, 47, 49–50, 54, 65, 131,
  139, 143, 144, 158, 202n42, 221n121
Treaty of Basle, 1–2, 177n2
truth, 109, 110, 130, 139
tyranny, 76

ubergang, 53
Uleman, Jennifer, 45, 186n7, 191n81
unconditioned, 144, 145
understanding, 18, 30, 32–33, 35–37, 51, 53–55,
  57–58, 61, 68, 108–9, 141, 144, 146,
  195n33
  faculty of, 19, 53, 60, 66–67, 138
unholy, unholiness, 29–30
universe, 11, 24, 69, 75, 101, 105, 132, 134, 145,
  148
universal, 12, 38, 44, 69, 136
  communication, 56
  law, 41, 43, 68, 84–85, 150
  monarchy, 88, 125, 154, 157
  moral law, 40, 54

religion, 127
right, 90
  subjectivity, 51, 56
Universal Natural History, 104
unnaturalness, 104
unpredictability, 78
unsocial sociability, 75–78, 100–101, 106, 118,
  171
utopian fantasy, 6

Vattel, Emer de, 89
vices, 125, 142
Vico, Giambattista, 219n84
violence, 73–74, 100, 116, 129
virtue, 37, 94–95, 97, 106–7, 110, 116, 123, 125,
  153
Virgin Mary, 163
Voegelin, Eric, 160
volition, 39–40
  faculty of, 46
Vorländer, Karl, 179n9

Waite, Geoffrey, 5, 179n14
Walker, R. B. J., 14–15, 178n7, 199n2
war, 2, 5–6, 8, 18, 66, 70, 74, 77, 85, 87–92, 99,
  114, 118, 125, 128, 139, 150, 154, 157, 162–63,
  167, 206n147
  absence of, 27, 94–95
Watson, Stephen, 32
Wattles, Jeffrey, 197n51, 198n61
Weber, Max, 14
Wendt, Alexander, 178n6
Wight, Martin, 6, 178n6, 180n17
Wilhelm II, Friedrich, 1
will, 34, 38–40, 45–47, 56, 66, 69, 71, 74, 107–8,
  143, 152, 154. *See also* free will
  of God, 65, 124, 148
wille, 46
Williams, Howard, 3, 23, 92, 97, 178n8, 179n16,
  180n16, 203n67, 204n109
Williams, Michael C., 17
willkür, 46
wisdom, 17, 22, 80–81, 113, 119–20, 130, 156, 159
wise creator, 21, 78, 80
Wolff, Christian, 141
Wood, Allen, 134, 137
Woolf, Leonard, 5–6, 179n15
world, 11, 25, 32–33, 49, 57, 60, 62, 64–65, 78,

Printed and bound by CPI Group (UK) Ltd, Croydon, CR0 4YY

10/06/2025

14686731-0001